RELATIONAL ORGANISATIONAL GESTALT

RELATIONAL ORGANISATIONAL GESTALT

An Emergent Approach to Organisational Development

Marie-Anne Chidiac

Routledge
Taylor & Francis Group

LONDON AND NEW YORK

First published 2018
by Routledge
2 Park Square, Milton Park, Abingdon, Oxon OX14 4RN

and by Routledge
711 Third Avenue, New York, NY 10017

Routledge is an imprint of the Taylor & Francis Group, an informa business

© 2018 Marie-Anne Chidiac

British Library Cataloguing-in-Publication Data
A catalogue record for this book is available from the British Library

Library of Congress Cataloging-in-Publication Data
A catalog record has been requested for this book

ISBN-13: 978-1-78220-523-4 (pbk)

Typeset in Palatino
by V Publishing Solutions Pvt Ltd., Chennai, India

CONTENTS

v

PART III: APPLYING GESTALT TO ORGANISATIONAL SETTINGS

ACKNOWLEDGEMENTS

This book has emerged from a field of generosity and collaboration. It is not an isolated entity but interconnects with and has been influenced by the work of many other gestalt and non-gestalt practitioners whose work and ideas I reference and build upon. I would like therefore to acknowledge and appreciate the wonderful teachings and support of the many people that have made this book possible.

For colleagues and friends who have kindly and patiently read and commented upon several chapters of this book in their various forms and generally supported me through discussion and creative challenges including Nicky Burton, Sally Denham-Vaughan, Lynda Osborne, and Charlotte Sills. My love and appreciation also goes to Zoha Nassif, my Lebanese friend and artist for her resolute belief in the power of creativity and her wonderful guidance with the design of the front cover.

Thank you to others on the faculty of the Relational Change ROG (relational organisational gestalt) programme who have supported either directly or indirectly the delivery of these ideas including Dian Marie Hosking, Sue Gammons, Kate Glenholmes, Mee-Yan Cheung-Judge, Rosalind Maxwell-Harrison, and Frans Meulmeester.

I appreciate and honour many teachers whom I have been privileged to both meet and read and who have left lasting impressions on my work. I would like to mention in particular Edwin Nevis, Sean Gaffney, Lynda Osborne, Phil Joyce, Lars Marmgrem, Malcolm Parlett, Joe Melnick, and Lynne Jacobs.

I feel lucky to have been able to work alongside some amazing individuals and organisations in various countries in the world. Some of them feature in this book although I have ensured to protect their identities, that case material is suitably disguised. This book is written because of you and your willingness to allow me to journey with you and share with me the ups and downs of organisational life.

I also thank *The British Gestalt Journal* and its editor Christine Stevens for her very early encouragement in writing this book and her generosity in sharing published articles. Also, my thanks to Gestalt Press, Deborah Ullman and Gordon Wheeler for use of material and their support of gestalt relational approaches.

I want to make a specific mention of Sally Denham-Vaughan who for many life reasons was not able to co-write this book with me. I have missed her in this writing project. As a dear friend, colleague and co-founder of Relational Change, we have together chewed, shaped, designed, co-trained, and especially had fun creating some of the ideas and concepts in this book. I am grateful to have her in my life and for her unwavering support.

Finally, and most especially, this book could not have been written without the love and active support of my husband Richard Barker and the tolerance and patience of my daughters Maria, Oriane, and Isabelle.

Dr. Marie-Anne Chidiac is an experienced change and OD consultant, coach, trainer, psychotherapist, and supervisor. She has over twenty years' experience leading change in both the public and private sectors. She is co-founder of Relational Change, an organisation that works to develop relational skills in individuals, teams, organisations, and communities. Marie-Anne is an accredited coach and associate of Ashridge Business School and holds a DPsych in public works with a focus on the synthesis of gestalt psychotherapy and organisational development.

FOREWORD

Dr. Andrew Day and Professor Charlotte Sills

We are delighted to share some of our thoughts and reactions to Marie-Anne Chidiac's book following our first read of it.

In many ways, this is a book of its time and an important contribution to both the field of gestalt and organisation development (OD). While there are plenty of books written from a gestalt orientation for therapists, there are fewer for practitioners in organisations. Furthermore, it is a rare book that clearly describes the subtleties of gestalt theory and its influences while keeping the beautiful, accessible, present moment of gestalt practice in the foreground in working with individuals, groups, and large systems. And yet the world today has need of just such an approach, one which does not flinch from the complexities of twenty-first century life; a real need of a book that describes a gestalt oriented approach to organisation development. This is the ambition which Marie-Anne has achieved in this rich and yet practical book, with its generous abundance of examples in every chapter bringing the ideas alive.

The "relational turn"

Over the past twenty-five years, the world has experienced a "relational turn" in the social sciences. The fields of psychology, organisation development, sociology, and psychotherapy have started to question their objective and reductionist assumptions and their focus on the "individual" or "the organisation" as the basic unit of analysis. This fundamental paradigm shift seeks to understand patterns of relationships, connections, and interdependencies between phenomena, rather than attempting to break things down into their component parts. And it is not just in the social sciences. The focus on processes of relating seems to have become central in the fields of philosophy, art, architecture, history—to say nothing of quantum physics. We look in awe at the prophetic words of Einstein (1950):

> A human being is part of the whole, called by us, "Universe," a part limited in time and space. He experiences himself, his thoughts and feelings as something separated from the rest, a kind of optical illusion of his consciousness.

And then more recently, Rovelli (2014) summarised some of the work of physicist Neils Bohr as "reality is only interaction".

Complexity science has revealed how patterns, stability, and order are emergent phenomena in both natural and social systems. Local interactions between agents spontaneously give rise to system-wide patterns, which are paradoxically both stable and unstable, ordered and disordered. This worldview reveals that our world is fundamentally uncertain: we cannot fully predict the future. It also challenges deterministic ways of perceiving the world, which assume that knowledge can help us control the world. Marie-Anne describes how gestalt practice has historically reflected, and indeed led the way in these new ways of thinking (see for example Jacobs, 2000). She builds on these foundations to develop a relational gestalt philosophy of organisation development, offering us a way of understanding change and development in organisations that is different from traditional *planned change* models of OD. The underlying assumption behind these models is that by using more appropriate methods of behaviour, OD practitioners can help leaders to change the organisation from one form to another that is more adapted to its environment. In contrast, Chidiac argues that change is an emergent process; it is unpredictable—with outcomes that cannot be pre-determined. Her writing therefore challenges many of the orthodoxies of OD theory and practice.

Chidiac starts by discussing her view of organisations. She sees them as communities of interactive processes, which she calls "living systems". She says that this requires:

> An organisational approach that can translate emergent and self-regulating insights from the complexity sciences into human action. This approach must support and embrace uncertainty and the paradox of the recognisable unknowable future and understand emergence and novelty as arising in relationship.

She then locates gestalt in its context—relational concepts that have been around for three-quarters of a century—and offers her model, relational organisational gestalt (ROG), as a coherent, cogent, and dynamic approach.

We are reminded of wider developments in organisation development, particularly the work of Gervase Bushe and Bob Marshak on dialogic OD. Dialogic OD, like relational gestalt, argues that change in organisations is a relational process and requires a change in the core narrative or discourse across the organisation. Bushe and Marshak talk about these developments as requiring a change in thinking and a way of being for practitioners; not just a set of new techniques. We would agree, and we feel that Chidiac really helps to capture and describe a different orientation to practice than is offered by many traditional books on consulting and change in organisations.

Much of what has been written relating to the application of gestalt theory has focused on work with individuals and groups, there has been less written about how gestalt principles can be applied to large systems change. As the book unfolds Marie-Anne moves from the individual to the organisational level, from the micro to the macro. Towards the end of the book, she presents a range of case studies of that illustrate how she has applied gestalt in working with large organisations. This theme is taken up by Sally Denham Vaughan in her thoughtfully inspiring chapter.

Relational practice

What really appeals to us from this way of understanding organisations and change is the invitation to notice and inquire into "what is" and all the messiness of the realities of organisational life. We and those we work with can never be in control of change and we can never be certain of what will happen next. We find it liberating, exciting, and challenging to let go of our assumptions about how organisations "should be" and to join a client system without strong beliefs about what is an effective organisation. We are put in mind of Wilfred Bion's exhortation to the psychoanalyst to enter the session aiming to be without memory of the past, or desire "for results, 'cure' or even understanding" (1967, p. 273). It is challenging because we carry so many assumptions about what organisations *should* look like, how they *should* function and how people *should* behave. If we really allow ourselves to notice organisational life, as it *is*, we sense and see much more of the complexity of relationships, emotions, and social patterns. What emerges is not the ordered and structured pictures that we learn from textbooks or theories but a richer, messier, and fluid gestalt. If we are practicing relational gestalt in organisations, then we also are inviting our clients to notice the full richness and complexities of their experience. We cannot fall back on a simple set of tools or techniques as every encounter will be different and we need to meet our clients where they are and help them to engage with the challenges that they encounter.

In encouraging practitioners to work relationally, Chidiac reminds us of the centrality of the "self" of the practitioner in the consulting work. Gestalt has always emphasised the importance of the practitioner's *presence* in their work and Chidiac develops this idea in the context of a relational frame. How we make contact with the client system, what we notice about how we show up and what is stirred up in us and how we express ourselves and our difference all matter. Our energetic availability and responsiveness to others and the situation support good "contact" in the present moment. It is the consultant's capacity to show up and make use of their immediate experience that makes a difference and supports growth and development. This is a very different orientation to much of what is still advocated in mainstream consulting where ideas of objectivity, impartiality, and methodology prevail and the significance of the consultant's being and embodied presence seems not to matter. If we think about consulting as a relational process then it becomes self-evident that how we engage with our client is going to matter.

Throughout the book, Chidiac underlines the power of heightening of awareness. We appreciate the subtlety of her differentiation between "directed" noticing and "emerging", which captures both the idea of focussing mindfully on a chosen aspect of the field and also allowing the field or ground to throw up figures as they happen. She really brings forward the notion that raising awareness leads to change. Indeed, relational organisational gestalt encourages the consultant to co-create experiments with clients, whose intention is to raise awareness and to enable those involved in the work to have a different experience which supports new learning. Some of her client stories are delightful examples of engaging an organisation in a sort of action inquiry into itself.

The centrality of experimentation has its origins in Kurt Lewin's action research and the early writings on gestalt by Perls, Hefferline, and Goodman (1951 [1994]). An experiment invites us into an immediate experience in the present rather than focusing on planning for a desired outcome or distant future. In her chapter on experiments, Chidiac brings their role to life with several examples of experiments from her work. This is a theme throughout the book. Chidiac introduces a central principle or idea, helps the reader to understand its importance and application in practice, then provides descriptions of how she has applied it in her practice.

Contributions to theory

The book has several specific concepts and models that appeal to us. We very much enjoy her model of the self in terms of a sea. It makes good sense of Perls et al's (1951 [1994]) model of id, ego, and personality functions which we have always found cumbersome—confusingly Freudian-yet-not and unhelpful. Chidiac's model provides a useful map for the organisational consultant to think about what she sees and experiences as she enters an organisation. It articulates a layer called "id"—separate from the level of habit and personality or of obvious dynamics (ego)—the traditional idea of organisational culture. Chidiac's "id" is lively and responsive, fuelled by the urges drives, tensions, needs, and dynamics of human beings in relationship with each other. We applaud this. One of our (few) criticisms of a relational approach is that it risks denying the essential animal nature of the human being. This model embraces it.

We are interested that she calls her model a "wave analogy". We think it would be better termed an "ocean(ic) analogy" which describes all levels of experience. As she says:

> The advantage of [...] [this] conceptualisation is that it is dynamic, constantly forming, reacting, shaping and being shaped by its environment. It also speaks to today's interconnected economy in which organisations (even large ones) are not islands but rather operate within a web of connections and need to adapt to these and their changing environments.

The wave or ocean analogy draws attention to the depth of our experiences and how much is going on beneath the surface in organisations that is outside of awareness. Most of the time we do not notice the pull of these currents. Chidiac offers some experiences from her consulting practice where the deeper currents influenced how employees saw and looked at their business and customers. She also offers exercises to help the reader to raise their awareness of the different levels of their experience and its dynamic nature.

Another element of a gestalt orientation which she brings to light in the book, is that of "holism" (Smuts, 1926). Attention is given to mind, body, and emotion—not just numbers or facts! The role of the consultant is not to solve the client's problem but to raise awareness of their behaviour, relationships, emotions, sensations, etc., and the wider relational field. The consultant's focus is on helping the individual, group or team to find a clear figure and make an adjustment that represents "good form". This is not an analytic solution that meets rational criteria or the needs of one set of stakeholders, such as management but an aesthetic and ethical adjustment which feels right to those present.

As practitioners ourselves, the book reminds us constantly how challenging and counter-cultural gestalt can feel in organisations. At the same time, as gestaltists—of which our friend and colleague Bill Critchley—often say: "Gestalt philosophy and method have a certain rightmindedness" (quoted in Parlett, 2000, p. 75). In its essence, it is an encouragement for clients to be more aware of how they work together and to notice how their needs are being met or not. Change itself is a natural, self-regulatory process that emerges as the individual or group becomes aware of itself.

And above all, perhaps, we love the abundance of examples in every chapter. Chidiac's ideas come alive in the generous accounts that she shares with the reader—and of course, for those who like models and acronyms, there are those aplenty!

PREFACE

From the search for certainty to the use of self

Having come to the consulting world from an engineering background, I was at first seduced by the certainties promised by many organisation development (OD) theories and nicely packaged methodologies and tools. I soon however experienced the mismatch that existed between the promises of change methodologies and what happened in practice. More often than not, the war stories emerging from organisational change projects were bloody, painful, and depicted drained and exhausted practitioners and organisations. So, this book stems from what these change theories didn't deliver and what I learnt in my journey as a gestalt change and OD practitioner.

In my first consulting experiences, the notable tension between the clients demanding set, pre-determined, fail-proof methodologies and procedures of work and the increasing complexity and uncertainty of change situations, meant that working in such environments often led to early burnout and a failure to realise promised benefits. Clients often wanted cultural and behavioural change led in the style of operational planned improvement projects and most consulting firms tried to deliver this through slick looking, one-size fits all, change methodologies.

On the one hand, we were asked for certainty of outcome and process and on the other, contemporary OD theories were telling us that managing complex change situations required something radically different, something that could not be planned for or pre-empted. What was needed was to open up the space for emergence, to relinquish our expert positions and allow new learning to come from our clients. However, more often than not, we would talk the language of co-emergence and collaboration but still behaved in the old consulting model of leading the client towards a pre-defined solution. The ideas and principles from emergent OD, although exciting and emboldening in terms of their potential, often left us in practice feeling uncertain and disempowered. I believe we mostly struggled with sitting with our own uncertainties and feeling unsure how to facilitate newness to emerge. For many of us, it felt unsafe to trust and believe in the self-organising abilities of our clients. After all, the client expected results and we needed to deliver them! It was a challenging time where co-emergence was wanted and desired and yet as practitioners we felt tool-less.

It is exactly in this context that I found and turned to gestalt. Stemming from a humanistic psychology, gestalt has at its heart the belief in self-organisation and growth and that emergence and newness stems from heightening awareness in the client. I found in gestalt a philosophy as well as a proven practice and set of skills which allowed me to work with emergence and complexity in a practical and relational way! What was even more helpful at the time was that gestalt provided a way of supporting me, the practitioner, by very explicitly placing the use of self and presence at the heart of its practice. I went from feeling tool-less to understanding that the most valuable tool was myself.

Aim of the book

My aim in writing this book is to make available in one place material that I have been teaching, with my colleague and friend Sally Denham-Vaughan, for the last twelve years on a variety of programmes on gestalt in organisations. Together we co-founded Relational Change, a not-for-profit organisation which supports the development of relational values and became a vehicle through which we could take this practice of relationality and emergence to organisations. Gestalt offers an OD approach that is practical, dynamic, and one that resources both the practitioner as well as the organisation. It invites us to better support ourselves when faced with the uncertainties and messiness of organisational life and so sustains the resilience of people to operate in often stressful and pressurised conditions. It is not a set methodology of "what to do", but rather a way of being, an experiential approach, which makes a significant shift in people's work and personal lives.

The issue with an experiential approach is that often people are busy with the immediacy of their experience and so the distance of writing feels much less appealing. However, I feel this book is needed to offer students and newcomers to the gestalt approach in organisations a brief pause amidst the aliveness of experience to chew, integrate, and reflect more on their theory base as organisational practitioners.

INTRODUCTION

The field of organisational development (OD) and change is becoming increasingly complex as one-size-fits-all methodologies do not adequately tackle the uncertainty and uniqueness of emergent change situations. As a relational and emergent approach, gestalt views individuals and organisations as embedded in their context, dependent on, and emerging from within a web of relationships and interactions. Gestalt therefore offers a way of managing the uncertainty by fostering relationships and inviting practitioners to actively seek the organisation's or the group's emergent issues and mobilising change around these.

Gestalt has its roots in the humanistic movement and holds at its core the notion that awareness in and of itself is a precursor to change. In working with organisations, groups or individuals, gestalt practitioners believe that by heightening awareness, maintaining, and creating conditions for dialogue, individuals are more likely to see possibilities for movement and take action as part of healthy self-regulation.

Gestalt and OD

The histories of both OD and gestalt have been closely intertwined since the early 1930s. They both derived their basic assumptions from theories evolved during the period of 1930–1965 a time dominated by liberalism in intellectual, social, political, economic, and technological thinking (Nevis, 1997).

OD grew out of experimentation and research in the aftermath of World War II. The post-war optimism was also fuelled by a reaction against the earlier mode of "Taylorism" (a term for the principles or practice of scientific work efficiency) in organisational practice which upheld the belief in scientific management during the first third of the twentieth century. Scientific management methods thought to optimise organisational tasks by reducing workers to machines with no consideration of the person behind the task. In contrast, the field of OD delved into the psychological and sociological orientations of the time focusing on the individual and workgroups.

Similarly, gestalt therapy theory developed as a reaction against Freudian doctrine and behaviourism (a school of psychology based on the belief that behaviours can be measured, trained, and changed). The founders of gestalt therapy theory in the 1940s and 1950s, Fritz Perls, Laura Perls, and Paul Goodman were in part motivated by what they deemed as the weakness of psychoanalytic and behaviourist theory; notably the lack of consideration of personal needs and emotions. So, gestalt sits firmly in the humanistic psychology camp which Callahan (2014, p. 16). describes as the "third force" as an alternative to both psychoanalysis and behaviourism.

The marriage of gestalt and OD seemed inevitable in the zeitgeist of the time where both fields were searching for ways to improve the human condition and free the individual from the oppression of a conservative society. Edwin Nevis, a contemporary of Fritz Perls, wrote about this time as a "golden age" because of the optimism and excitement of people leading them to seek ways to broaden their awareness of themselves as well as their organisational existence (Nevis, 1997, p. 113). It is therefore no surprise that gestalt has been at the forefront of psychological approaches applied to organisational development and change in organisations.

The application of gestalt to organisations

Although best known as a therapeutic approach, gestalt has been applied to non-therapeutic contexts since the 1950s and has had considerable influence on OD, consulting, coaching, and facilitation practices.

Beyond the organisational boundaries however and as shown in Table I.1 below, it is helpful to note that gestalt has also been applied in community-building and social change.

There are therefore many flavours of gestalt organisational practitioners, and the European certification of GPO (gestalt practitioner in organisations) issued by the European Association of Gestalt Therapy (EAGT) does not identify a specific field of organisational application. What unifies gestalt organisational practitioners are key assumptions around how change happens in individuals and larger systems. Essential to these assumptions are notions of awareness, dialogue, aiming for the appropriate balance of challenge and support and the practitioner's use of self as an instrument of change.

Table I.1 The application of gestalt to different contexts.

Application	Practitioner researchers
Coaching	Denham-Vaughan et al. (2010, 2012); Leary-Joyce (2014); Bluckert (2015); Francis and Parlett (2016), Siminovitch (2017)
Group work and facilitation	Bentley (2000), Barber (2012), Gaffney (2013),
Leadership development and management	Nevis et al. (2003); Elsner & Farrands (2012); Marmgren (2014); Clark et al. (2014); Rask (2014), Congram (2015)
Organisational development and consulting	Nevis (1987); Rainey Tolbert (2004); Maurer (2005); Meulmeester (2006); Critchely et al. (2007); Chidiac (2013, 2017)
Social change & community building	Lukensmeyer (1997); Levine Bar-Yoseph (2005); Melnick and Nevis (2009), Fairfield (2013); Parlett (2015)

This book: relational organisational gestalt

Although gestalt in its philosophy has always been deeply relational, gestalt in organisations has matured alongside gestalt theory in acknowledging the importance of relationality in its application and practice. It is significant that this book very deliberately emphasises the term relational in its title *Relational Organisational Gestalt (ROG)*, as it provides a particular understanding of relationality within organisational gestalt practice. As will be explored in the chapters that follow, "relational" here acknowledges the inter-connectedness of people, events, situations and contexts and that it is the relationships existing between or amongst them that offers maximum possibility for change. ROG therefore embraces the complexity of influences present in any situation at a given moment and that change can only be emergent and unpredictable. In doing so, it offers a transformative, integral, and bespoke methodology for working with complexity and supporting the practitioner in doing so.

Central to the concept of a gestalt change intervention is that practitioners and clients work collaboratively and learn together from the experience of change. This is a practical, action-orientated, and relational approach that incorporates shared inquiry and evaluation of outcomes on an ongoing basis. Whatever their specialisation, gestalt practitioners also possess a high ability to develop the positive relationships required to support this learning process.

* * *

The journey through the book takes the reader through three distinct parts.

- Part   I: Understanding emergent and relational approaches.
- Part II: Gestalt concepts and practices.
- Part III: Applying gestalt to organisational settings.

Part I begins by exploring commonly held views of how change happens by contrasting the gestalt held view of organisations as relational living systems with the still prevalent notion of organisations as machines (Chapter One). This is then followed by an overview of gestalt's history as well as assumptions and characteristics of a relational organisational gestalt approach (Chapter Two). Part I then concludes with presenting in Chapter Three, a gestalt view of an organisational "self" which captures the emergent, dynamic, and responsive view of organisations in gestalt.

Part II is then structured around four key relational abilities which underpin gestalt work in organisations: practitioner presence, sensing, supporting, and sustaining. Chapter Four starts off this part of the book by outlining a relational and ethical notion of *presence* which is foundational to what in gestalt is the practitioner's main instrument—their use-of-self, and which allows practitioners to be responsive to emergent issues and situations.

Chapters Five and Six then focus on the skills of *sensing*, that support practitioners to explore and make meaning of the experience of the client group or organisation they are working with. Chapter Five first covers the skill of raising awareness through phenomenological inquiry while, Chapter Six describes two key gestalt conceptual frameworks that guide our understanding of experience; field theory and the cycle of experience (CoE).

Whilst awareness and sensing lead to meaning-making, *supporting* movement to sustainable action also requires enabling and safe conditions. And so, Chapters Seven and Eight explore ways to support action through the notion of dialogic change, and propose a gestalt based framework for dialogue in organisations. Chapter Nine then describes the stance and artistry of gestalt interventions. In gestalt, *sustaining* change requires an assimilation of experience which is most rapidly accessed through experimentation (in Chapter Ten) and attending to unfinished business and endings (in Chapter Eleven).

Although every chapter in the book offers guidance through experiential exercises as well as examples, Part III of the book focuses on the application of gestalt to differing organisational settings. It starts by addressing in Chapter Twelve some of the queries commonly encountered when people begin to introduce gestalt into their work and then offers in Chapters Thirteen to Sixteen case studies and illustrations of using gestalt to support different types of OD interventions such as coaching, leadership development, working with a family business, and a merger situation.

This book as a relational and emerging dialogue

This book has arisen from numerous exchanges and conversations as well as endless hours of practice with generous organisational clients who have shared their struggles and successes and allowed me and other practitioners to journey alongside them for a while.

Having emerged from dialogue, the wish is that this book contributes in turn to an ongoing dialogue into approaches to change in organisations. The hope is that it puts the relational organisational gestalt contribution to the evolving field of OD in focus, and in so doing, supports OD practitioners in their continued quest for emergent and relational approaches as a way of ethically addressing the growing complexity and uncertainty of organisational life.

PART I

UNDERSTANDING EMERGENT AND RELATIONAL APPROACHES

This first part introduces gestalt as an emergent, relational, and dialogic approach to change and situates gestalt within the evolving and expanding OD field of practice. As a change approach based on a humanistic orientation, gestalt views organisations as relational living systems with the capacity to self-organise, evolve, and emerge in response to changes in their environment. This position is in contrast to many OD and change approaches which still view organisations as machines whose cogs (individuals and groups) can be made to predictably slot into place for effective performance. This first part will therefore start by outlining the key differences in beliefs between organisations as machines and living systems, before providing an overview of gestalt, its history and assumptions as an emergent, relational and dialogic approach to change. Part I will then conclude with a view of organisations based on the gestalt theory of self.

CHAPTER ONE

From organisations as machines to living systems

The aim of science is to seek the simplest explanations of complex facts. We are apt to fall into the error of thinking that the facts are simple because simplicity is the goal of our quest. The guiding motto in the life of every natural philosopher should be, "Seek simplicity and distrust it".

—*Whitehead*, 1920

Whatever their orientation, change practitioners hold beliefs, values, and assumptions about how change takes place. This specific attitude is influenced by the practitioner's experiences and learnings but also by the predominant paradigms of the time. For many today, this is still the modernistic culture influenced by a century of scientific thinking; a culture which invites us to perceive our physical world as an aggregate of separate entities that come together as cogs in a machine. This attitude endures despite the realisation that all entities in this world, including humans, are thoroughly relational and are both composed of, and nested within, complex networks of creative dynamic interrelationships (Spretnak, 2011). This latter post-modern perspective calls instead for us to view organisations as relational living systems and bring this thinking to bear in the way we understand organisational processes and behaviours.

We witness still the predominance of modernistic thinking in the areas of OD and change management. Although ideas around complexity theories and emergence have, since the 1980s, had some impact on OD literature, these seem to be rarely applied still to change programmes. HR and/or OD functions within organisations are still pushing against cultures that view organisations as machines, people as cogs and business management systems as a control process. The greatest challenge lies in letting go of planned approaches to change, where the movement is assumed to be towards a known, often predetermined, future state. Many OD and change approaches struggle with embracing emergence and sit with the uncertainty of exploring true novelty in change and a movement towards an unknowable future.

Understanding therefore the modernistic lens—with its scientific and interlocking mechanistic assumptions—is also key to understanding the transition that is occurring slowly but surely towards an interconnected and relational view of organisations as relational living systems. This chapter will therefore contrast these two conceptualisations of organisations as machines and living systems and how they hold important and very differing beliefs about management systems, processes and leadership behaviours and especially how best change can be achieved and sustained. The chapter will conclude with situating gestalt as a needed relational and emergent OD approach, aligned to post-modern change practices and bringing experience and know-how to facilitate this in the personal and intersubjective domain.

Organisations as machines

The influence of modernistic thinking

Fundamental assumptions about the nature of reality in western culture can be traced back to the classical Greek philosophers' emphasis on rational thought and notions of atomism (that the physical world is composed of small, indivisible atoms which are invisible and collide and combine to form our world). The basis for a reductionist approach was set where rationality demanded we categorise our world according to differing forms and functions and in so doing lost the more comprehensive view of reality.

This view was then revived during the Renaissance and embraced by the scientific revolution in the sixteenth and seventeenth centuries and later applied to social theory as well. In the eighteenth century a new mechanistic way of looking at the world (called the "new mechanical philosophy") was embraced and was applied to every life perspective—even faith. Belief in God, Voltaire argued, did not require faith, since reasoning from observation could be used to infer the existence of a supreme being. A rational man, Voltaire claimed, only had to rely on the evidence of his senses to see how the "clockwork of the universe cannot exist without a clockmaker".

And so today, three hundred years later, we are still influenced by these images of the world as a great clock and hold the belief in predictable and controlled processes in organisations. There is something ultimately reassuring in this simple belief of cause and effect and that organisations and people can also be engineered into efficient solutions. Frederick Taylor, an engineer and the originator of Taylorism (which is a term for the principles or practice of scientific management and work efficiency), was one of the early management gurus as he legitimised the right of managers to run their business in the most productive and profitable way irrespective of the views of the employees. For Taylor, the power of science and the authority of logic and reason led him to "scientific management" and the view of organisations as machines. This metaphor is still very present in much of the beliefs and widely accepted truisms about how change happens in organisations. Some of these myths of management life will be discussed next as they influence our perception of how organisations operate and change. Before that, you might want to reflect on your own assumptions about how change happens.

Suggestion

Ask yourself about your own assumptions and beliefs about how change takes place. What are the most effective ways to bring about change in yourself and others? How does this apply to your workplace? What trends do you observe in your work in organisations? How do these principles or ideas about change guide your work?

The myth of planning and top-down management as the only way of managing change

Planning itself can be a helpful and useful coordinating activity and yet the belief that creating an action plan itself leads to change is still widely held. Underlying this belief is the supposition that the only obstacle to change is a cognitive knowing of what needs to be changed. And so, organisations often spend inordinate amount of time in trying to "understand the problem" and then break it down to its smallest component to resolve it.

Chasing the "problem" and breaking it down to manageable chunks fits with a perspective of an organisation as a machine and doesn't support managers to embrace change that may result from creativity, opportunity or improvement. This is after all, the relationship we have with machines and tools in our lives. Would we for example, think of improving the effectiveness of a washing machine unless it looked broken? Or, get a new coffee machine unless the current one wasn't performing as anticipated?

This top-down approach to change through deconstructing and planning also brings about the issue of "motivating the troops" who have not been involved in most decision making and yet are expected nonetheless to carry out instructions or implement change plans decided upon by senior executives. In most organisations, the issue of motivation is managed through performance management and a carrot and stick approach. The assumption here is that the lure of an attractive salary or that the power of criticism and fear will motivate change. This disregards the need of human beings for positive and growthful connections in their workplace and speaks more to the mechanistic worldview. A view where people in organisations are perceived as discrete, fundamentally separate, mostly self-contained entities, and workplace relationships are seen as extraneous to the capabilities of a person.

The myth of the leader-hero at the helm

Another widespread truism around change is that it will be successful only if led by the top. As a result, leadership has come under scrutiny ever since the foundations of organisational development theory and the metaphor of the leader as a "lone hero" is imbued in our popular folklore. A good example of this is the praise for Rudy Guliani, the former mayor of New York who was recognised as the epitome of what a leader should be following the terrorist attack on New-York in September 2001.

The expectation is still for leaders to act as captains of their organisations and pull "change levers" and "drive" the organisation out of the chaotic seas to new and more exciting horizons. He or she is the one who courageously takes charge in a moment of crisis and independently makes decisions that save the world. This leadership model implies that for change to happen, the leader needs to be a larger-than-life individual who sets the "right" direction, empowers and motivates co-workers and changes behaviours all in one go. And do this alone because admitting vulnerability means you are not the man or woman for the job. This expectation often places leaders in an untenable and isolated position.

The myth that emotions are problematic and have no place in organisations

The topic of emotions within organisations is still viewed as inappropriate and as having no place in a mechanistic context. Emotions don't make sense or support the worker-cogs to be more efficient or predictable. Emotional display rules exist in every workplace and include for instance expectations of being pleasant, expressing a minimum of hostility and negative emotions (Cropanzano, et al., 1993). Emotional displays at work are often perceived as problematic and must not intrude for example on the rationally built incentives that motivate people in organisations to perform and stick to common goals. In a change project too, negative reactions to the proposed change are often termed "resistance" and as such a problem to be resolved or removed.

Organisations as living systems

What do we mean by living systems

A new understanding of organisations has emerged from the sciences (systems theory, chaos theory, and especially complexity) as well as from postmodern thinking arising in a variety of fields such as sociology, literature, psychology, physics, biology, cybernetics, and linguistics. These areas of studies have significantly influenced the theoretical and conceptual underpinnings of OD approaches. Some would like to view these influences on OD as separate and distinct theoretical bases as they arose from different fields of work and study. The cross-pollination across disciplines doesn't however support such a purist approach and it is exactly this inter-breeding that best underpins a new understanding of organisations in the post-modernity era.

This new understanding is best captured by the metaphor of organisations as living systems and stands in stark contrast to the mechanistic view that arose from a century of modernity.

But what is meant by living systems?

First, it acknowledges the interconnected nature of organisations. Such a view invites us away from a causal perspective, to embrace and appreciate the complex dynamics within human phenomenon and structures. We can no longer rely on mechanistic predictability and control. This view was shaped from many ideas such as general systems theory (Bertalanffy, 1968) as well as field theory (Lewin, 1951).

Second, a living system is an organisation that is itself alive. This is *not* to describe organisations as "biological" systems, but rather to say that they are infused with consciousness and seem to have properties we attribute to living systems. Not only are organisations populated by living human beings but viewing an organisation as alive reminds us that living systems are located within, and are responsive to, their environment. To be alive is also to be dynamic in our behaviour and hold the potential for growth and renewal. Rather than static, organisations are therefore seen as complex and emergent systems with their own life force and some would say, purpose.

Suggestion

How do the organisations you know behave more as living beings than machines? What feels familiar and what is your reaction to it? Where would you place yourself as an organisational practitioner/manager on the continuum of organisations as machines and living systems? What feels more or less comfortable?

The remainder of this section will summarise the key beliefs and assumptions underlying the metaphor of organisations as living systems and how these impact the work of change practitioners.

A postmodern perspective

Modernity is viewed as a period in which reason dominates and so modernist knowledge such as science is therefore seen as resting on solid and irrefutable foundations. In Postmodernity, we find a weakening of reason, a breaking down of homogeneous, unifying models of knowledge (Montuori, 1998). In other words, knowledge becomes relative and contextual, and any pretence at linear progressive development is removed.

The postmodern condition appears as we find a succession of failures in our "modernist" thoughts and practices. Old and established business practices seem unsuccessful, as the economy and organisations appears more confusing, chaotic, and complex. In other words, more human! Organisations contain all aspects of human life which can often be messy, irrational as well as emotional and confusing. There is nothing orderly or predictable about human beings and viewing them as cogs or machines just does not fit.

Postmodern thinking is found in various philosophies or theories of knowledge such as for example constructivism, social constructivism, and hermeneutics. The common ground of these theories is that they stand in opposition to a positivist view of the world which is the belief that valid knowledge is only derived from observable data and interpreted through reason and logic. Instead in postmodernistic thinking, knowledge or reality is a co-construction which is created and evolves *in* relationship. We therefore cannot observe a phenomenon, without changing and being changed by it which is a perspective that is also supported by quantum physics (Sassoli de Bianchi, 2015). Viewing organisations through this lens means accepting the multiplicity of realities present at any one time. Any change process must therefore include a continuous inquiry into the differing interpretations of the change amongst the various stakeholder groups.

The other aspect of a postmodern perspective is for managers or consultants to accept that they co-create change rather than direct it. So, the change process is not set but one that evolves in relationship between all parts of the organisation. This provides the space for an emerging narrative of the change which can be constantly shaped by stories, metaphors, and conversations; constantly shaped by relationship. The narrative of an organisation as a living system is therefore constantly in flux, and results from the human interactions and relationships taking place at every moment.

Organisations are embedded in a complex network of relationships

Instead of looking for basic building blocks, life scientists studying living organisms took a new tack: they started to look at wholes rather than parts, at processes rather than substances. They found that these wholes—be they cells, bodies, ecosystems, or even the planet itself—are not just a group of disparate entities, but are dynamically organised and balanced "systems" that are interdependent in the way they behave and exchange information. They saw that each element is part of a wider pattern, a pattern that connects and evolves by noticeable principles. The discernment of these principles gave rise to general systems theory and that black-boxing elements of a system to solve a problem is an increasingly risky approach. For example, whilst we may have believed in a mechanistic worldview that outsourcing the HR function has no noticeable impact on the rest of the organisation, in a relational and interconnected system we know that this will change overall patterns with the organisation. These may be patterns of beliefs, communication, sense-making or emotion.

The modernistic view of organisations has largely been environment-free. In other words, when thinking of an organisation's environment or context, we might focus only on that small part of the environment which we can directly identify as relevant to the organisation, e.g., competition, consumer preferences, or the stock market. The "environment" is therefore perceived as fundamentally "other", and the relationship to the "other", is something to be dominated or viewed in terms of power relations. An organisation as a living system however, is one which reclaims all aspect of its environment and views it as a part of itself. This more "ecological" view highlights the role of our embeddedness in a context, our ability to learn from it and contribute to it, and the need to listen and learn from divergent perspectives. We are creating our worlds in the context of an environment which is creating us.

This deeply interconnected view of organisations is even more relevant in today's rapidly changing environments where there is a fierce pressure to adapt to environmental change. It is necessary for all businesses to recognise what is their business ecosystem—whether from a process perspective (industrial synergies, for instance) or a people perspective (co-creation and shared innovation, for instance). Companies of the future are ones that view their organisation as a living, dynamic, emergent organism connecting within a living, dynamic, emergent ecosystem. Organisations and their related ecosystem are interdependent and their health and resilience is mutual. This brings a shift from linear, atomised, supply-chain thinking to interconnected, holistic, ecosystem thinking (Hutchins, 2012).

Finally, the interconnection of living systems also brings an ethical realisation: that we are intricately and unescapably linked to each other and our environment. This recognition is fundamental and alters our perceptions of who we are, what resources we really need and, that an ethical future is based on our ability to collaborate, compromise and act together.

Organisations as complex and emergent systems

A fundamental aspect of all living organisms is their capability to adapt. Viewing organisations as living systems is recognising they have the capacity to self-organise and move towards greater complexity and order as needed.

This outlook on organisations has emerged from the translation of complexity and chaos theory to organisations and leadership. It supports the view that creative and unpredictable responses arise from the emergent dynamic relationships within the organisation and from its dynamic relationships with its environment. Self-organising systems will respond intelligently to the need for change and organise themselves into adaptive patterns and structures without any externally imposed plan or direction. The role of the change agent therefore is not to drive the change but create the conditions necessary to support and foster this self-organising property.

The individual within the living system

In talking of living systems, we might imagine that the person has a lesser role and that there is a primacy of the whole over the single individual. In which case, what is the role of leadership?

Unlike machines that need a single clock worker to wind up the mechanism, a living system is dependent on the leadership of each particular individual at every level. Each individual is part of the whole and can't stand "apart from" and as such will influence the properties of the whole. There is no observer position in this view of organisations and each person has an impact. The individual is therefore very important in this concept as more is expected of her or him than "being told what to do". Building such leadership capability is still an important aspect of adaptive and self-organising companies.

The notion of a hero leader who holds the answers and can solve all problems or challenges is also a myth. The complexity and interconnectedness of organisations make it impossible for a leader to be "in control" and yet this is still our expectation, our desire for heroes. Wheatley and Frieze (2011) write instead about leaders as "hosts" who offer the best conditions for people to work together, a leader that collaborates, empowers, and provides coherence to ensure the overall system is vibrant and thriving. In a postmodern and relational perspective, nurturing the self-reflexive capability of individuals will enable them to provide to others (employees or co-workers) the vital relational supports that ensures well-being and health (Denham-Vaughan & Chidiac, 2009, 2016).

The need for emergent and relational OD approaches

OD and change approaches echo the dichotomy in thinking between the modernistic and post-modern mindsets. In the ethos of organisations as machines, planned approaches to change dominate. The latter typically involve well-defined sequential steps put in place once decision-makers identify a need for change (Burns, 2006; Livne-Tarandach & Bartunek, 2009). The belief in this case is that the organisation will move towards a pre-determined and known future state.

In the face of rising complexity and connectivity of a global and competitive environment, organisations do however increasingly recognise the need to balance their traditional planned, structural change methods with the unpredictability of newer emergent approaches (Liebhart & Garcia-Lorenzo, 2010). There is an understanding that pre-determined outcomes cannot be guaranteed in a dynamic environment and so, even 'planned' change will be "emergent".

Fundamental to an emergent approach is the acceptance that change is unpredictable, often unintentional and involves an element of unplanned self-organisation (Weick & Quinn, 1999). Although this may be acknowledged, emergent change approaches have often in practice either been mis-understood or applied in ways that still strive for certainty. Some writers argue that although complexity theory offers many insights that are appealing as they reflect aspects of social and economic phenomena, the translation of these into human action and behaviour is still at an early stage (Levy, 2000). Stacey et al. (2000) for example, write that in systems thinking and also in the translation of the complexity sciences to human action, most practitioners still use rationalist or formative frameworks. The latter assumes that individuals are called to realise their full potential as human beings if "hygiene factors" such as a sense of mission, inspiring visions and organisational designs (p. 162) are in place. The former rationalist perspective assumes that all goals are chosen by self-motivated reasoning autonomous humans in order to realise their chosen aims. In both frameworks the emphasis is always on the individual not the relationship and assumes a predefined process of individual behaviour. Stacey, et al., (ibid) go on to write that what is needed is a "relationship psychology" (p. 182) which "provides a cogent view of individual and collective identities emerging in interaction".

What is needed therefore is an organisational approach that can translate emergent and self-regulating insights from the complexity sciences into human action. This approach must support and embrace uncertainty and the paradox of the recognisable unknowable future and understand emergence and novelty as arising in relationship. This book contends that relational organisational gestalt offers such an approach.

Summary

This chapter noted the dominance still of positivist and modernistic thinking in the view of organisations as machine and, contrasted this with a more complex and interconnected post-modern perspective of organisations as relational living systems. The latter view better supports the reality, connectivity, and increasing complexity of organisations that need to respond and rapidly adapt to changing environments.

Viewing organisations as dynamic living systems requires however a revisiting of the more traditional planned and predictable approaches to change towards an approach to human action and behaviour that is both emergent and relational. This chapter ends by setting the scene for the remainder of the book and placing relational gestalt as a theory and practice base that both invites and works with emergence. The chapter that follows will expand on this by providing an overview of gestalt, its history, influences and key change assumptions and characteristics.

CHAPTER TWO

Gestalt as a relational and emergent approach

Gestalt [...] is systematically relational in its underlying theory and methodology. A relational perspective is so central to the theory of gestalt [...] that without it there is no coherent core of gestalt

—*Yontef*, 2002, p. 15

G estalt is an approach that focuses on exploring the needs and tensions within individuals and teams as a way of facilitating movement towards change. It is primarily an inquiry into the lived experience of a person, team or organisation and as such cannot be pre-empted or its outcomes pre-defined. It is therefore principally an "emergent" approach.

Although gestalt theory, which emerged in the 1950s, contains numerous references to a modernist mode of thinking (Robine, 2011, p. 38), it also introduced new postmodern ideas based on field theory (Lewin, 1926) which recognises the interconnectedness of all things, as well as a view of selfhood that is fluid, dynamic, and constantly changing in contact with others and the environment. This places gestalt at the heart of what is called "postmodernism" which mean that it views reality as emerging and evolving within a web of relationships. We can't therefore extricate the person or team from their context nor assume that the gestalt practitioner is an independent observer. Gestalt is therefore a "relational" approach in the sense that it works with awareness of the impact of relationships both within the client system and between client and practitioner.

An overview of gestalt as an emergent and relational approach to managing change will be further unpacked in this chapter. This will be done through an understanding of the historical and philosophical roots of gestalt and by providing the reader with an overview of the key assumptions and distinctive characteristics of a gestalt approach to change management.

Influences on the field of organisational gestalt

To better understand the field of organisational gestalt today, it may be helpful to know how the gestalt premises and principles have evolved and have both influenced and been influenced by other OD and change management thoughts. Figure 2.1 attempts to capture some of the

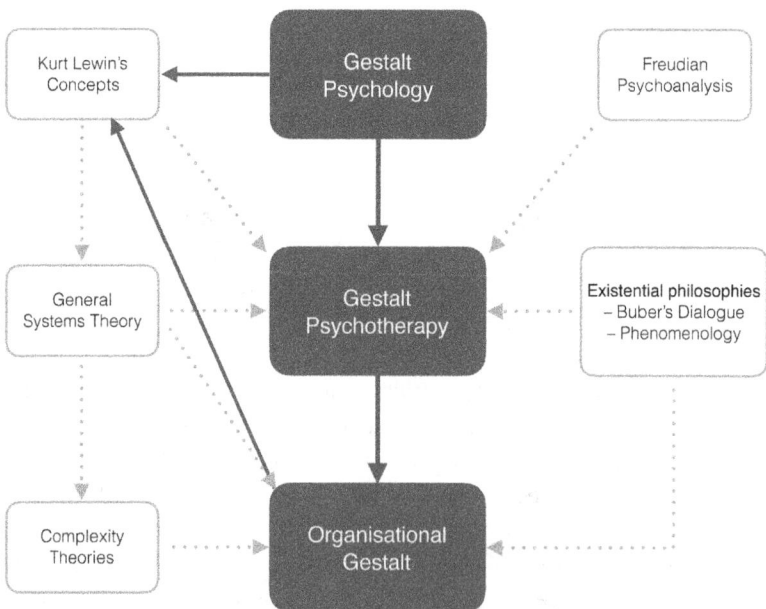

Figure 2.1. Influences on contemporary organisational gestalt.

influences on modern organisational gestalt and how it has emerged as a separate discipline from both gestalt psychology and gestalt psychotherapy.

Gestalt psychology

The German word *Gestalt* remains confusing to many as it has no equivalent in English and can only be loosely translated as "organised whole". It originates from a psychology movement founded in 1912 in Germany that focused on researching the laws of human perception. The central principle of gestalt psychology is that human beings structure what they perceive into meaningful and organised wholes. So, in looking at an image of disconnected shapes, most people will attempt unconsciously to organise the image into something complete and meaningful to them—a clear 'figure' emerges from the "ground" of possibilities.

This tendency towards meaning-making is a fundamental aspect of understanding human experience. In gestalt, understanding what an individual or group is making *figural* and what is left in *ground* is an essential aspect of understanding their experience. As unique individuals, there is a multitude of ways in which we can make meaning of what is around us and the gestalt figure/ground theory highlights this multiplicity of "realities".

To illustrate this further, take a look at the image in Figure 2.2. What do you see? Most of us will be able to alternate between the image of the

Figure 2.2. Figure and ground optical illusion (shutterstock, stock photo id: 257554651).

man's profile and the man facing us. Out of these only two possibilities, perhaps one stands out to you more than the other. What meaning does this hold for you if at all?

This rather simple illusion exemplifies the difficulties faced in organisations when a group come to discuss their financial results or any other organisational data. It would be safe to assume that each person will configure and make meaning of the information in their own particular way. Reaching a joint meaning (or joint figure) often requires dialogue to unravel the various interpretations present as well as willingness from individuals to shift or compromise on their understanding of reality.

* * *

Many of the roots of OD are traceable to the thinking of Kurt Lewin (1935, 1936, 1948, 1951), a German gestalt psychologist who emigrated to the United States in the 1930s to escape Nazi Germany. Lewin gave the field of OD some of its most essential concepts such as field theory, group dynamics, and action research. His work has had a major impact on gestalt psychotherapy and organisational work, notably his notion of field theory.

What is often less known is that Lewin was particularly influenced by gestalt psychology ideas whilst studying at Berlin University between 1924 and 1926. In particular, the notion of *unfinished business* or the *Zeigarnick* effect (Zeigarnick, 1938)—named after the gestalt psychologist Bluma Zeigarnick- was a major input into his thinking on field theory. The Zeigarnick effect states that there is a tendency or "need" to complete a task once it has been initiated and the lack of closure that stems from an unfinished task promotes some continued cognitive effort. The often-quoted story of Bluma Zeigarnick that led to her noticing this phenomenon starts on a cold autumn day in a coffee shop in Vienna. Sitting with a large group of university students, she observed that despite the number of people in their group, the waiter seemed to remember all orders for tea or coffee which were in the process of being served. Once completed however, the waiter did not retain that information even for a short period. Back in the laboratory, Zeigarnik decided to test the theory on her students. She set them a range of tasks such as solving puzzles and stringing beads. In some tasks, she allowed them to finish; in others, she interrupted them half-way through. Afterwards, she discovered that the students were twice as likely to remember the interrupted tasks as the completed ones.

For Lewin, this seemed to prove his theory of psycho-dynamics and eventually led to his notion of field theory. The latter states that human behaviour is a function of *both* the person's psychological needs as well as the needs (i.e., pressures or demands) of the physical environment. According to Lewin (1926), the need organises the field so that what is perceived in the person's field is meaningful in some way to either help or hinder the satisfaction of those needs.

So, the waiter's memory was driven not by his personal want to remember but by the demands and tensions of his environment which required him to recall the orders in order to get paid. Although simplistic today, field theory stood at the time in stark contrast with Freudian understanding of behaviours which stemmed exclusively from internal drives. In other words, Lewin was stating that the whole psychological field—which he called the "lifespace" (Lewin, 1951)—within which people acted had to be viewed, in order to understand behaviour.

Gestalt psychotherapy

Although they share similar names, gestalt psychology and gestalt psychotherapy are distinct disciplines. There is no doubt however that the basic methodology of gestalt therapy is descended philosophically from gestalt psychology (Yontef, 1982; Wheeler, 1991). The founders of gestalt psychotherapy drew upon several disciplines including psychoanalysis, Reichian character analysis, existential philosophy (in particular phenomenology and Martin Buber's dialogue), Eastern religion as well as gestalt psychology and Lewin's work (Smith, 1976; Barlow, 1981).

One of the more significant contributions of Perls, Hefferline, and Goodman (1951), the founders of gestalt psychotherapy, was the joining of various ideas and concepts into a coherent practice of need satisfaction. Starting with Lewin's insight that individual needs (both personal and driven by our environment) determine or configure our field (i.e., how we construct and make meaning of the world around us), then gestalt evolved as a practice of bringing into awareness emergent needs in order to better satisfy them. This process of need fulfilment is seen as a self-regulating process in gestalt and depicted as the cycle of experience (Zinker, 1977).

The early days of gestalt therapy were full of the excitement as they pioneered ideas that differed vastly from the old psychoanalytic drive theory. Emphasis was then on direct experience and active experimentation, trust in organismic self-regulation and ecological interdependence of person and environment (Yontef, 1993). As gestalt therapy grew however, more emphasis was placed on attending to and listening to the client's experience, and the methodology of work moved towards an emphasis on dialogic relating (the method and stance that facilitates interrelatedness) through the work of Hycner and Jacobs (1995) in particular.

Organisational gestalt

It is only from the 1950s with people like Edwin Nevis and Richard Wallen who had a foot in both the organisational camp and psychology (Nevis attended lectures with gestalt psychologists Goldstein and Wertheimer and was a student of Fritz Perls) that the theories of gestalt started being applied to organisational contexts.

Fritz Perls was very influenced by Holism which is the idea that systems (physical, biological, chemical, social, economic, mental, linguistic, etc.) and their properties should be viewed as wholes, not as collections of parts. In the latter half of the twentieth century, holism led to systems thinking and its derivatives, like the sciences of chaos and complexity. It was a natural step therefore for gestalt practitioners to embrace the systems view of organisations as living systems interacting with their environment. As such some gestalt psychotherapy concepts were directly transferable. Edwin Nevis (1987) in his seminal book *Organizational Consulting: A Gestalt Approach* showed how the gestalt notions of cycle of experience and figure/ground were found to work as well at the level of groups and organisations. More information around the cycle and its use in practice can be found in Chapter Six. The gestalt practitioner would for example track the movement of a group through the various stages of the cycle and heightens awareness of the process of change. Gestalt practitioners in organisations are therefore often referred to as "awareness agents" rather than "change agents" as change in gestalt begins with Awareness.

Building on the evolution of contemporary gestalt therapy theory, gestalt organisational practitioners have also emphasised the importance of working phenomenologically (by tracking and staying close to the client experience) and with dialogue. Both aspects of working phenomenologically and with dialogue will be expanded upon in Part II.

It is important also to acknowledge the influence of complexity theories on the application of gestalt in organisations. The field of complexity has introduced into organisational development important concepts which find echo in gestalt theory and practice. In particular it provides a scientific foundation for understating the mechanism of self-regulating systems which gestalt adopts as the basis for its change model but doesn't explain what actually happens in the process of self-regulation (Marmgren, 1998). Complexity and more particularly the ideas derived from complex adaptive systems (CAS) have therefore provided a way of understanding the intricacies of emergent change through self-organising processes. This complements well the gestalt relational and dialogic skills which have been developed through decades of working with human change to support emergence and self-regulation.

It is worth noting that the organisational application of gestalt has matured since its inception and this book brings together ideas and concepts which are best described as relational organisational gestalt (ROG). The greater emphasis on "relational" is of particular significance as it signals a distinct shift from a predominantly systemic view to one that emphasises the dialogic and relational aspects of gestalt theory balancing the impact of the individual as well as the larger system.

Relational organisational gestalt assumptions and characteristics

It is helpful to position the field of relational organisational gestalt (ROG) by highlighting some of the fundamental and distinctive features of its theory and practice in relation to some more classic OD and change management features. This is not intended as an exhaustive overview of ROG but aims to give readers an overall flavour of the distinctiveness of the gestalt approach. The differentiating characteristics are summarised in the table below and will be expanded upon and discussed throughout Part II and III of the book.

Behaviour can only be understood as a function of the relational field

Influenced by Lewin's notions of groups and field theory, gestalt views the person embedded in his or her context, and so recognises that people cannot be validly understood apart from their environment or "field".

Table 2.1. Classic OD *vs.* relational organisational gestalt assumptions.

Classic OD	Relational organisational gestalt
Individual, group or organisational behaviour is knowable, predictable and controllable.	Individual, group and organisational behaviour is a function of the relational field in which they are embedded.
Change is episodic, planned and can be reduced or abstracted to an isolated person or system.	Change is a constant; it is emergent, relational and happens through dialogue.
Facts and data lead to change.	Heightening awareness in the present moment leads to change.
Change is driven by experts and top-down.	Change is co-emergent and requires a balance of challenge and support. Change is both top-down and bottom-up.
The practitioner is a subject matter expert and applies methodologies and tools to bring about change.	The practitioner uses their self as an instrument of change.
Change is assessed against a predefined model of what a "good" (leader, team or organisation) looks like.	Change is guided by aesthetic and embodied knowledge as well as explicit knowledge.

This contrasts with the more conventional viewpoint that people exist as separate and self-contained entities but also have relations with others. In gestalt, this isolated individual is only an abstraction, a reduction that cannot capture the dynamic relationship between person and environment. Similarly, group behaviour cannot be understood apart from the wider organisation or community it sits in, and the organisation itself is inextricably linked to its wider social, economic and cultural ecosystem.

The term "field" (derived from Lewin's field theory) is an informing metaphor to capture all the complex interrelated influences and events that effect individuals, groups or organisations at any one moment in time. For an individual for example, the field contains both "external" social forces and 'internal' personal drives and needs that are all interacting and affecting each other. In organisations the tendency is often to ignore the personal or emotional lifespaces and attribute behaviour only to the immediate present moment and work-related influences.

Trying to separate these intermingling forces and examining them separately would mean dropping into the reductionist trap.

The influence of the historical field is also often underestimated. When for example exploring the constant conflict between two departments in an organisation, it is helpful to look into historical events and experiences that have shaped the existing dynamics. We often find that past conflicts or organisational issues (that may even pre-ate individuals currently in post) have shaped a habitual narrative and way of behaving between the two teams.

Change is a constant; it is emergent, relational and happens through dialogue

Gestalt theory views a person's sense of self as fluid and changing with every interaction rather than rigid and predetermined by their past narrative. We are therefore constantly impacting and being impacted through our relationships and interactions with our environment and changing (both ourselves and others) in that process. Similarly, an organisation is constantly changing as it reacts and interacts within itself and with its customers, suppliers, investors etc.

So, change is a naturally occurring and ongoing phenomenon that we cannot control through fixed ideas, theories or plans. This view is fundamentally different to approaches to change which are bound to set methodologies based on abstract models of behaviour or organisation. For gestalt practitioners, change is co-created, emerges in the moment, and cannot be anticipated or planned for. This is at odds with so much organisational life where meetings or workshops are planned to the last minute and agenda timings are adhered to as a sign of successful and well-run meetings. Little space is made for the emergent moment-to-moment process or for a non-organised conversation and the creativity that can arise from that free-flowing exchange.

As an illustration of this, I sometimes ask a new group to introduce themselves in turn but first to write down what they plan to say in their introduction. I then ask them to put the paper aside and clarify that they are not constrained by what they wrote. People find that those who speak first often stay closer to their written introduction whilst others end up modifying what they say substantially as they take in other people's words as well as the mood and energy in the room. It may seem obvious for this to happen and yet the impact of others and our context is rarely acknowledged in our organisations. We often behave as if change is an individual and isolated process which is consciously chosen and acted upon whilst our experience shows us that it is an emergent and relational process.

In gestalt, the practice of dialogue is viewed as enabling change. It is both a stance towards others as well as a conscious sharing of ourselves which enables something new and unexpected to emerge. As is explored in Chapter Eight, fostering the conditions for dialogue is not always easy in organisational settings as pressure for outcome and action dominates.

Heightening awareness in the present moment leads to change

Gestalt holds a belief in the self-organising capabilities of individuals and systems. This belief derives originally from the concept of homeostasis (Ginger, 2007, p. 112) which refers to the individual's ability to modify their internal environment to ensure stability when responding to changes in the external environment. Although stability is not always guaranteed and largely dependent on the resilience of the system, complexity theories have shown that conditions for self-organisation can be nurtured in individuals as well as groups and larger organisations.

In gestalt the primary driver for self-organising is that of need satisfaction or responding to the most imperative need of the moment. For instance, the most urgent need for a working group might be clarity around a new situation or a deadline for action. The inability to prioritise and agree the most urgent need leads to an ineffective response to the situation in the moment. The working group might be busy with internal debates or even action but these are unlikely to lead to a satisfying outcome as they are not focused on what matters most at this point in time.

Supporting individuals and systems therefore regain a sense of their most pressing need and acting on it is what gestalt views as the process of *heightening awareness*. Ways in which awareness is raised may include an inquiry into the current experience of an individual or group which in gestalt is termed phenomenological inquiry (see Chapter Five), or through experimentation (see Chapter Ten).

Change is co-emergent and requires a balance of challenge and support

Laura Perls (1978) believed that as gestalt practitioners we need to provide as much support as necessary and as little as possible. This position encapsulates the importance in gestalt of holding a balance between challenge and support.

Lynne Jacobs (2006) described "support" as that which enables the other to take the next step. This does not imply a necessary move into action but as Denham-Vaughan (2010, p. 43) writes, support may simply be that which accompanies the other. It is a sense of being alongside to allow or facilitate the unfolding needed for change to occur. In working with groups, we can see this support role in its most basic practice in the chairing of meetings, attending to time and agenda items and in its more complex form, in containing the process of a meeting and dynamics of a group to make it safe enough for demanding conversations to take place.

Challenge on the other hand could be defined as that which agitates/provokes or incites a response or reaction. It need not be a confrontative or provocative stance but could as Nevis (1987, p. 128) writes, also come in the guise of a subtler evocative presence. A challenge in gestalt has a quality of liveliness. It demands attention and tends to introduce an element of newness into a situation or context. As a practitioner, I can choose for example, to challenge a client through sharing my feelings about the mood in the room "there seems to be little energy after your announcement", or a statement about what I observed in a particular interaction.

Maintaining the equilibrium between challenge and support is part of the artfulness of the gestalt practitioner. It is like riding a bicycle and knowing when to accelerate, push hard to get over a steeper hill or a long boring flat road, or alternatively slow down to better navigate tight turns and road bumps. The skills of presence, phenomenological inquiry, and dialogue which are covered in Part II are key to this practice and artistry.

Too much support would be safe but probably boring and little stilted; while too much challenge might be thrillingly anarchic but perhaps offensive or dangerous. The equilibrium of both is analogous to the complexity concept of being at the "edge of chaos" (Kauffman, 1993). The latter refers to a transition space, thought to exist within a wide variety of systems, between order, stability, predictability on one hand,

and disorder, chaos and unpredictability on the other. This transition space of being on the edge of chaos is similar to the gestalt notion of safe emergency (Perls, Hefferline, & Goodman, 1951 [1994], p. 64) and the point at which intervention is most likely to be effective (gestalt interventions and safe emergency are described more fully in Chapter Nine).

The practitioner uses their self as an instrument of change

Nevis defines the "use of self" as the way in which one acts upon one's observations, values, feelings, and so forth, in order to have an effect on the other (Nevis, 1987, p. 125). In other words, making use of oneself as an instrument of change means allowing one's sensations and feelings (as well as one's cognitive knowing) to inform and support richer and potentially more insightful interventions within client systems.

The approach of a gestalt practitioner does not therefore rely on a methodology, but rather transcends any particular technique or tool used. It has more to do with the presence of the individual as they respond or intervene in the "here-and-now" of the situation. A facilitator for instance makes hundreds of in-the-moment decisions whilst facilitating a group's process, such as whether to comment on a leader's particular behaviour or on the entire group's inability to agree; whether to share (or not) an observation of a particular dynamic, or whether to reveal their experience of the tension in the room or the tonality in an interpersonal discussion. These choices are not pre-decided or thought out in advance. They emerge in the moment and rely on the facilitator's ability to assess what would be of most benefit to the individual or group given a particular situation.

The way a practitioner makes use of him or herself to inform their interventions cannot be captured or replicated. It is specific to them. It is linked to the person's internal process: what they sense, feel, notice and respond to. Making use-of-self in an organisational setting therefore requires us to attend to all our senses, and use this information to inform our choices and decisions. The more attuned we can be to what is going on within and around us, and the more clarity we achieve about this data, the more effective our interventions.

Change is guided by aesthetic as well as explicit knowledge

Gestalt holds a belief that human beings, groups, and organisations will self-organise according to the best possible outcome given prevailing conditions. This notion of what is "best" is more often an aesthetic rather than an intellectual response to a situation. For example, we often feel when a meeting or decision is "good" even when we don't have an external benchmark to judge it against. We can sense when a discussion is going well even when no concrete outcomes have been reached, or when a group is beginning to engage and work well together rather than stuck in a quagmire. When a team struggles successfully through a task or difficult situation, the experience feels whole, complete, right, good, and beautiful. The reverse is also true. The stuckness of a team that can't agree and where obstacles and frustrations dominate interactions is aesthetically unpleasant to experience or witness.

We are therefore sensitive to intrinsic sensed qualities of energy and vitality that are often hard to pinpoint or articulate. In gestalt this type of sensing is termed aesthetic as it has more to do with emotional and embodied responses to the situation rather than intellectual ones. In prioritising a holistic approach to awareness, gestalt offers a more inclusive approach to what is valid knowledge. And so, tacit knowledge that corresponds to sensory/aesthetic knowing is as valuable to people and organisations as intellectual/explicit knowing.

Gestalt theory and practice does not therefore hold an external criterion of what "good" is whether for an individual, team or organisation. It does not present an exacting measure or model of what successful change should look like or how organisational elements need to align for a good outcome. It does however embrace an assessment of change as an intrinsic aesthetic criterion which engages the whole of the person; not just the mind but the physical, emotional, intellectual, and even spiritual aspects of self. In gestalt this is called "*good form*" (Zinker, 1994) which refers to the process of change as an aesthetic expression of creating a new well-formed figure which arises from the web of existing elements and yet stands as a vibrant shape of newness.

Capturing this newness through metaphors, images as well as words is a way of naming and embedding the experience of change. For instance, when trying to heighten awareness of the prevailing culture within an organisation, I might ask a team to embody their organisation as an object or animal, explore how they would move, sound and speak. The resulting metaphors not only speak much louder than words about the characteristics and nuances of the organisational culture but communicate an aesthetical narrative of how individuals experience their organisation. Sharing these metaphors is a powerful way of heightening awareness of "what is" in a non-defensive way.

Summary

Through a brief history of gestalt and its influences provided in this chapter, we can see the long intertwining of OD and gestalt theory. The application of the latter to the context of change and organisations is not new. Yet the renewed interest in is application stems from a recognition that today's OD and change approaches need to respond to more complex and uncertain situations. Relational organisational gestalt (ROG) answers this challenge and reiterates the key assumptions and characteristics of gestalt practice emphasising the relational, emergent and dialogic elements of practice.

It is finally interesting to note that gestalt sits mid-way between the diagnostic OD and dialogic OD continuum identified by Bushe (2013). The latter distinguished two major forms of OD practice where: diagnostic OD process is "driven by diagnosing how to objectively align or realign organisational elements (strategies, structure, systems, people, practice, etc.) with the demands of a broader environment as suggested by open systems theory" (Marshak & Bushe, 2013) whilst, dialogic OD is a more fluid socially constructed perspective on change where actions result from prevailing narratives, stories, metaphors and conversations through which people make meaning of their experience (ibid).

Although gestalt includes a diagnostic process and can be viewed from within the more traditional action research frame, it also holds any diagnostic assumption lightly allowing room for emergence and newness. The practitioner therefore is not an expert but a "convener" that co-creates, through awareness raising, the conditions for emergent change.

CHAPTER THREE

The organisational self: a gestalt view of organisational functioning

Selves can only exist in definite relationships to other selves. No hard-and-fast line can be drawn between ourselves and the selves of the others, since our own selves exist and enter as such into our experience only in so far as the selves of the others exist and enter as such into our experience also.

—*Mead*, 1934, p. 164

Rather than a holistic view of organisations as complex, interactive entities, the pull towards a simplified, categorised understanding of how organisations function is still very present. Various models aim to break down the major components in a bid to better manage or control events and people. Most dissections are along the lines of "process", "people", "structure", or "IT" with the illusion that these components can be managed separately

The illusion would be similar to trying to explain human beings as a set of arms, legs, head, heart, etc., and loses the sense and intricacy of the whole "self". Similarly, organisations need to be viewed as whole selves and gestalt offers a way of understanding this based on its theory of self.

Previous chapters have highlighted the importance of viewing organisations as living systems and how gestalt has evolved as a reaction against the reductive, behaviourist understanding of people and organisations. This chapter will now outline a gestalt view of an organisational self and how this supports change practitioners in thinking about their interventions with people, groups and organisations.

The "self" in gestalt

To anchor their work, all organisational practitioners need a set of assumptions about how change comes about. Lewin (1951) wrote of needing to "unfreeze" forces in a system to bring about change before a new system "equilibrium" could be found. Other theories of change such as learning organisations (Senge, 1990), self-organising systems (Wheatley, 1999), and complex adaptive systems (Olson & Eoyang, 2001) to name a few; all provide a different shift in perspective that has led to innovation in OD practice.

Gestalt similarly offers a different and useful perspective on organisations and change. This view emerges from the notion of self in gestalt theory and can inform the way we engage with organisations (Chidiac & Denham-Vaughan, 2009).

In gestalt, our sense of self emerges at every moment from our interaction with others and the environment. The self is therefore constantly changing and adjusting according to the situation within which it finds itself. It is fluid and dynamic, responsive to the environment, and experiencing changing needs and goals as the situation changes.

The purpose of the self however, is to organise this emerging and changing experience to make it meaningful. This meaning making process is termed "self-functioning" and is accompanied by the "self-structures" of "id", "ego", and "personality" (Perls, et al., 1951 [1994]). Unlike the Freudian concepts of id, ego, and super-ego, or the Jungian concepts of self, these three aspects of self (id, ego, and personality) are not fixed structures or psychic demands, but ways of relating to the world. These "self-functioning" aspects contribute in different ways to our meaning-making process and therefore resulting behaviour.

- The id function is the most receptive state of the self. In id functioning, often our needs, wants or interests are not yet in conscious awareness or have not been clearly grasped or languaged. If I were entering a group or organisation for example, this phase might describe my initial sense of being overwhelmed, not knowing any norms or groundrules, and lacking a sense of the culture. As id functions develop, meaning begins to coalesce and at this point we begin to consciously grasp our individual personhood within that particular world. In other words, I start to gain a hold on what this particular place and moment in time means to me and what are my needs. I may ask myself "what does this smell, wallpaper or logo mean to me?"

- The ego function is the clear identification of a figure of interest. Put more simply, it is the choice we make in responding to our needs, wants or interests. It is what we say or do, often involving action imperatives and a sense of "knowing" or familiarity. It describes the moments when I start to ask myself and/or others those questions that I have decided are important. That is, I let go of any impressions of the wallpaper or logo, but decide that the smell in the hallway quite clearly reminds me of a restaurant with too much fried foods that I didn't like. I also decide that given how strongly this impacts on me, I make a choice in how I will respond to my dislike and therefore my course of action.

- Finally, the personality function is the enduring or slow-moving aspect of self. It is our narrative or story and contains the meaning we have made from the accumulation of our experience. As such it forms a ground which can organise all other aspects of self. If we wish to be truly open to emerging impressions and sensations, we need to be vigilant to the tendency of our personality function to organise experience in habitual ways whereby we behave in very predictable patterns, asking similar questions, making similar interventions, etc. This will specifically impact our healthy id functioning and considerably reduce our ability to be creative and in tune with the moment.

In practice, it is impossible to see these self-structures separately; they are intimately intertwined in an indivisible and ongoing process through which we contact and engage with the world.

The gestalt concept of self provides us with a relational framework for interacting with the world, one in which we impact on, and are impacted by, all what is around us. Furthermore, it takes account of emergent, out of awareness processes (Id), as well as more conscious choices or actions (Ego) and enduring aspects of ourselves (personality).

An organisational self

As complex systems, organisations—like individual people or groups—can also be meaningfully viewed through the lens of the gestalt theory of self. That is, they are also formed within a network of emerging relationships and depend on those relationships. They are also constantly changing and shifting as these relationships change. Rather than understanding an organisation in light of what it "does", a "self" view invites us to perceive organisations as constantly emerging and responding to the multiple nonlinear relationships and influences happening at any one time. The extent however of this fluidity of self and responsiveness is contingent on the organisation's historical experiences and narrative.

The view of the organisation as self is best captured through a wave metaphor shown in Figure 3.1 where:

• The actual body of the wave (or ego function) is the most visible part of self-functioning in terms of what the organisation says or does- its resulting action. At an organisational level, this would include for example the organisation's hierarchy or structure, its vision/mission, strategy, goals as well as procedures and processes. Also visible are often the clearly identified influences on an organisation (e.g., supplier pressures, policies, etc.) which are represented in the model as the surface wind that influences resulting action. As organisational practitioners or consultants, this is what we are most often called

Wave as Ego
Above the surface, visible, what we say we do – the resulting action

Sea Waters as Id
Less visible, unacknowledged dynamics, connected to local currents and flows

Seabed as Personality
Sedimented but changing slowly with time - the culture and narrative

Figure 3.1. The organisation as self—a wave analogy.

in to support: the more clearly visible or articulated aspect of the organisation's ego functioning.

- The sea waters below the wave (or id function) are the less visible influences or dynamics of an organisation. These are usually less in awareness (or even unconscious) and not articulated by the organisation. Typically, these internal dynamics or external influences would not be recognised by the organisation and may include for example, unwritten rules, internal tensions, covert power struggles or even undetected external influences such as changing stakeholder or customer needs. For instance, we can sometimes notice in organisations with very flat structures, which pride themselves in not having much formal hierarchy, that there often exist unwritten rules of behaviour which define an implicit, unarticulated hierarchy. These may manifest in informal groupings (going for drinks after work) or complex circles of influence.

- The seabed (or personality function) is the more "sedimented" ways of being of an organisation which are typically linked to the prevailing narrative and culture. In gestalt theory, the personality function is the enduring or slow-moving aspect of self. It is our narrative or story and contains the meaning we have made from the accumulation of our experience. It is easy to see how the seabed/personality function forms a ground that can contribute to organising other aspects of self. The story or history of a group or organisation is often what shapes its distinct rules, values and way of being—the "way things are done around here" and we can often see this reflected in many details in that organisation from who gets allocated a parking slot or office, or even in the layout and positioning of desks within a department.

The advantage of the wave conceptualisation is that it is dynamic, constantly forming, reacting, shaping, and being shaped by its environment. It also speaks to today's interconnected economy in which organisations (even large ones) are not isolated but rather operate within a web of connections and need to adapt to these and their changing environments. In that sense we can recognise that the id function (sea waters) is a combination of both internal dynamics (swirls in the seawaters) or external influences (underwater currents). Similarly, the ego function (body of the wave) will be shaped by visible external pressures (local winds) as well as the swirls and currents in the sea waters or indeed the shape or density of the seabed.

Experiential exercise

Take a moment to consider an organisation (or department, or team) that you know well. Reflect on the following questions.

1. What is your sense of the internal dynamics of this organisation/ group (e.g., interpersonal tensions, lack of clarity or alignment, sense of stuckness or inaction)? [Id function]
2. What are the external influences you are aware of that may not be fully acknowledged or responded to in the organisation/group (e.g., changing customer, key stakeholder needs)? [Id function]
3. What is the history, culture, values or myths of the organisation/group (e.g., what stories/events do people talk about or mention, what are the unwritten rules or repeating patterns)? [Personality function]
4. For each of the above questions, how do you see your answers shape or impact resulting behaviour in the organisation/group? How does this compare to how the organisation/group presents itself in terms of what is said and done (e.g., goals, mission/vision statement, key processes)?

From this exercise, you will begin to appreciate that the starting point for change in gestalt is heightening awareness of all influences particularly those that are "below the surface", unacknowledged or unnamed. As we have covered in Chapter Two, awareness leads to change. Supported organisations, teams, and individuals when presented with what influences their action and behaviour, are likely to choose differently. As gestalt practitioners we therefore focus primarily on raising awareness of both id and personality functioning and make links to how this is impacting resulting action—i.e., the body of the wave.

Very often the work of managers or OD practitioners centres on what needs to be fixed, put right or achieved and the wave itself (the resulting action or behaviour) is what is most noticeable and focused on. Consultants are often called in when processes are broken or the strategy is not providing desired outcomes. Most organisational interventions then focus on fixing the wave, remaining at the level of what is said, done or clearly articulated such as restructuring or re-engineering processes. Experience suggests however that just attending to the rational and visible aspects of change does not lead to sustainable interventions.

In gestalt, we appreciate that as human beings in organisations, it is often the less rational or visible dynamics that impact behaviour.

Attending therefore to the inter-personal, emotional, and less articulated aspects of our meaning making processes allows us to understand more effectively our behaviour and therefore the resulting shape of the wave. This wave metaphor shows how the shape or face of the wave, i.e., the resulting behaviour and action of an organisation, department or team, emerges as a function of the internal dynamics and external environment as well as the ingrained narrative and culture of the business.

Example one: shallow waters

Two years after privatisation, a public-sector organisation was beginning to see its profitability decline. The CEO encouraged his team to launch change initiatives in a bid to cut costs and satisfy shareholders. In response to the CEO's call for action, senior managers mobilised rapidly, moving to action with a flood of activity which focused primarily on fixing the bottom-line profit through leaner operations and headcount reductions. Given the CEO's autocratic style, there was little challenge or questioning of his call to action. Used also to a dominant position in the market place, the organisation did not attend enough to the maturing service requirements in their customers which were being served by smaller competing businesses. The organisation's response was thus fixated on the visible problem rather than sense the id or sea waters to explore internal dynamics or external influences that might be at play.

In this example, we can view this organisation as having insufficient sensing of its id functioning—and in the metaphor, the sea waters are shallow and both internal dynamics and external influences are not detected. We know that in shallow waters, the wave is shaped by the structure of the seabed and so unsurprisingly without sensing into the present context or situation, the initiatives of senior managers were based largely on their historical narrative: "how things used to be".

And so, poor attendance to the organisation's id function (shallow waters)—in terms of internal dynamics (swirls in the seawaters) or external influences (underwater currents) will result in a "desensitised" organisation and one that is not able to adapt to its changing environment. Wollants (2012) writes of the importance of attending and sensing into the "id of the situation" or in other words "what is given, what there is out there waiting to be uncovered and what calls for the client's attention, implicitly informing him about what the situation implies for him and what it demands of him" (ibid, p. 105).

Example two: sedimented seabed

Encyclopedia Britannica is a typical and well-known example of an organisation that suffered from poor attendance to its changing environment and customer needs. It was slow to react and adapt—stopping its weighty thirty-two-volume print edition to focus on digital expansion quite late amid rising competition from other websites such as Wikipedia. It is fair to say that the organisation was well aware of the changing customer requirements and the rise of the digital marketplace as it launched a digital version of the encyclopaedia. What was more difficult to let go of, was their own expertise over content and the acknowledgment of a more collaborative online construction of knowledge which Wikipedia built on. In the case of *Encyclopedia Britannica*, the sea waters were not shallow as the organisation was well aware or changing external landscape but the power of the culture or narrative was so strong, the seabed too sedimented or rigid and resistant to change.

A rocky and rigid seabed will hugely influence the shape of the wave and unless this ocean floor is loosened somewhat, it results in an entrenched organisational memory and prevailing narrative. As Govindarajan and Trimble writes: "Deeply rooted memory may be great for preservation, but if it is not tamed sufficiently, it gets in the way of creation" (2011, p. 110). If the ground of the narrative or personality function is too rigid, then assimilating change is difficult. We know that the elasticity of an organisation's culture and dominant narrative—the malleability or plasticity of its seabed—is linked to its ability to learn and experiment with newness.

So, while poor attendance to an organisation's id function reduces adaptive capacity, an entrenched narrative or culture (personality function) is also an impediment to change. Organisational practitioners or managers often hear resistance to change being expressed as "this is how things are done here". This entrenched position or rigidity of the personality function within an organisation or team needs attention. If it is over-ridden or ignored, change will not be sustained. For example, we often witness the benefits of large process re-engineering projects decline after the consultants have left. The change in behaviour needed to support the new processes is often not embraced, and so historical or cultural ways of being, and of making meaning, are still in place and hindering the change effort.

Example three: malleable seabed

At Google, employees are encouraged to innovate. The Google "70-20-10" rule directs engineers to spend seventy percent of their time on core business tasks and twenty per cent on related projects, but allows them to spend ten percent of their time pursuing their own ideas (Jaruzelski & Dehoff, 2010; Steiber, 2014). This rule has been pivotal to Google's success as it has encouraged employees to experiment and develop new products that might never have seen the light of day. So, Google's internal processes themselves encourage innovation and change. The seabed in this case is very malleable as the company expects the next product/innovation to sustain and even transform the business.

Often business literature implies that the malleability, speed, responsiveness of companies like Google is the way forward for all organisations. Today fast and speedy responses to stay ahead of the game or of perceived threats are admired and encouraged. But what if an organisation's culture is not geared for this pace of change? What if this pace of response, of decision making, of mobilisation is in fact not consistent with the overall values of the organisation or what it believes in or holds dear? Many employees of the British National Health Service (NHS) for example, would see in the increasing change initiatives over the last decade an erosion of what they had originally come into the organisation for: the passion for service and the values that attracted them. A balance in this case is needed between preserving the positive narrative and values within the organisation whilst improving service often hampered by an overly rigid seabed. In many non-western cultures as well, a quickness to mobilise or lack of full consensus building is more often than not seen as rash and a sign of not having listened or consulted enough. The wave metaphor does not therefore imply that a sandy seabed is best, more responsive or that bottomless depth of seawater is more effective. Rather it is the overall coherence of the organisation (the way the different self-functions interrelate) that needs to be considered as well as its embeddedness in its existing context and situation.

Implications for practice of a gestalt organisational self-perspective

One consequence of the view of an organisation as an interconnected living organism is that its sense of self is not static. Organisational life is constantly being shaped at every moment by a multitude of influences both past and present, both internal and external to the perceived boundary of that organisation. All aspects of an organisation (id, ego, and personality) are interconnected and so an intervention in any part will impact the totality of the organisation's self.

As we have mentioned earlier, some change approaches operate and intervene primarily at the surface of the wave (ego function); in the realm of what is explicit, rational, and measurable. The strength of gestalt is however in exploring what is below the surface of the wave and bringing the human dynamics and implied processes to awareness. A gestalt practitioner would therefore typically invite individuals, teams or organisations to uncover the implicit and possibly unconscious to support new, different and more aware movements to action.

Improvement in organisations often linked to particular measures or KPIs (key performance indicators). For instance, a decrease in a customer satisfaction measure may typically lead to diagnosis of processes, technology or even behaviours that contribute to that particular measure. Underlying such an approach is the assumption of linear cause and effect linkages and that any problem or issue can be deconstructed and fixed. In some conditions of stability or where the main issues are linked solely to technology or process, then such an approach may indeed yield good results. When dealing with people and behavioural change, they often do not.

So, when change issues are well known, requirements clearly articulated, and the problems easily solvable or at least the endpoint plainly identifiable, then a gestalt approach may seem redundant. The intervention needed is at the surface or body of the wave. We could argue that in those environments, there is little need to create conditions for a new self-organising solution to emerge as the endpoint is known. Gestalt is most suitable however when we want to delve below the surface of the wave, when a different change strategy is needed, one that is more implicit, embodied and emergent.

Despite failure rates in planned change projects as high as seventy per cent (Sackmann, et al., 2009), "conscious, planned change [is perceived] as infinitely preferable to unconscious, emergent change" (Livne-Tarandach & Bartunek, 2009, p. 11). The need for certainty and the anxiety in stepping towards the unknown, leads most change initiatives to adopt traditional planned change management strategies. There is therefore an inherent tension in the type of OD and change work that delve below the surface of the wave. It requires a balance between simultaneously supporting and soothing the anxiety of a leader (and practitioner) and inviting them to take a leap of faith; to trust that with increased awareness and dialogue comes more coherent and sustainable change.

For most people in organisations including many OD practitioners, this starting position can be seen as disruptive and uncomfortable. So, when is a gestalt emergent approach most needed or warranted given the higher level of anxiety that it might generate compared to pre-arranged, sequential and a more conscious approach?

Here, it is useful to introduce Rittell and Webber's (1973) typology of "tame" and "wicked" problems. A tame problem is one that may be complicated but holds only a limited degree of uncertainty and a standard procedure should solve the problem. Examples would include: timetabling the railways, building a nuclear plant or planned heart surgery. A wicked problem on the other hand, is complex rather than complicated. In other words, there is no predictability to it and no clear relationship between cause and effect. A key characteristic of wicked problems are the interconnected nature of these problems which we may struggle to define or contain.

When considering situations and problems involving human beings or organisations as complex and adaptive, we are necessarily in the realm of wicked problems. The complex nature of the "selfing" process precludes predictability and so any standardised approach will fail or be unsustainable. Key characteristics of wicked and tame problems (ibid) are summarised in Table 3.1.

If we believe that sustainable organisational change is fundamentally linked to behavioural change, then an emergent gestalt approach is needed and suitable. And so rather than polarising emergent and planned approaches to change, they are best viewed as a dialectic. In other words, effective change requires a to-ing and fro-ing between designed intent and disorganised newness. In inviting clients or organisations to work below the surface of the wave requires practitioners to

Table 3.1. The distinction between wicked and tame problems (Rittell & Webber, 1973).

Wicked	Tame
No definitive formulation to the problem. There is always more than one explanation of the problem.	Characteristics are known. The boundaries of the problem can be articulated or defined.
There is no idealised end state to arrive at.	The end state can be articulated.
Every wicked problem is a symptom of another problem. There is a high level of interconnectedness.	The tame problem can be considered in isolation from its context or situation.
There is no template to follow. Every wicked problem is unique.	Similar problem has been solved or tackled before.

come up for air at regular interval and check the client's anxiety, meaning making as well as meet their need for mobilisation and action.

Key relational gestalt abilities

Based on the above conceptualisation of an organisational self, key relational gestalt abilities stand out as essential to support good enough organisational "selfing". The latter is often referred to in gestalt as "good form", a sort of aesthetic harmony between ego, id and personality functions so that behaviour and action are in response to emergent needs and dynamics arising from the sea waters and ocean floor.

These relational abilities shown in Figure 3.2 superimposed on the wave metaphor are as follows:

- Sensing ability—as the stance or activities that track and stay responsive to all three aspect of the organisation's self-functioning (id, ego, and personality). Although quantitative data is often useful to track and measure in organisations (particularly in ego functioning), sensing here is more particularly the ability to notice and heighten awareness of interpersonal and subjective processes.
- Supporting ability—as the stance or activities that enables the movement from awareness into new action and change. Knowing what needs to change doesn't always lead to change. Organisations like

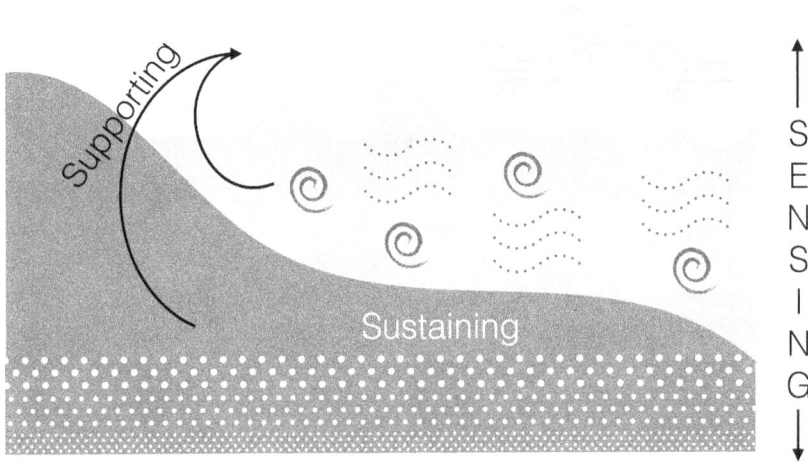

Figure 3.2. Key relational abilities and the wave metaphor.

teams or individuals require often the right conditions for emergent change to flourish. Supporting is what accompanies and makes that movement from awareness to change possible.

• Sustaining ability—as the stance or activities that crystallise change and new learning. These address the often more entrenched or slow-moving aspect of self: the personality function. Recognising that for change to be sustainable, new learning needs to be reflected upon, chewed, embedded, and embodied. Sustainability is achieved when newness becomes habit.

These three organising abilities rely on a fourth: the instrumentality of the practitioner. What is meant by this is not only the knowledge of the gestalt practitioner but their *presence* in the client system and how their use of self as instruments of change is an integral part of any intervention.

These four interlinked elements (practitioner presence, sensing, supporting, sustaining) will be explored in Part II of this book. Separating them may seem like a reduction of a greater whole, of a gestalting process as of course none of these abilities can stand alone. They are intricately interwoven and dependent of each other and come together as steps of a dance in the work of gestalt practitioners. The hope is that they provide some structure to what follows in Part II as the particular skills and philosophy behind gestalt organisational work are unpacked.

Summary

There is nothing possibly more responsive, adaptive and emergent as our selfing process as we encounter and interact with the world. This chapter has put forward a view of an "organisational self" derived from gestalt theory and practice which captures the complexity, adaptability, and responsiveness of organisations. The view of an organisation as a wave illustrates how gestalt work is mostly focused on what happens below the surface, both in the present moment (id) and historical experiences (personality), and which shapes organisations.

This positions gestalt as an intervention which supports emergent change by exploring the less explicit or unaware aspects of organisational life. As such it supports practitioners to work with the complexity of human dynamics and recognise that even planned change situations are emergent as they take account of the uniqueness of individuals and situations.

This chapter ends with the naming of four key relational gestalt abilities (practitioner presence, sensing, supporting, sustaining), which will be explored in Part II of the book.

PART II

GESTALT CONCEPTS AND PRACTICES

This part of the book separates out and explores the abilities which underpin gestalt work in organisations. These abilities are described as *sensing* and heightening awareness of organisational processes, *supporting* action that emerges from that awareness and finally, *sustaining* change as it crystallises into a new way of being. These are not intended as sequential steps or a methodology of action but rather a loose road-map or guide to working with people in organisations. Each ability is intricately linked to the other and so they need to be viewed as elements of a whole, or individual notes in a musical structure. Balancing time and emphasis between each ability is what creates the tune and harmony of the work.

Central to the use of these abilities in a gestalt way is the notion of "presence". This part of the book will therefore begin by outlining in

Chapter Four what is meant by presence and situating it as a relational process. Each ability will then be explored in turn in the remainder of Part II. The application of these abilities to various OD interventions such as coaching, consulting or facilitation will be illustrated through examples.

Presence

Presence is not just a theoretical exploration—fascinating though it may be—but an essential pre-condition to gestalt work. At the heart of gestalt as Perls, Hefferline, and Goodman (1951 [1994]) write, is meeting the other at the "contact boundary" (p. xviii) which is a journey into the unknown, an opening to emergence. It is where we impact and influence others in ways that we could not have anticipated or foreseen. Staying steady, supported, and responsive in that space is the gift of presence.

CHAPTER FOUR

A relational orientation and ethical presence

P resence can be positioned at the heart of the gestalt approach because it is a core condition for the effective instrumentality of the practitioner, which in gestalt is called the "use-of-self". We have explored in previous chapters how the gestalt approach does not rest on a methodology of action but is responsive to the uniqueness of a situation and that responsiveness is a distinctive ingredient of a practitioner's presence.

This chapter will first explore the evasive and somewhat mysterious connotations surrounding the word "presence" before providing a gestalt based view of presence as "energetic availability and fluid responsiveness" (Chidiac & Denham-Vaughan, 2007). This definition clearly positions presence as a relational process, one that is strongly situated and takes place through connection and relationship rather than just an acquired skill or attribute. What is meant by "relational" in this context will also be explained and links made between a relational orientation and an ethical presence.

Finally, this chapter will propose a conceptual framework (CARES model) which attempts to unravel the self-dimensions of "being present" into five key attitudes and skills. This is not meant as a recipe for presence but rather a route map for practitioners to reflect on aspects they need to hone in themselves in being more relationally and ethically present.

Being present: energetic availability and fluid responsiveness

When people in organisations are asked about the qualities they most appreciate in managers, coaches, consultants or facilitators they had worked with, the answers seem invariably to centre on attributes that go beyond the ability of these individuals to do their job. Comments like: "It is something about how they were: people listen to them" or, "It is the unusual and yet accurate observations they made", or even "it is the way they listened and understood our problem" seem to focus on what is often referred to as the practitioner's presence. This intangible quality of presence remains largely ill-defined. Some try and explain it by focusing on given skills or qualities in the person: good listening and communication skills, attractive stature, articulate and attractive speech or accent, etc. Yet these elements of skill or style don't seem to capture the essence of presence.

In researching the notion of presence (Chidiac & Denham-Vaughan, 2007), it was important to address both the experience of "being with" presence as well as what it felt like to be present in oneself. Being with presence holds an intense attraction. It is a feeling of having captured the interest of the other and having been given it easily. "I notice you noticing me, and I feel seen." Meeting people with presence, arouses a sense of having their full attention, of being attentively listened to and met in a way that is deeply enthralling.

Alternatively, when feeling present, people report a sense of feeling well resourced and engaged with what is around them. This could be described as a state of being grounded or centred from which I can choose to just "be"; or feel moved to act and intervene. It need not be a place of certainty in the outcome or influence as can be seen in the following account of a facilitator's sense of presence at the start of a workshop.

A facilitator's description of feeling present

I have been asked by my client, the head of a business unit to facilitate an away day for his leadership team. Team dynamics and behaviours have been putting a strain on the effectiveness of his team to carry out their day-to-day job, and my client wanted to take some time away from their daily routines to address the issues. I could still hear my client's voice fretting over the phone yesterday evening, his nervousness about the day still present despite several meetings—getting this right was important to him.

I arrive early, familiarise myself with the surroundings of my work today. With no one there yet, I can start configuring the physical space, moving furniture, opening windows, placing flip-charts to best support myself and the day's process.

The music is starting, excitement and anxiety mix as the sounds of Abba rises in the recesses of my mind … "Mamma Mia, here we go again …!" I feel energised and ready for the day.

The participants arrive, I breathe deeply and feel my body relax and tune into the music of the moment. Check in has already started each person declaring themselves in the way they walk in the room, greet others or not. Some continue on with their phone conversations, just waving before settling down and opening their laptop. I could fill in the words implicit in the behaviours … "I didn't want to come to this meeting", "It is a waste of time", "I'm too busy for this!"

I go through the day's agenda and ask for expectations and ground rules, inviting each one to check in verbally—and where possible name any reservations they might have about the day. This for them is already different from a regular meeting and I notice looks of apprehension and interest.

I attend to my own feelings and how each person impacts me. The words flow in the background whilst I notice the challenge in a person's voice or the invitation in another's smile. As a facilitator, this is the work of establishing a working alliance as the group gets to know me as a facilitator as I model the parameters of my role as I see it.

Simultaneously, I need to gauge the impact of my style and way of being on this new group. Am I taking too much space in this field, do I need to step back and let the group come forward? Are the boundaries I am undoubtedly setting safe or restrictive?

> Whilst this intimate and relational knowing unfolds, I shuttle between my awareness of it and my need to attend to the wider process and task of the meeting.
>
> I know there are too many levels to attend to simultaneously and I need to trust that I remain available enough to deal with aspect that I might have missed. What anchors and liberates me is the confidence of knowing who I am in this context and what I am trying to do or my intent in this moment. Worrying about the content of what I am delivering restricts me in attending fully to what is happening around me.
>
> I feel mostly carried by the sense of the task as it unfolds, keeping it on track. I remain attentive to the inhalation and exhalation of the group as they attend to the task, how are they breathing, what are energy levels like both as a group and within that as individuals as they choose to differentiate themselves. I am aware of my client as he starts to relax into the process.

In this example of a first-person account of feeling present, we can notice energy in the readiness and intent of the facilitator, as well as their responsiveness to what emerges. This dialectic of stepping forward and shaping as well as letting go and allowing space is at the heart of presence. As shown in Table 4.1 below, this state can be captured in the combination of "energetic availability and fluid responsiveness" (ibid). It is a wholly relational concept as it arises from the current environment and lived moment. It cannot be rehearsed, and yet it must be planned for, in so far as one musters all of one's resources prior to setting out on a trip.

Table 4.1. Presence as energetic availability and fluid responsiveness.

	Energetic availability	Fluid responsiveness
As I experience presence in others	Feeling deeply attracted by presence in others. Feeling noticed and seen by the other.	Being listened to and fully understood. Feeling held/safe and with a person that is well resourced.
As I experience my own presence	Alert yet calm. Attentive to, and connecting with, others and the situation around me.	Knowing what I know liberates me to focus on others, on what emerges in the situation.

Presence as a relational and ethical process

What stood out most clearly from this research is the understanding of presence as a relational process. But what do we mean by relationality?

What does "relational" mean?

The word "relational" is increasingly widely used in organisational development (OD), psychotherapy, coaching, leadership as well as in everyday conversation. What is meant by "relational" in this book transcends the usually polarised view of either attending to the other or being of service to others, versus seeing the other as a resource to satisfy one's own needs. Rather as described by Denham-Vaughan and Chidiac (2013), it is based on a key post-modern concept: the idea that rather than individual things, events or people being the main, sometimes only, focus of attention, it is the relationships existing between or amongst them that offers maximum possibility for change.

This can be viewed in organisational development for example, as a move away from viewing organisational issues arising only from the organisation's shortfall or the manager's incompetence to a broader focus on the relationships they have, (both with others and between them) and the situation and context in which these connections arise.

As Denham-Vaughan and Chidiac (ibid, p. 101) write, "the quality of our relationships powerfully define and shape the 'quality' of us as individuals, (be that individual people, teams, organisations or communities)". Indeed, neurobiological research, (e.g., Siegel, 2007), reveals that our developing brains, although genetically informed, are very heavily influenced by our relationships with others throughout our lives. Similarly, it is well documented (e.g., Kotter & Heskett, 1992; Truskie, 1999; Alvesson, 2002) that these foundational webs of relationships and interactions within an organisation determine the emerging sense of culture and identity, and has a profound impact on resulting productivity and performance.

This relational paradigm is captured in the SOS Model (Denham-Vaughan & Chidiac, 2013) which proposes that a relational stance is one that finds a balance between the three interrelated elements illustrated in Figure 4.1:

- Self; which can be seen as either the individual, group, community or organisation;

CONTEXT

self

other   situation

CULTURE

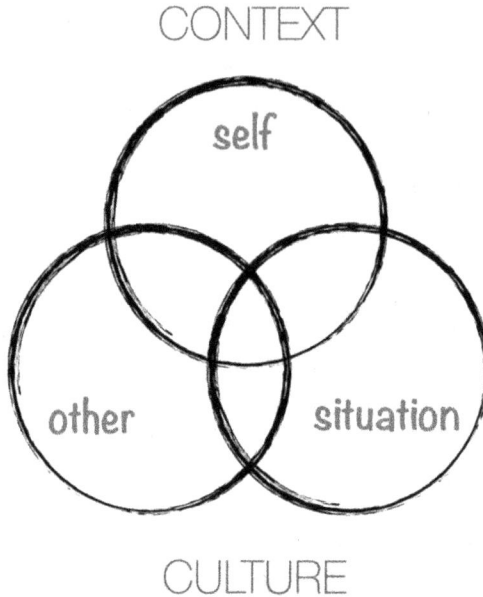

Figure 4.1. The SOS (self, other, situation) model.

- Other; as the "other" in the relationship at any given moment. When self-reflecting, this can be the "other within the self", or for a business this can be competitors or allies from whom they differentiate.
- Situation is the particular set of happenings occurring in any given moment. In a workshop for example, this could be the conflict arising between two participants, or the unexpected absence of a key member of the team.

As seen in Figure 4.1, these three lenses of self, other, and situation do not sit in a vacuum but are embedded in a given context and culture. Situation is a temporal happening which we respond to in the moment whilst context and culture are often less in awareness, more in ground, but nonetheless exert a continuous influence on our behaviours, beliefs and values.

Relational presence

Presence therefore as a relational process, is an energetic availability and fluid responsiveness to our self, to others and to the situation in

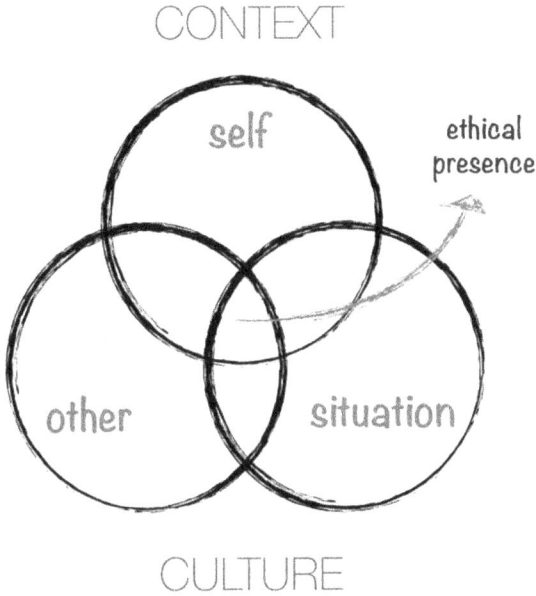

Figure 4.2. Ethical presence at the centre of the SOS model.

the present moment. So, as shown in Figure 4.2 locating presence at the heart of the "SOS" framework is a natural step. Presence is a state of being fully embodied, resonant with others and the current context and ready to creatively respond. In this state we bring all of our future potential, and previous experience, into the present moment to innovate and co-emerge with the situation.

Viewing presence as embedded in and dependent on culture and context is also useful. This moves us away from picturing set attributes of presence across cultures. Global leaders for example fully understand the usefulness to adapt and calibrate their style and presence to the prevailing norms and cultural expectations. The example of Steve Ballmer (ex-CEO of Microsoft) below is a good illustration of how presence is contextual and cultural.

Some may remember Steve Ballmer the previous CEO of global giant Microsoft. If not, a quick google search on "Steve Ballmer going crazy" would show you a clip of Ballmer running on a stage and hopping around while squealing, screaming, and making other various high-pitched noises after being introduced at a Microsoft worker's meeting.

> The question is: do you think the then-CEO of Microsoft had "presence"?
>
> When asking a British audience, most people would promptly answer by the negative and yet, for the audience at the time, Ballmer was totally appropriate in his responsiveness to people's expectations of him. Although one might argue that he had not attended sufficiently to his self-awareness (he was clearly panting and heavily out of breath!), his behaviour was in tune with the culture and context and seemed to energise his audience.

An ethical dimension

When the three lenses of self, other, and situation are all operating in ways that respond to the demand qualities of context and culture, then we are most "present". Inherent in this relational model is an acknowledgment of our interconnectedness as human beings living together and increasingly dependent on collaboration for the survival of our planet and future generations. Indeed "SOS" is also a globally recognised distress call and a reminder that we are all interconnected, vulnerable and in need of help and support.

So implicit in the realisation of interdependence and relationality are deeply held values about presence as it is defined here. Energetic availability is a genuine openness to all aspects of the other (including his or her difference), rather than a pretence of openness or availability that is conditional on an acceptance of the other as long as they agree or align with us. In the example of sects with deeply charismatic leaders, we can see how a yearning to belong and be accepted can lead to total confluence with what the leader desires or preaches. It is also clear that some personalities, performers or politicians also hold the ability for fluid responsiveness or "resonance". A stand-up comic for example, attunes to his or her audience and fluidly responds to the shifting mood in the room. Similarly, a skilled politician or chairman is able to read the atmosphere of a meeting and respond appropriately to reach his or her agenda or preferred outcome.

So being ethically present is a state of mind to cultivate when working in organisations: whether individuals are in the role that identifies with potentially more power and control or less. Presence comes with authenticity as well as clarity of intent: an ethical stance in service of the other. This is why personal preparation is a key element of presence. In paying attention to our impact and responding to it, ethical presence serves as an antidote to toxic enactments leading to shame, guilt, abuse, fear or even trauma.

The CARES model

For organisational practitioners, presence is the primary condition for the use-of-self with intent. When asked to describe a moment of being fully present, most people recount experiencing themselves differently. Individuals speak of vibrancy, aliveness, feeling both connected, and strangely settled. These characteristics of presence experienced from the first-person perspective are captured here in the CARES model (shown in Figure 4.3) where CARES stands for:

- C—Connection
- A—Authenticity
- R—Range
- E—Embodied sensing
- S—Self support

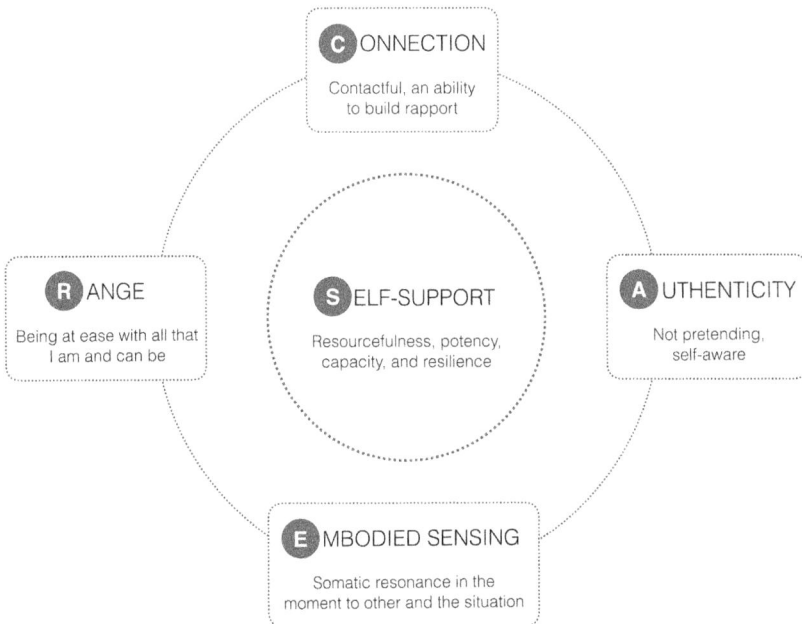

Figure 4.3. The CARES model.

Although these characteristics can only represent a subjective view of presence—in the sense that we can never fully capture the experience of others—they stand here in the hope of providing practitioners some frame against which they can reflect and work on their own presence.

Connection

Reflecting on the work of Martin Buber, Friedman (1955) notes that at the heart of connection to other is "making present". He writes: "Making the other present means to 'imagine' the real, to imagine quite concretely what another man is wishing, feeling, perceiving and thinking [...]. It is through this making present that we grasp another as a self" (ibid, p. 82).

The ability to establish connection relies fundamentally on understanding the world, thoughts, and feelings of the other person. As human beings however, we only have access to our own experience and cannot have a direct knowing of what is happening for others. So, connecting rests primarily on our ability to extrapolate from our own experience into the experience of others. This attitude or stance has been described by many, notably as empathy (Carl Rogers) or inclusion (Martin Buber), and is one which we all respond to favourably as it is an important part of a healthy social and emotional development. When faced with empathy or even unexpected kindness, we feel seen, understood, and made special by the availability of the other person to us. In organisations we often find this stance in company chairmen who make the time and space to learn the name and some detail of each person they come across. Even knowing that this might be part of their job, it still is an impactful and powerful connection.

Researchers from the Max Planck institute identified a part of the brain that recognises a lack of empathy and autocorrects the tendency of human beings to be egocentric (Silani, et al., 2013). When this brain region doesn't function properly—or when we have to make particularly quick decisions—researchers found one's ability for empathy is dramatically reduced. So, although connection and empathy may be natural, nurturing it helps. To be most present, we need to make ourselves available to the "connection" and willing to make space in our busy lives and days to slow down enough to make "that bold swinging [...] into the life of the other" (Buber, in Agassi, 1999, p. 82).

To develop our ability to empathise and connect, we need enough self-knowledge to find what we have in common with the other, to resonate even at an emotional level with the other person. Many people in organisations often assume they need to leave their feelings at the door when they come to work. The belief that emotion has no space in the workplace is a key inhibiting factor in being present to ourselves and others and establishing valuable connections that anchor us as emotional being, and support the work we do.

Finally, empathy and connection are not always easy to achieve, particularly at a time of conflict or when people feel they have nothing in common with another person. These are times to challenge ourselves and recognise that we are all connected in some way to each other through our basic humanity. So, what are aspects of the other person you can admire or what aspects of their weakness can you also relate to?

Experiential exercise

Think about someone with whom you want to establish a better connection. It could be a boss, colleague or a friend. On a piece of paper, write down in about 10 minutes all the information that you know about this person under the following headings:

- Work—this person's work life, responsibilities, problems, etc.
- Home—this person's family life, responsibilities, problems, etc.
- Past—this person's history, what they may have struggled with or difficulties they might have encountered
- Dreams—this person's hopes, dreams, goals and aspirations

When you are done writing, read what you wrote aloud imagining that you are this person and that you are reading about your own life (try reading inserting "I" or "my" in the sentences). Also, be curious about the aspects of this person's life that you have little or no information for.

How does this make you feel? Does it increase your level of empathy towards this person? Could you imagine reacting to him or her differently in the future?

Authenticity

Most people would readily agree that pretending or "faking" is not just unattractive but evokes both suspicion and fear. We tend however to react intuitively in a positive way to people we feel are authentic or genuine. A study conducted at Bangor University in Wales (Heerey & Crossley, 2013) showed that people can generally distinguish when others are being genuine. The study paired strangers getting to know one another and monitored their reactions to both genuine and polite smiles. It found that the subjects responded much more quickly to genuine smiles than polite smiles, and viewed the genuine smiles as valued social reward.

Authenticity is not a personality trait that can be learnt or acquired but more to do with how we choose to "be'" with ourselves and with others. In leadership literature for example, "authentic leadership" emphasises the need to nurture genuine and fair relationships between leaders and followers and, for leaders to "know themselves". Research on the notion of authenticity seems to come back to two main components: first the ability to be self-aware and act "in accord with one's true self" (Kernis, 2003, p. 13) and second, a striving for openness and honesty in relationship.

Developing self-awareness is never ending and the topic can consume pages of definition; it is not a destination to be attained but a journey to be travelled. Self-awareness is the process of acknowledging both our strengths and weaknesses and being active in seeking opportunities to do so. This level of openness and introspection is not often seen in organisational cultures but when found is prized and impactful. A leader inviting comments from her team about her leadership style after hearing that staff were unsure about how to approach her is an example of authentic meeting.

Honesty and openness on the other hand, have at times been misunderstood as an invitation to say what is on one's mind irrespective of impact or how appropriate (or not) this may be to the given situation. For example, in a consulting firm that wanted to embrace authentic leadership and the giving and receiving of feedback, the uttering of the words "Let me give you some feedback" was occasionally a pre-cursor to a bullying or destructive voicing of opinion.

So being authentic is not about being/behaving in the same way at all times, but being responsive to the demands of the situation. It is about bringing the fullness of oneself to each moment. Hycner and Jacobs (1995) who explored dialogic relating in gestalt viewed this as *genuine and unreserved* communication and as a key element of participation in dialogue. As a gestalt practitioner, I might therefore also choose to self-disclose aspects of my own experience if this supports connection and an authentic way of being.

Range

Fluid responsiveness is best captured in the image of dancers, moving with and in response to the music that paces and holds them. As the music varies from classical to contemporary, rock or folk music we might notice a different responsiveness, more or less flow in the figure of the dance. This could be put down to physical abilities or dancing skill but it is also the unique subjectivity of each dancer that responds to the music. Each person's individual style, preferences, and experience means they will resonate with different types of music and be more responsive to them.

Similarly, as individuals, we each find ourselves more responsive to certain energetic attributes in others, the way they talk, move, look or hold themselves. As facilitators or coaches for example, we might notice we are more at ease with certain types of groups that may be calmer or louder, that ask many questions or not, that express anger or repress it. This preference and responsiveness is invariably linked to our own personal range which has been formed through our early development and experience.

As gestalt awareness raising agents, we are often called to provide or notice what is missing in the client system (Rainey & Jones, 2014, p. 116), and therefore need to respond to a wide spectrum of people and situations. So, our "range'" is an essential component of our presence. For instance, by being overly challenging or explicit as a facilitator with a group of Japanese managers, I may miss the more subtle messages being expressed. Similarly, a facilitator's own discomfort with anger and conflict may result in those feelings not being voiced in the group or being expressed in less transparent and constructive ways. Nevis (1987) offers ideas about developing range by looking at "evocative" vs "provocative" (as shown in Table 4.2) styles or modes of intervention.

Table 4.2. Different modes of intervention (adapted from Nevis 1987, p. 128).

Evocative mode	Provocative mode
• Behaviour that shows or enhances your way of being in the world' and use a bullet like other entries.	• Actions that make something happen; cause something to occur.
• Behaviour that raises the client's awareness but the response is something the client chooses.	• An active, directed intervention to force someone to attend to something specific.
• Behaviour creating conditions—such as trust, hope, safety, vision—that allow excitement or interest to grow in others and draws them out.	• Actions that contravene under-standings or contracts among people.
• Display of skills or values with-out disrupting the functioning of the client system.	• Actions that interrupt the nor-mal functioning of the client procedures or structures.
• Actions that do not compel a particular response.	• The other can hardly avoid responding; must react.

By developing our range, we are more able to calibrate our presence and meet the client where they are. Range is what allows us to be fluidly responsive to what we attune to and more choiceful in our use of self. This does not mean being confluent or similar to our client in temperament or style. In fact, Hanafin (2004), a gestalt practitioner, cautions us that we must not be too similar else we run the risk of being absorbed by the client. Nor should we be too different and run the risk of being ejected by the client. The key is to titrate our presence and attend to what he calls the "perceived weirdness index" (PWI) (ibid, p. 28) to reach that perfect place of acceptance and challenge.

Experiential exercise

Take a piece of paper and divide it into two columns. In the first column A (which we shall call the "I am" column), write down a series of characteristics or statements about yourself at work in. For example, "I am loyal, I am accurate, I am conscientious, etc.", do not limit yourself and put down as many characteristics or statements you feel apply to you.

Next, look down the list and combine them if overlapping and whittle them down to six-eight characteristics or statements.

Now, in the second column, write the qualities or statements that would start with "I am not …". These need not always be the opposite qualities to those in column A. So, for example, when looking at the statement, "I am independent", the "I am not" statement might be "I am not needy or vulnerable" rather than "I am dependent". So, check and see what feels right for you.

Once you have finished, read back the two lists inverting the "I am" with "I am not". Notice what sensations and feelings arise as you do this and pay attention to those statements that feel most challenging to say. What do they say about your range at work? What aspects of yourself might you be disowning or rejecting? What is the benefit and loss of viewing yourself in this way?

Embodied sensing

Embodiment in this context refers to the state of experiencing the body and "embodied sensing" is the capacity to experience others and the world around us through embodiment, through an attentive awareness of our body sensations, feelings and sensory information.

As Kepner (2003, p. 7) points out, our culture has disconnected bodily life from our sense of ourselves, from our identified "I". Noticing our bodies and sensations is not part of what most of us attend to in our working or professional lives. In fact, social media and virtual connecting is moving us even further away from our embodiment and we seem to spend more time refining our online profiles rather than attending to what we feel or sense in our bodies.

Embodiment or embodying as Parlett (2015) writes is "about living fully as a whole body-mind-energy system […]. We think, talk, puzzle things out […] but it is through our physical bodies that we actually (bump into, take hold of, smell, touch) the physical world around us" (p. 137). So, our bodies are the primary way in which we encounter and experience the world and as Barber (2012, p. 45) writes, are pools "in which all else is reflected". Attending to our embodiment and sensing through our body, is therefore a way in gestalt in which we access information, and a different type of knowing, about the world around us. As a coach, facilitator or leader embodied sensing is a primary way of attuning to myself, others and the situation around me.

Example

Upon meeting a new coachee, I may notice an unusual feeling of heaviness in my chest or unease in my stomach. By being curious about these new sensations, I allow myself to wonder at how they might be echoing what is happening for my coachee, or expressing an aspect of the dynamic in the room. Rather than disconnect and keep going with the coaching session, I might make a statement about what is going on for me that is contextually appropriate and opens a space for the coachee to relate to these feelings or sensations and bring something new to our joint awareness.

Daniel Kahneman (2011) in his famous book *Thinking, Fast and Slow*, writes how his research has shown that we apprehend the world in two radically opposed ways, employing two fundamentally different modes of thought: "system 1" and "system 2". System 1 is fast; it's intuitive, associative, metaphorical, automatic, impressionistic, and it can't be switched off. System 2 is slow, deliberate, and effortful. Its operation requires attention. To set it going now, ask yourself, "What is 13 × 27?" and see how it hogs attention. Kahneman argues that we mostly wrongly identify with system 2 whilst in fact, we are mostly noting and making sense of the world from system 1 as an intuitive and embodied response to what is around us. System 1 is a vital tool perfected via evolution that allows us to detect and instantly react to, for instance, hostile facial expressions. Automatically your body puts itself on guard even before a cognitive knowing is possible. System 1 can't be switched off. Although system 1 might not be one hundred per cent reliable or correct (although it can be for individuals whose experience is such that they can safely react from intuition), it is always there and is worth paying attention to it as a useful data source.

So, paying attention to our embodiment, to our sensations, impressions, intuitions, and gut feelings is as important for gestalt practitioners as attending to more cognitive or intellectual knowing. Embodied sensing is therefore an invitation to slow down enough to pay attention to this different awareness and let it inform us as a valid source of information, and to learn to read our embodiment as a facilitative antennae on the world. This also links to the notion of "presencing" by Senge et al. (2004) who view presencing as a new way of learning, one that allows for deeper seeing or awareness through inward focus.

Support

Support is very deliberately placed at the centre of the CARES model as it speaks to our ability to be energetically available to others but especially to ourselves. Support here has two facets:

1. Support that arises, as embodied human beings, from our mental and physical well-being and our resilience in facing situations.
2. Support which comes from acknowledging our resourcefulness, authority and trust that we can be impactful and make a difference.

This book will not dwell on the masses of research which shows the importance of our physical and emotional well-being on our effectiveness and performance. Feeling well and steady in ourselves is easier in stress-free and relaxing situations, but the key question for most of us is how to attend to our well-being when facing life challenges such as coping with a sick child or simply feeling anxious or overwhelmed by a certain aspect of our work. Part of the answer lies in our ability to be resilient. Siegel (1999) views resilience as finding the optimal zone of arousal where we are able to manage and even thrive and respond to the demands of everyday life without getting thrown off course. It is essential to recognise the signs of when we find ourselves out of this zone—often referred to as the window of tolerance (WoT) (Siegel, 1999; Ogden, et al., 2006)—and also how to get ourselves back within it. In stepping out of our WoT (shown in Figure 4.4) during periods of stress, we generally are less able to reflect, think rationally and make decisions calmly. Instead, we tend to respond at a physiological level by either becoming hyper-aroused or hypo-aroused; both states indicating a less supported or resilient self.

Support flows therefore from resourcing ourselves in whatever way feels effective to us and which will depend on our unique self and approach to living. Remembering especially that key relationships as well as healthy living or rest are also important aspects of resourcing ourselves.

The second aspect of support comes from feeling well grounded physically, intellectually, and ethically. Archimedes, the famous Greek mathematician and inventor is purported to have famously said: "Give

HYPER-AROUSAL   Emotional overwhelm, panic, feeling unsafe, angry, racing thoughts, anxiety, etc.

OPTIMAL AROUSAL ZONE   WINDOW OF TOLERANCE

↑

↓

HYPO-AROUSAL   Numb, no feelings or energy, can't think, shut down, ashamed, disconnected, depression, etc.

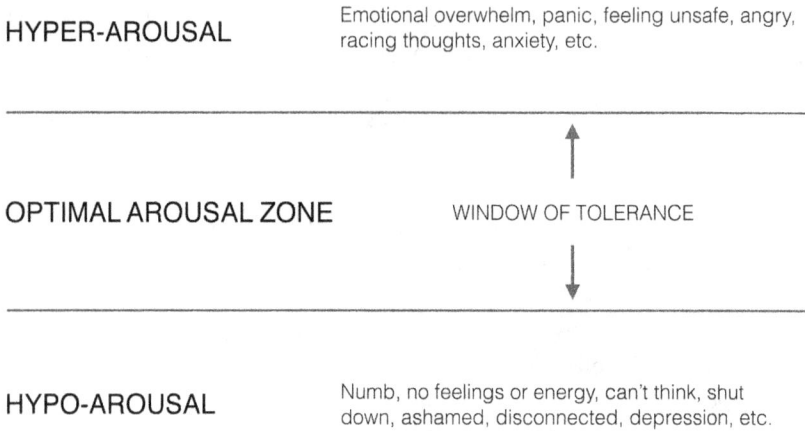

Figure 4.4. The window of tolerance (adapted from Siegel, 1999; Ogden, et al., 2006).

me a ground to stand on and I will change the world". Feeling grounded and solid in where we stand and what we do, is an essential component of presence. It is sometimes described as personal power (with a small p), the sort of power that comes from inner steadiness and from living your values and philosophy. Nevis (1987), in his book on gestalt organisational consulting, describes presence as the living embodiment of knowledge as it includes one's personal assumptions, believed to be essential to bring about change and influence.

Experiential Exercise

Think of a moment or situation in your life when you felt supported in yourself. You knew what you were doing and you were doing it well, you felt "in flow" both available and responsive to the situation you were in. Stay with this feeling for a little while and explore it. What does that feel like in your body? What emotions are present? What images and/or thoughts come to mind?

Now attend to what supported you to be in that place? What made it possible? How resourced were you feeling? How would you rate your physical and emotional well-being at that time in your life?

List the top three elements of relational support which stand out for you. How often do you have these in your work and life?

Summary

To support the deliberate use-of-self in gestalt requires practitioners to be present. Rather than a set skill, presence was defined in this chapter as a fundamentally relational and ethical process which arises from the situation and the relating between self and other. This chapter acknowledges that the act of presence is demanding and requires from practitioners to attend to specific aspects of their being. The later are captured in the CARES model which stands for connection, authenticity, range, embodied sensing, and support. It is important that the CARES model is not viewed as an attempt to deconstruct the flow of presence but rather provide practitioners concrete points on which to focus whilst recognising that the whole is greater than the sum of the parts and the experience of being present is unique to each individual.

Sensing

Sensing is the starting point of any intervention. It is the practitioner's stance of listening, curious noticing, full attentiveness to, and exploration of what the individual, group or organisation is expressing. Sensing is our attempt as organisational practitioners to comprehend in every possible way the experience of the client, group or organisation we are working with. This type of knowing in gestalt is not limited to quantitative data (e.g., survey results, performance measures or indicators) or what is in conscious awareness (e.g., stated goals, mission statements, process maps, etc.) but sensing in gestalt is more particularly the ability to track and heighten awareness of implicit or unawares interpersonal and subjective processes.

Therefore, the skill of sensing rests primarily on the practitioner's ability to track and raise awareness of the ongoing process or experience of an individual, group or organisation. Raising awareness through phenomenological inquiry is a key gestalt skill that will be covered first in Chapter Five. Chapter Six will then describe two important gestalt conceptual frameworks that guide our understanding of experience; field theory and the cycle of experience (CoE). The latter is a simple and powerful orienting map for understanding the flow of experience and awareness and tracking this in our clients.

Raising awareness and phenomenological inquiry

Awareness is the spontaneous sensing of what arises in you—of what you are doing, feeling, planning.

—*Perls*, et al., 1951 [1994], p. 323

The previous chapter described presence as being "energetically available and fluidly responsive" to ourselves, to others and the situation in which we find ourselves. Awareness facilitates presence. It is the route through which we can grasp our own experience, our authenticity and connection to others and our embodied sensing of situations.

The term awareness and self-awareness are notoriously ambiguous and philosophical, psychological and neuroscientific literatures are filled with competing, conflicting, and complementary definitions (Zahavi, 2005, p. 13). In gestalt, awareness is not just about thinking, reflecting or introspecting but also includes a quality of non-verbal knowing. As Yontef (1993, pp. 144–145) writes, "awareness is a form of experience which can be loosely defined as being in touch with one's existence, with *what is* [...] the person who is aware knows what he does, how he does it, that he has alternatives and that he chooses to be as he is" (emphasis in original).

Joyce and Sills (2014) suggest that awareness can be viewed as a continuum with sleep at one end (where awareness is minimal) and full self-awareness at the other, where we feel "a sense of connection, spontaneity and freedom" (ibid, p. 30). This later state is akin to what the psychologist Mihaly Csikszentmihalyi, (1990) has termed 'flow', a mental state of operation in which a person performing an activity is fully immersed in a feeling of energised focus, full involvement, and enjoyment in the process of the activity.

With awareness, gestalt holds that we are most in touch with what we need and are therefore in the best position to self-organise to meet that need. Awareness is therefore a cornerstone of gestalt and raising awareness is a central task of the gestalt practitioner. As was highlighted in Chapter Two, raising awareness leads to change as it supports an individual, group or organisation to surface what is most figural to them in that moment, their most pressing issue or need and take action around that.

A gestalt practitioner working with an individual, group or organisation could choose to focus on a particular aspect of functioning and raise awareness of id, ego or personality (see Chapter Three for more information about aspects of self-functioning). Table 5.1 below shows

Table 5.1. Aspects of self-functioning within individuals, groups, and organizations.

	Individual	*Group*	*Organisation*
Ego	Intent, goals, behaviours	Intent, goals/ objectives, team behaviours	Vision, strategy, policies, procedures, processes
Id	Feelings, embodied sensations	Group dynamics, inter-personal issues	Power struggles, rumours, un-acknowledged influences
Personality	Historical narrative, life/ work experiences so far	Group experience so far, individual experiences of groups	Organisational narrative and culture

typical areas of focus in exploring the experience of individuals, groups and organisations. Most OD practitioners would be familiar with a number of tools, psychometrics or interventions to raise awareness of ego functioning in particular, as it is more accessible to analytical frameworks or tools. What is the strength of gestalt practitioners, however is to uncover or raise awareness of id and personality functioning which are habitually less in conscious awareness. The primary gestalt skill for this is a type of inquiry called phenomenology, which stays close to the experience of the client system and which will be covered later in this chapter.

Awareness raising

As the starting point of sensing, raising awareness is about intuiting and beginning to understand what is going on for the client, be it a person, group or organisation. It is the origin and base point of knowing from which all interventions emerge.

This arguably is a starting point for many OD approaches which would look at a diagnostic or assessment phase before commencing the work. However, rather than a traditional diagnostic approach where the consultant identifies the illness or dysfunction to better treat the system, a gestalt awareness raising process is more akin to a joint diagnostic intervention where client and practitioner uncover together what most needs attending to. Rather than adopt an expert stance, a gestalt practitioner immerses him or herself in the system, holds back from deciding unilaterally upon figures of work and trusts that the most pressing need will surface by paying attention and exploring what is in their own awareness and that of their client. The basic assumption in this approach is that key figures of interest that need work will crystallise as awareness is raised around various aspects of functioning.

Example

Following an initial check-in, a team coach makes the following awareness raising intervention:

COACH: I notice that you all seem to sit in the same places each time we meet. [Coach names what is in their own awareness]

TEAM MEMBER 1:   I guess we are used to it. [Deflecting away from staying with that awareness]

COACH: What happens for you when I notice this behaviour? Can we stay with this for a moment? [The coach invites the group to pay attention to this piece of data]

Some uncomfortable silence ...

TEAM MEMBER 2:   It makes me think of reasons why this is our behaviour ... probably that some of us are more comfortable with particular individuals and less with others

TEAM MEMBER 3:   There are clearly sub-groups in the team ...

COACH: As you now name this, what are the reactions in the room?

TEAM MEMBER 1:   ... I think we all know this but it is the first time anyone has actually said it ...

TEAM MEMBER 2:   It is good to name it.

The team coach then checks agreement on the figure of work that emerged and supports the team to find ways of exploring it.

An important distinction is made in gestalt between open, undirected and active, directed awareness (Nevis, 1987, pp. 110–111) shown in Table 5.2. The distinction is in the stance, intent, and approach of the practitioner as he or she raises awareness in the client. Directed awareness describes the procedures most often used in OD interventions based on structured or guided questioning of members of the clients system, whilst open, undirected awareness "attempts to hold hypothesis formation in abeyance for a longer period of time [...] and is an attempt to reduce bias and remain as naive as possible while engaged in diagnosis" (ibid).

Although both approaches have a place, gestalt favours the more open and receptive stance of undirected awareness. The outcome is not predetermined and the practitioner not attached to follow a particular structure or method, rather they can attend to what emerges in the moment and to what stands out and grabs their attention and that of their client. The practitioner thus follows the flow of energy and trusts that what is most pressing or needed will be followed.

Hanafin (2004) notes how helpful it is for him to think about himself as an awareness agent rather than a change agent as this allows him to generate more options for approaching a situation rather than getting locked into a particular outcome or approach.

Table 5.2. Directed and undirected awareness (Nevis, 1987).

Active, directed awareness	Open, undirected awareness
Going to the world	Letting the world come to you
Forcing something to emerge	Waiting for something to emerge
Use a structure/framework to guide what you wish to see, hear, etc.	Investigate without being organised or "prejudiced" in any way as to what you wish to see, hear, etc.
Focused questioning: strive for a narrow, sharp field of vision	Widest peripheral vision: little foreground and everything of equal importance
Attend to things in terms of knowledge of how they work, what is present and missing in a normative sense	Naïve about how things work; hope to find something new about how things work
Searching use of sensory modalities	Receptive use of sensory modalities
Work supported by content values and conceptual base	Values are process-oriented, tend to be content-free

Exploring awareness

Staying in the here-and-now

Awareness raising stays close to the present-moment experience of the client. This present moment or here-and-now focus in gestalt is an important aspect of raising awareness.

> Work in the "here and now" has the greatest power in bringing about change. (Stern, 2004, p. 3)

Awareness is both knowing and being (Joyce & Sills, 2014, p. 31), and so only reflecting or "talking about" does not invite a full experiencing of awareness which is a much more powerful driver for change. So, for example, when suggesting to a management team that they pay attention to the tension between two sub-groups within the team, the invitation is that they both "know" and acknowledge the tension and that they attend to the experience of it in the present moment. It is staying with the full experience of tension, what it feels like at an embodied level and in relationship with others in the room that presents the opportunity for change and difference. A cognitive reflecting on the "tension" alone is not enough. Dan Zahavi, a philosopher distinguishes between reflective and experiential awareness and states that "experiential life is not an object and any investigation that seeks to grasp it as an object is consequently bound to fail" (Zahavi, 2005, p. 78). Staying in the here-and-now whilst tracking the unfolding of ongoing experience is what supports the heightening of awareness beyond the reflective and cognitive dimension.

Accepting that all awareness, however small, may be relevant

Stepping into the mode of awareness agent, what becomes immediately obvious is that there is a lot to notice. In trusting self-organising principles, what is most relevant is what stands out to the practitioner or client and what seems to hold most energy or interest in the moment.

Whilst it may not always be immediately clear how a particular awareness is relevant to the ongoing process, it is helpful to make a mental note of it as it could be significant in relation to either the practitioner or the client process. For example, upon entering an organisation for the first time, a practitioner may notice feeling overwhelmed by the layers of bureaucracy and identity checks faced by an 'outsider'. This awareness could offer insight into the trust levels within the organisation and how they deal with suppliers and clients. All awareness, however small, may be meaningful and connected in some way to the ongoing situation. A gestalt practitioner remains open to being impacted and monitors their experience trusting that this awareness, like a fractal, may be illustrating an aspect of the whole.

Awareness is noticing what *is* present as well as what is *missing*. Noting that a coaching client may seem for example, more distant or less engaged in the process than he has been so far is also relevant. This allows the practitioner to lead with active curiosity. What is missing in a meeting, what is minimised or simply avoided? The gestalt practitioner will often name and share what stands out for him or her as a way of raising awareness in the client. The freedom to follow intuition and explore that is central to awareness raising is a key difference between gestalt and using pre-determined diagnostic organisational models such as the Weisbord six box model (1976) or the McKinsey "seven s model" (Waterman, et al., 1980). The latter models funnel the attention of the practitioner into predefined categories and in so doing may miss other types of relevant data such as the practitioner's own awareness, key patterns or even coincidences.

Avoiding the expert trap and holding hypotheses lightly

One of Edwin Nevis', the father of gestalt OD, favourite interventions when raising awareness in a client, was "isn't that interesting"! A gentle man, he would smile and nod displaying interest and curiosity that would invite the other person to consider again what they said or did. This type of awareness raising requires relinquishing the expert position and is similar to what Schein (2013) calls the "humble inquiry".

Heightening awareness in clients often requires practitioners to lead from a genuine position of not knowing, to let themselves be truly surprised and interested in what might come next. The process of raising awareness is one of joining the dots in a way that is new and different for the client, making linkages and new hypothesis about what is happening. Nevis (1987) writes that the practitioner will need to find the right balance "between an uninterrupted flow of awareness and translation of the data of awareness into workable hypothesis" (p. 107). This balance and moment of choice is one that will co-emerge between client and practitioner.

Practitioner's own self-awareness

To intervene and raise awareness in clients, a gestalt practitioner needs to work at heightening their own awareness. Presence and use-of-self relies on the practitioner's ability to be aware of their own process, of what is happening around them as well as the meaning they make of their experience. Attending and staying open to our self-reflexive world is a pre-requisite of working as a gestalt practitioner. There are a variety of ways or approaches to develop self-awareness and for many of us it is a never-ending journey of self-study, education and experience. At its most basic, it is a noticing of what Perls (1969) called the three zones of awareness: the inner, outer, and middle zones.

- The *outer* zone of awareness is what we usually are most noticing of in the outside world. Typically, this is what we glean through our senses; what we hear, see, smell, etc., and what we most attend to in what is around us.

- The *inner* zone of awareness is the world of our feelings and sensations. How aware are we of what is happening in our bodies and our emotional world. How easy is it for us to attune to an embodied sensation, and how familiar are we in attending to, naming or recognising feelings.

- The *middle* zone of awareness is mostly represented by our internal voice, what we tell ourselves or what we think. Experiences in the middles zone include thoughts, beliefs, narrative memories, interpretations or fantasies.

Exercise

This exercise is to get you to focus in succession on your different zones of awareness. You could do this alone or with a partner. In turn, whilst facing each other, make the following three statements:

- What I notice is … . (outer zone)
- What I feel is … . (inner zone)
- What I think/imagine is … . (middle zone)

Continue for ten minutes or until you run out of statements.

Be aware of the statements you find more or less easy to articulate. Do you have a zone of awareness you rely on more heavily than others?

This exercise should have given you a sense of what is your habitual or dominant zone of awareness, or in other words, what type of awareness do you rely most heavily on. It is typical for many highly effective managers or consultants to have a greater reliance on what they think. If that is the case, it would be interesting if you could try and focus on the other two zones in your working life and notice if you become aware of new or different kind of information.

When you are next in a meeting and you can afford a few minutes of personal focus, take the opportunity to attend to these three zones of awareness. How does what you feel inform you, or provide you particular insight about the meeting?

The phenomenological method of inquiry

A central way of heightening awareness of a client is to stay close and inquire into their ongoing experience. This method of inquiry is called phenomenological and is a key skill in gestalt practice. The phenomenological approach requires the practitioner to track and stay as close to the client's experience as possible, to stay in the present moment and withhold, as much as possible, any interpretation or judgment. The phenomenological method was first developed by Edmund Husserl (1931) as a way of investigating the nature of existence and how we perceive things. It is a discipline to identify and enhance direct, immediate experience and to reduce the distortion of bias and prior learning.

Ernesto Spinelli (1989) identified three rules within the method. The first is *bracketing*, where the practitioner is asked to suspend preconceptions and approach things in a fresh, open, and welcoming way as if coming upon something totally new. The second is *description*, where the practitioner allows the client or situation to speak for itself and describes what is immediately obvious. The third is *horizontalisation*, where all aspects of the client or situation which are noticed are given equal importance.

Bracketing

Bracketing for Husserl (1931) is the suspension of all judgments and beliefs in order that the phenomena can be fully focused upon and understood. Staying close to a client's experience requires a practitioner to put aside, at least temporarily, their own subjectivity in terms of past knowledge or experiences that may influence their perception.

A consultant, who has for example experienced a bad merger situation, would in this method, put aside their feelings when listening to a leadership team debating the option of a merger. Retaining openness as an essential component of bracketing means allowing the team to explore this possibility unencumbered by the consultant's personal assumptions, biases or beliefs.

There is a debate on whether bracketing is possible and whether it is conceivable at all for human beings to suspend meaning. In phenomenological thought, the traditional view termed "transcendental phenomenology" holds that there is such a thing as "pure" perception whilst "existential phenomenology", informed by Heidegger's philosophy, talk of the "myth of immaculate perception" (Sapriel, 1998). Gestalt in its field theoretical belief of the interconnectedness of all things subscribes to existential phenomenological thinking and to the view that bias and meaning making can never be totally withheld or controlled enough. This is aligned with neuroscientific research that shows that we draw heavily on our memory and past experience to make sense of even the simplest sensory information.

Exercise

Consider the following statements. What is your immediate reaction, emotion or judgment/thinking to each? Even with very little information you can see how quickly you form an opinion ...

- The finance director of a large company has decided to work a four-day week.
- The CEO of a multi-national oil company resigns as his homosexual affair is made public.
- Hoshi, a Japanese colleague, is resigning her job as her engagement to an office co-worker is made public.

Bracketing therefore is more of an attitude than a technique. In its simplest form, this means accepting that there are multiple realities and that they are all valid! So, the manager's reality is not more valid or objective or true than the employee's or indeed the consultant's perception more valid than the client's. It relies therefore on the practitioner's self-awareness to keep exploring and challenging their personal assumptions, feelings, and thinking. Gestalt practitioners accept that there is no pure perception but we can view bracketing as an attempt to identify and acknowledge the preconceptions, judgements, and attitudes that we inevitably carry with us in the work environment. This is why it is essential for gestalt practitioners to support their practice through regular supervision of their work.

Tracking and description

The skill of *description* involves staying with what is immediately obvious in one's awareness and describing it rather than interpreting or meaning making. In description, the practitioner confines herself to describing what she notices (sees, hears, senses, etc.), perceives the client saying or doing *without interpreting*, and what she is currently experiencing herself. The challenge here is to stay with concrete experience to allow the coachee or group to stay with their lived experience rather than become more cognitively engaged and "talk about". Fairfield (2004) in describing his use of the phenomenological method with groups writes: "The more concrete is my focus, the more straightforward the experience. The more abstract is my focus, the more reflective the experience" (p. 346).

Example

Facilitator's description of staying phenomenological.

During a break in a day long workshop with a team, I observe two group members Sue and Jack in what appears to be a skirmish. I can't be sure this is the case and need to bracket that assumption. As the group resumes, I stay with what I am observing. Sue's dismissive hand gesture and turning her face away from Jack. They are speaking in a low, rapid, and clipped manner. They seem angry: I notice Sue's pursed lips and Jack's frown. Their faces appear tense, rigid, flushed. I'm aware of a tightness in my chest and a hushed silence in the rest of the group. I am no longer tracking what else is happening in the room and decide to make an intervention addressing both Sue and Jack:

"You are both looking away from each other following that exchange." "It is nothing", Jack replies abruptly. I suspect this is a deflection and wonder for a moment at sharing my own experience of tension and discomfort following their exchange. I look around and notice Brian's face looking solemn and intently watching both Sue and Jack as if wanting to interject. As this catches my attention, I decide to check my perception: "Brian, I notice you watching both Sue and Jack and wonder if you wanted to say anything to them?" "I do", Brian replies and proceeds to challenge both Sue and Jack on their habitual skirmishing and its impact on the team.

A practitioner will not describe out loud every aspect of what they notice. The flow of awareness can be overwhelming if named in its entirety and the practitioner will need to decide what to voice in terms of the emerging figures of interest. In so doing, he or she will need to be following the unfolding movement or process of the client over time. This tracking activity would be noticing what might be immediately obvious in the individual or group such as:

- Vocal changes (e.g., voice tone, pace, cadence, volume, rhythm, emotional quality)—"I notice that your voice lowers as you reflect on the merger."

- Posture or embodied tension—"As you think about this problem, your body seems to get very still."
- Facial expression—"I notice the smiles between the two of you in the group, how do you imagine this impacts others?"
- Movement—"As you speak to your team about this, your right-hand fists up."
- Eye contact—"We've been talking about redundancies for the past 30mns and I notice you mainly look out of the window."
- Subtle changes (e.g., facial flushing, breathing)—"When you are about to speak, your breathing gets shallower."
- Non-verbal vocalisations—"There is a lot of sighing every time topic X gets mentioned, would anyone like to put words to the sighing?"
- Energy shifts or moods—"The energy in the room seems to have dropped as soon as X started her presentation—what is going on?"

Other aspects of the experience of an individual or group may not be directly noticeable or accessible to a phenomenological concrete description and so the practitioner might need to directly inquire about these. Figure 5.1 shows the five building blocks of present moment

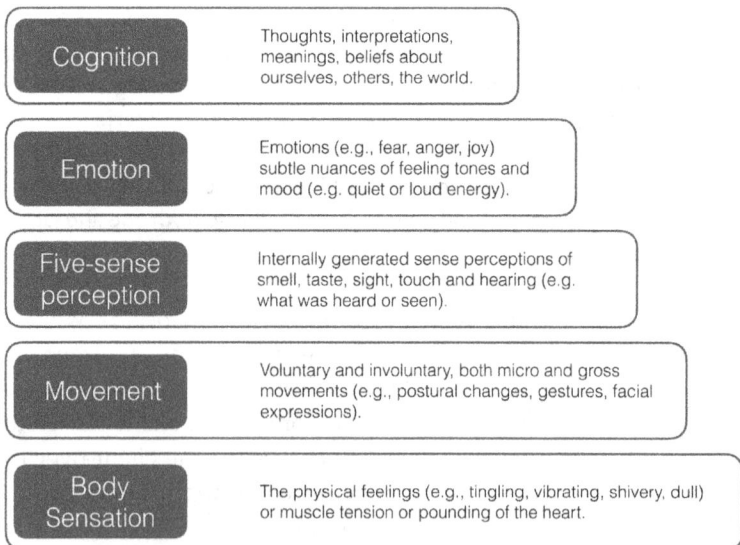

Cognition	Thoughts, interpretations, meanings, beliefs about ourselves, others, the world.
Emotion	Emotions (e.g., fear, anger, joy) subtle nuances of feeling tones and mood (e.g. quiet or loud energy).
Five-sense perception	Internally generated sense perceptions of smell, taste, sight, touch and hearing (e.g. what was heard or seen).
Movement	Voluntary and involuntary, both micro and gross movements (e.g., postural changes, gestures, facial expressions).
Body Sensation	The physical feelings (e.g., tingling, vibrating, shivery, dull) or muscle tension or pounding of the heart.

Figure 5.1. The five building blocks of present moment experience (adapted from Ogden, et al., 2006).

experience (Ogden et al., 2006). Tracking an individual or group present moment experience could involve inquiring into all five core organisers of experience (cognition, emotion, five-sense perception, movement and body sensation). It is worth remembering however that although this is a powerful technique to heighten awareness of the client's process, it may also leave individuals feeling exposed or shamed by the experience of someone noticing their process in such detail. Practitioners need to be careful to ensure that the client is open to such intervention and will not feel under gratuitous scrutiny.

Horizontalisation

This rule states that in each present moment, everything that happens should potentially be considered as equally important as anything else. The rule of horizontalisation (or equalisation) directs the practitioner not to ignore anything they become aware of and to give equal weighting to all phenomena in a given situation. Everything is potentially relevant to the unfolding experience in the moment and rather than be hasty in formulating a hypothesis or explanation, the practitioner needs to stay open to other ways of making meaning.

Example

COACHEE: I have been thinking what to bring and I really want to talk about how to deal with my team in this change process. I need a plan.

COACH: That would be fine of course. I notice you have your notebook ready with you today.

COACHEE: Well, I need to write down what we come up with today and have something concrete to take action on. It shouldn't have taken me so long to come up with the answer.

COACH: How is it for you not to know or have the answer?

COACHEE: It is frustrating and makes me feel I'm the wrong person for the job. I feel the CEO is losing confidence in me. Not sure how I can sort that out though …

COACH: Rather than a plan, perhaps we need first to look at your frustration with yourself and perception of what is expected of you. How would that be?

In the example above, the coach gave equal weight to the coachee's request for a plan and to noticing the readiness of the notebook. This allowed an unexpected new figure to emerge around the coachee's self-doubt and relationship with his CEO.

Horizontalising is often about naming what is obvious to the practitioner and trusting that by using themselves as an instrument in the co-emergent process, the client will signal if it is meaningful for them too. By noticing and naming the obvious, practitioners can help clients attend to aspects of their experience they are unaware of or, which over time have become implicit and less attended to.

Horizontalising is often a leap into uncertainty and not knowing, risking the client being puzzled, confused or shamed at the practitioner self-disclosing what they notice or what stood out for them. Again, as for the practice of description, self-disclosure should be done carefully with thoughtfulness of its impact rather than provocatively.

Summary

Awareness leads to change. This short yet powerful principle of gestalt work emphasises the importance given in gestalt to both the practitioner's own self-awareness as well as the fundamental skill of awareness raising. The latter in particular is often the starting point of the sensing activity in gestalt and relies on the phenomenological method of inquiry into the lived experience of an individual, group or organisation. Through bracketing, description, and horizontalisation, the practitioner notices, tracks, and accompanies the client through their journey of awareness and change.

CHAPTER SIX

Field theory and the cycle of experience

> We conceptualize organization as analogous to a living organism, and we hypothesize that the Cycle of Experience and the figure-ground paradigm holds at this larger system level as it does for the individual.
>
> —*Nevis*, 1987, p. 30

Gestalt holds that all systems (and individuals) when engaging with their environments are subject to two key fundamental influences which shape experience. The first is a field theoretical perspective (derived from Lewin's (1951) work on field theory) and states that our perception and behaviour is never untainted or "pure" but influenced and connected to everything else. The second is that experience, despite its interconnectedness and large number of influences, still follows a certain sequence or cycle driven by the urge to self-regulate. These two notions come together in the gestalt map called the cycle of experience (CoE). The latter captures the flow of experience subjected to both the complex factors within the field and the urge of any organism to self-regulate to meet its needs.

This chapter will explore how working within a field theoretical frame and with an understanding of the CoE as an orienting principle, provides the practitioner with a route map that guides and facilitate their sensing stance.

Field theory

As we have seen in Chapter Two, Kurt Lewin's work on field theory has been a major influence on both gestalt and OD. Field theory holds that people or groups can never be considered in isolation of their context or situation as all influences come into play to shape behaviour. Lewin (1951, p. 240) defined "the field" as "the totality of coexisting facts which are conceived of as mutually interdependent". At its most basic, this is an indication to practitioners to be aware of all background influences always present in any situation. In working with a group of middle managers on their operational effectiveness, a practitioner can't for example, ignore the influence of the chairman of the business being accused of fraud. Although seemingly unrelated in a causal way, field theory invites us to consider that the situation and wider context—as an integral part of the "field"—will shape behaviours, thoughts and feelings in the team and will need to be considered.

It is also a relational perspective which recognises that we are always in *relationship* with others, our experience both shaping and being shaped by people and events—both in the present and from past experiences. The web of influences that shape experience of the present moment is complex and in understanding our clients, we need not neglect or minimise potentially relevant aspects of their *field*. The term "field" in this case refers to all possible physical and psychological influences such as body, mind, emotional, current and historical situations, cultural, social, economic, spiritual or political influences. Working in a culturally diverse team for instance, we immediately notice the importance of framing communication through the lens of culture. The impact of culture, in this case, is obvious and transparent whilst other more subtle influences such as gender, experience or inter-personal dynamics could get minimised or forgotten.

Figure and ground

If field theory invites us to stay open to all influences, how to know what, out of "everything" that could potentially be considered, is most important to clients? Gestalt psychology which has deeply influenced Kurt Lewin's ideas on field theory provide us with the answer in its notion of "figure and ground". At any one time, the field is organised into "figure" and "ground" and describing this notion, the founders of gestalt theory write:

> The sign of spontaneous attention and concentration is the progressive forming of a figure/ground, whether the situation be one of sensing something, making a plan, imagining, remembering, or practical activity. If both attention and excitement are present and working together, the object of attention becomes more and more a unified, bright, sharp figure against a more and more empty, unnoticed, uninteresting ground. This form of unified figure against an empty ground has been called a "good gestalt". (Perls, Hefferline, & Goodman, 1951 [1994], p. 304)

Figure 6.1 shows two well-known gestalt psychology figure-ground images depicting the interchanging image of the old and young woman (Boring, 1930) and the Rubin Vase (Rubin, 1915 [1958]) which alternates between the image of a vase and two faces. These images vividly demonstrate how we organise our perception into a specific figure, letting other possibilities merge into ground. Gestalt tells us that the figure is what interests us at the time and so is a function of our most pressing need in that moment. For example, if we are hungry we tend to be alert

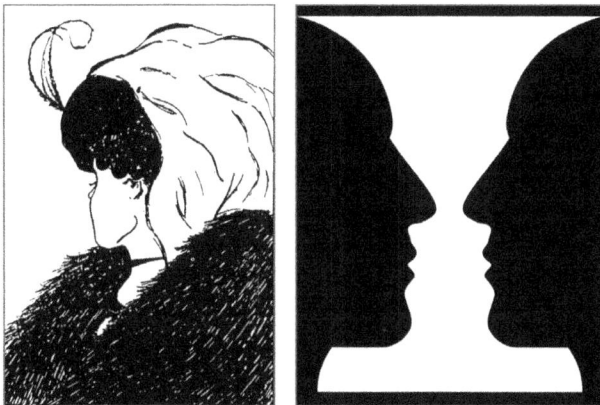

Figure 6.1. Figure and ground images.

to spotting food within an environment and all other influences (e.g., other people, paintings on the wall, etc.) stay in ground. What is often missed in the figure/ground notion is that each figure emerges from a particular ground. So, whilst valuable to attend to the emerging figure, i.e., what is most vivid or present to our clients, it is also important to attend to aspects of the ground from which this figure has risen. How have aspects of ground shaped and influenced the choice of figure?

Example

At the third session with a team I was coaching through a large transformation project, I stepped in expecting the main focus of work for the upcoming session to be the resignation of two of its members. Upon starting, it became apparent that the team changes were less vivid than a disruptive conflict between two remaining members of the team. The figure of the work was the presenting conflict and yet, the overall project context and the resignation of team members could not be forgotten as key aspects of the ground impacting existing behaviour. The challenge as a practitioner was therefore to keep shuttling attention between the client's immediate figure and the ground from which it emerged—constantly remaining open to possible connections and influences. How is the conflict influenced by the project development and the changes in the team? How much is it purely an interpersonal issue? All connections need to be made to heighten awareness and sensing into the presenting issue or problem.

In bringing this field theoretical view into practice, it is helpful to keep in focus all dimensions of the SOS model (described in Chapter Four), as varying aspects of the field through which to sense and understand behaviour and experience. That is why this approach is also termed field-relational as it emphasises our immersion in a web of relationships, constantly impacting and being impacted by others and events.

- First, a self or first person "phenomenal field" dimension which recognises that the way a person (or group) organise their experience is dependent on their own history and narrative.
- Second, the "other" or relational field recognises that experience is being mutually influenced by others at every moment in time and so, behaviour is always co-emergent. So, a team's behaviour for

example, cannot be understood separately from their interaction with other teams or individuals.

• Third, is the "situation" or particular event which will shape experience and resulting behaviour. An organisational re-structure for instance, will influence the behaviour of all staff, even those who are not directly impacted by the change.

• Fourth, what is often referred to as the "larger field" or overall context, culture, economic, and political moods will also impact and influence experience.

A field relational view therefore challenges the practitioner to stay open to all these influences, shuttling in their inquiry and curiosity between the varying levels of the SOS model in trying to understand and make meaning of their client's and their own experience. This is not about finding the root cause of behaviour through logical analysis of cause and effect but staying open to undirected awareness (described in Chapter Five) and all possible influences. It is in fact the lack of reduction in sensing that allows freedom for data and meaning to emerge. Nevis (1980) compared this style of working to be closer to the way the well-known television detective Columbo operates, rather than Sherlock Holmes' style. He writes:

> Columbo may be said to act like a sponge, immersing himself in his milieu and waiting for important clues to be drawn to him, like iron filings being drawn to a magnet. Holmes resembles a finely trained hunting dog who attacks his settings, and he never rests until he has put the pieces together in his mind. Holmes uses his mind to "force" data to emerge and make sense; Columbo teaches or coaxes the people and environment involved to "give up" data as he makes contact with them. Holmes educates himself by being in control of his environment; Colombo allows himself to be educated. It is interesting to note that it is an infrequent occurrence when Holmes makes close, personal contact with the villain; Columbo's method rests largely upon repeated personal contacts. (Nevis, 1980, p. 5)

The cycle of experience

In 1947, Perls introduced what would become the cycle of experience as a process of homeostasis or the ability of an organismic system to regulate and maintain its internal equilibrium and stability (Perls, 1947). Perls expanded this notion of physiological self-regulation to apply to psychological, mental, and emotional balance. This notion was later further developed by others (Zinker, 1977; Polsters, 1973) to describe the flow of experience in key stages. Zinker (1977) and Nevis (1987) then crystallised the concept of figure/ground and the human compulsion towards need satisfaction into a simple yet powerful metaphor named the cycle of experience (CoE).

The CoE thus became a way of phenomenologically tracking individual or group process through the formation, interruption or completion of emerging figures. The cycle (shown in Figure 6.2) tracks how as human beings we experience and respond to a disturbance, stimulus or need in our field by first noting it (sensation), making meaning of it (awareness/recognition), preparing our response to the stimulus (mobilisation), taking action which results in some contact/change taking place followed by a phase of satisfaction/resolution before moving away (withdrawal/closure) into ground ready for another cycle. Following withdrawal, the individual returns to a place of openness and receptivity to what comes next which Perls (1951 [1994], p. 138) has called the fertile void. It is a space of creativity and "bountiful emptiness" where all options within the ground are possible.

Table 6.1 provides an example of how an individual's response to hunger maps onto the CoE. Of course, this boundaried individual

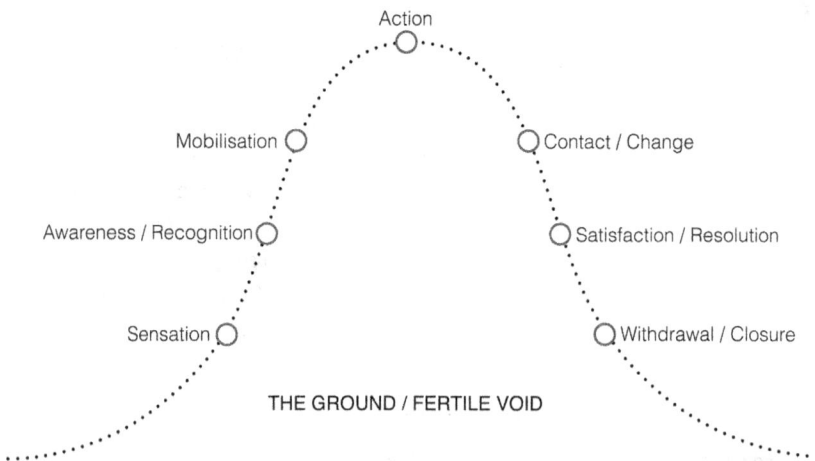

Figure 6.2. The cycle of experience.

experience is quite simple and reality is more complex. Usually, for individuals, groups or organisations, multiple figures are forming, vying for attention at any given moment and triggering a rapid and intricate selection process to decide which need will be attended to. The choice will depend on the urgency of the need but also on the level of support available for that need to be addressed. For example, if a team is experiencing internal conflict, it might not be safe enough for an individual to express dissent or disagreement. In this case, the voicing of opinion (as a figure) does not have enough support for it to emerge and thus will stay in ground.

It is worth noting that in gestalt terminology, the word awareness if used both to mean conscious realisation as well as to signify the part of the cycle where a clear figure of interest emerges. The term recognition

Table 6.1. Stages within the cycle of experience.

	Description	Example
Sensation	Noticing an emerging need, feeling or sensation—the arising figure.	I am aware of a sensation in my stomach.
Awareness/ recognition	Recognising and sharpening the figure/need or meaning/ making and prioritising it over other needs.	I recognise it as hunger.
Mobilisation	Planning, energising, and assessing support for satisfying the need.	I think of what I want to eat and what is possible.
Action	Taking action either through expressing, movement, or experimenting.	I go to the fridge and choose an apple.
Contact/ change	Resolving, completing, a shift or change occurs.	I eat it.
Resolution/ satisfaction	Integrating the change, accepting, learning, feeling satisfied.	I notice my hunger is satisfied.
Withdrawal/ closure	Disengaging, letting go, moving away.	The need has been met, I can let go and attend to something else.

adopted by Joyce and Sills (2014) has therefore been added to that part of the cycle to avoid confusion. In field theory terms, awareness/recognition is a point of creative organisation of the field into figure and ground. The figure in the field begins to sharpen, comes into conscious awareness prompting typically the start of a more mobilised active "doing" phase. It is helpful to integrate this model back to its original theoretical baseline in gestalt's theory of self (described in Chapter Three) and draw a horizontal line at this point (see Figure 6.3) recognising that the area below the line corresponds to id functioning, whilst the part of the cycle above the line is the more aware ego functioning. Many organisational clients attend exclusively to ego functioning as doing, mobilisation, action are typically valued and encouraged in these contexts. Gestalt practitioners thus bring the recognition of the interdependence of id and ego functioning, of doing and being. One cannot exist without the other. For organisations to thrive both stances and behaviours are needed.

The gestalt CoE offers therefore the OD practitioner a type of diagnostic lens on the individual, group or organisation under consideration. The word diagnosis here is used lightly without a judgement or bias to 'complete the cycle' as a sign of effectiveness or health. Fairfield (2004) warns us that rushing our clients towards satisfaction or resolution does not support a phenomenological attitude and risks shutting out new possibilities or choices that are enriching and enlivening.

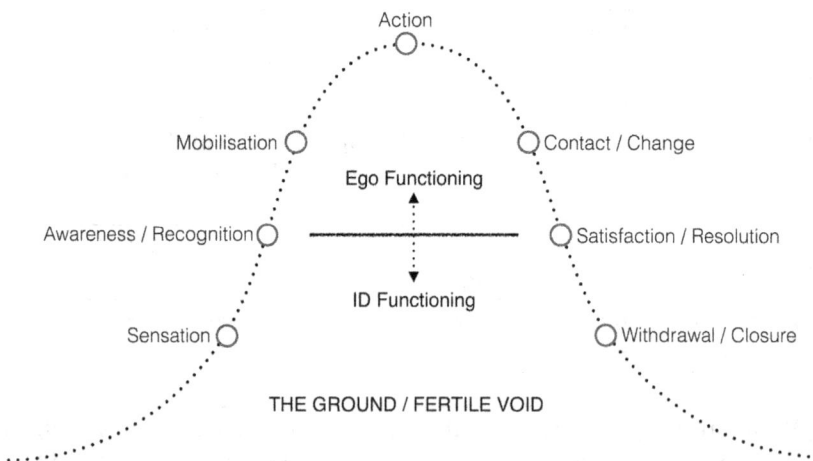

Figure 6.3. Self functions and the CoE.

So, staying with a phenomenological exploration of where our clients are on the CoE (even if stuck) encourages considerations of the various supports needed for the completion of the sequence. The question to ask is: What is missing that might support my client or group to take the next step on the cycle?

Example

Richard, a newly appointed department head, is being coached following a difficult transition from being a team member to stepping into the new position. His immediate boss is concerned that although knowing and understanding the business, Richard seems reluctant to make decisions (even simple ones), or define a new strategic direction for his department.

His gestalt coach explores with Richard his process using the CoE and together they notice Richard's stuckness at a particular point in the cycle. Having worked in the business for many years, he knows and can sense the issues (sensation stage), can see the most pressing figures or needs that must be attended to (awareness stage), he asks his team to explore all possible options to deal with arising issues (mobilisation stage) but is always reluctant to decide on a particular course of action. This stuckness between mobilisation and action seem to be particularly emphasised in the process of completing the new strategic direction. In exploring this, Richard recognises he feels unsupported by his previous team members imagining some are resentful that he got the job over them. He also feels the pressure of his boss to "hit the ground running" because he has been in the business for such a long time and doesn't feel able to ask for his help. Not moving to action feels safer for Richard and a way of avoiding both tackling his team issues and his relationship with his boss. The coaching agenda can now be agreed to address both these points.

The CoE in groups

Working with groups, gestalt theory maintains that a healthy group process and experience flows from an agreed upon figure (Nevis, 1987, p. 31). In other words, individuals within the group must agree a common figure of interest around which energy can be mobilised and action taken to reach a satisfying resolution. This seems to be stating a truism for most organisations for which goal setting is a standard process. Gestalt theory emphasises however the need for this goal or common figure to arise or respond to the needs of the organisation as a whole.

A joint figure cannot be determined by a few and imposed on others but must, in order to reach a satisfying and sustainable outcome, emerge from dialogue in which all those concerned can have a voice. A common group figure may however often require that individuals either compromise or decide to prioritise different needs to respond to the overall need of the group. Of course, not every organisational decision can be taken or goal set through consensus, and choices must be made around which goals or decisions require the investment in time and dialogue to ensure a common figure and better flow of experience.

Tracking the CoE in groups becomes more complex as both individual and group cycles must be considered. It is often helpful to recognise when facilitating, where the members of a group are at in terms of the different stages of the cycle of experience (as seen in Figure 6.4). At any given moment in time, some group members may be mobilised and ready to move into action whilst others have not yet a clear figure or awareness of the issue. Using the CoE as a diagnostic tool in these instances permits dialogue around the positioning of individuals on the cycle as well as the need for a common agreed figure to emerge for clear and sustainable action to be taken.

In facilitating a group, it is often tempting to only focus on the CoE of the group as a whole, and make assumptions about the group's

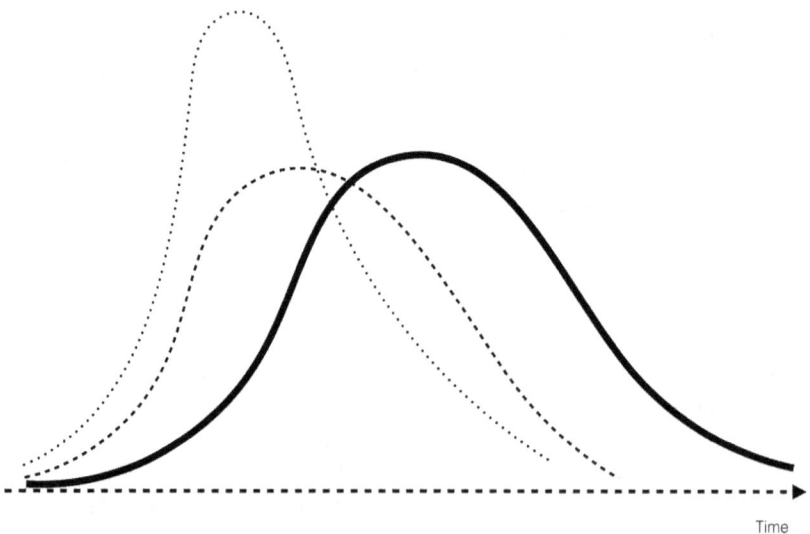

Time

Figure 6.4. The overlapping cycle of different members of a group.

experience as a homogenous entity bypassing where individuals may be in terms of their personal flow of experience. This system's approach although a useful abstraction at times, also loses the impact of the individual phenomenological experiences present in the room and risks reducing the CoE to a heuristic tool. The facilitator needs to weave in and out of the group and individual CoEs, attending artfully to the balance between both and the complexity and uncertainty this holds.

A cohesive flow of experience in groups is also reliant on the quality of dialogue among the members of the group. This also means that group participants need to be supported enough to attend both to their self-awareness as well as to noticing, hearing from, and responding to others. These skills of dialogue are essential to the gestalt approach and will be covered in more detail in Chapter Eight.

Moderations to contact

The CoE in healthy and well supported processes becomes a unified sequence of phases. When the phases do not follow each other in a smooth and flowing fashion, this is thought to be due to particular habitual patterns of relating. These patterns were originally presented as "interruptions to contact" however, this implied that there was an optimum or good way to go through the cycle and that all interruptions were negative. A number of gestalt writers (such as Mackewn, 1997; Wheeler, 1991) challenged this, arguing instead that an interruption could be beneficial or detrimental depending on the situation, and were better seen as adaptations or "creative adjustments" (Perls, et al., 1951 [1994], p. 5) to situations and renamed "moderations". Indeed, in certain environments interrupting an emergent need to complete is a perfectly healthy and useful process. An example of this could be feeling angry with a boss or colleague, and holding one's anger back rather than giving in to the need to give it full expression.

So, these points of stuckness or ways of "moderating" our experience are not "bad" or obstacles to be removed but instead point to possible opportunities for greater support to be provided. Table 6.2 provides an overview of the key moderations to contact in gestalt theory alongside illustrative examples at the individual and group levels. In some organisations for example, a common moderation is when much gets planned but little implemented (retroflection); or the reverse is true where

Table 6.2. Moderations to contact in gestalt.

	Brief definition	Individual example	Group example
Introjecting	"Swallowing" whole opinions and judgements without checking whether they fit the current situation. People tell us they are introjecting when they use a lot of "shoulds" and "musts".	A manager that holds the belief that they "always have to know what to do next".	A group rejecting a possible option as it doesn't fit "how we do things around here".
Projection	Placing onto others specific attributes. These may be aspects of ourselves which we may have disowned.	A manager who believes she is the only one struggling in her job and everyone else is finding it easy.	A department that accuses another of being manipulative and not transparent; "they never play fair" whilst adopting themselves questionable tactics.
Retroflection	Holding back impulses to act.	A person that stops himself from speaking first or disagreeing in a meeting.	A team that is over-cautious, plans endlessly thus holding back movement to act in case they get it wrong.

(Continued)

Table 6.2. (Continued).

	Brief definition	*Individual example*	*Group example*
Self-monitoring	A kind of inner dialogue that is constantly monitoring thoughts, feelings and behaviours. It is a way of focusing on oneself that inhibits spontaneity as well as a "here and now" relating to others.	Individual that is habitually excessively self-critical about what he does or says.	A leadership team that is over concerned about how they will come across to their staff which inhibits action to take place.
Confluence	Merging or over-adapting to others. Could be as a way of expressing closeness or as a way of offsetting a fear of rejection.	Individual that always waits for others to speak before expressing a similar opinion.	Often seen in teams where the leader surrounds himself with "yes-men".
Desensitising	Shutting down awareness of sensation in the present moment. Often utilised as a defence from fear of being overwhelmed by situation or feeling.	Individual that is habitually unaware of what they need (or often feel) about a given situation.	A team that does not sense new data in their environment but forms a figure based on historical rather than present situation.
Deflecting	Changing the subject, misunderstanding or re-defining what has been said are among the many ways of deflecting.	An individual that changes the subject at hand—particularly when the discussion become difficult in some way.	A team that avoids facing difficult questions or dynamics through excessive humour or laughter.

in some businesses, the impulse is to jump to action with little or not enough planning (impulsivity which is the polarity of retroflection). The CoE and moderations are useful diagnostic means to raise awareness in people, teams and organisations of habitual patterns of behaviour.

Each moderation describes a pattern of behaviour that was either formed in a previous experience, or signals a lack of support in the field to enable the individual or group to complete the cycle. For example, an individual that has been bullied by a previous boss might habitually deflect away from any signs of conflict or disagreement with his current employer. Or, when faced with a dissatisfied or angry customer, a sales representative may tend to become confluent in an attempt to appease rather than name what they really think is the problem. Again, these moderations only become problematic if habitual and out of awareness. Identifying these and bringing them into our client's awareness is part of the sensing task of a gestalt practitioner.

Exercise

Consider each moderation in Table 6.2, do any look particularly familiar to you? Can you recognise them in yourself or others? Spend a few moments thinking of particular examples for each of these in your own life or practice.

Next, think of a key client; what are the key moderations to contact that they might have? What does this tell you about their process and where they might get stuck on the CoE?

Summary

This chapter has addressed two fundamental conceptual frameworks for the gestalt practitioner which guide both our comprehension of experience and ways in which we can track and diagnose the quality of contact and experience in the moment. Field theory invites us to stay open to the uncertainty and complexity of our interconnectedness and not dismiss possible influences, whilst the CoE is an orienting principle that can our sensing in the moment. It would be too easy to use these frameworks as diagnostic tools of how things should be. The invitation however is to view them as co-diagnostic frames that stay close to the client's experience, without judgement, and which support meaningful discussion of process and change.

Supporting

Previous chapters have heightened the importance of *sensing* in the gestalt change approach. We have seen how *sensing* activities build awareness of the most pressing figure to be attended to by individuals, groups or organisations. Arriving at this clear figure is however only one aspect of what is needed in organisational work to support effective outcome or action. Indeed, in complex change situations, knowing what is needed does not necessarily mean knowing how to achieve it.

A balancing act between letting situations unfold and driving action is the artistry of organisational work. The next three chapters attend to the artistry of *supporting*, beginning with Chapter Seven by guest author Sally Denham-Vaughan who contrasts Will-based (more driven and linear) change strategies with the notion of grace based (more emergent and dialogic) change approaches and acknowledges the need for a threshold or liminal position as a core condition for supporting effective action. An enabling condition to achieving this liminal position is the practice of dialogue and relational support, which is then outlined in Chapter Eight. Finally, this section on *supporting* concludes with a chapter on the art of interventions to enable co-emergent movement and sustainable change.

CHAPTER SEVEN

At the threshold: meditations on will, grace, and liminal space*

Sally Denham-Vaughan

The existence of an integral principal in gestalt theory between two contrasting forces; "will/directed action" and "grace/ receptivity" was first proposed in an article in 2005 (Denham-Vaughan, 2005). With regard to how we individually operate, the article suggested that these two forces acting together produce a creative tension that radically configures how we interact with everything around us. In this chapter, the notion of will and grace is extended to describe an integral relational gestalt approach to organisational development. In particular, the proposal is that contemporary relational OD includes a focus on active co-emergence with stakeholders and the environment, and in this way can be described as a highly ethical and dialogic form of intervening with organisations. This chapter suggests the approach is particularly relevant in today's fast moving, challenging and increasingly global organisations where situations are complex, dynamic and fluid.

---

*Permission from Sally Denham-Vaughan to include her input in Chapter Seven as well as Chapter Thirteen which was co-written and previously published in a fuller version in a Gestalt Press book.

Contact and change: a brief reminder

Many writers would argue that since its inception, gestalt has been "relational". Indeed, the very notion of "contact" depends on the concept of one variable, classically "organism", coming up against another, classically "environment", (see Perls, 1973 for further discussion). It is at this meeting point that the contact boundary arises and all change is proposed to occur. As has been outlined in earlier chapters, this is described as the structuring of the field via emergence of a "figure" against a "ground": this process itself being commonly called the "cycle of experience" or "contact sequence". A version of the cycle is shown diagrammatically in Figure 7.1 and has been outlined in Chapter Six. The reader will notice that the last stage of withdrawal/closure is represented here as two separate stages to emphasise the reflecting and stepping back from the contact experience.

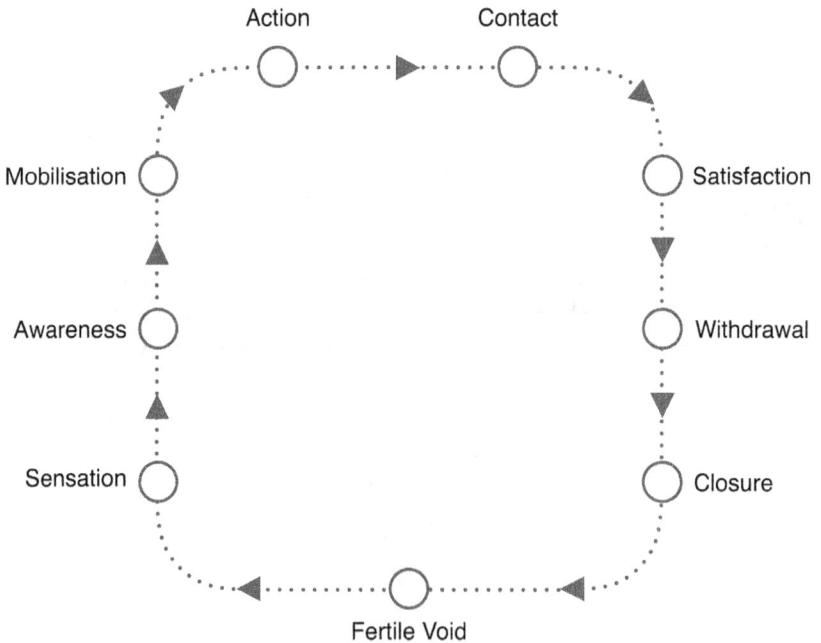

Figure 7.1. The gestalt cycle of experience.

Will and grace applied to organisational life

Given then that according to gestalt theory, change occurs at the "contact boundary", let us also accept that this "change" occurs in a multitude of different forms. "Change" can feel quick, slow, laborious, difficult, chaotic, messy, elegant, wrong, beautiful, creative, exciting, and so on; there is probably no end to the variety of terms we could use to reflect our experience of the variety of forms of change.

When outlining the dual processes of will and grace, the suggestion is that all these forms of change can be captured by an ever-present mix, (dialectic), of these two very different, but related, "movements" occurring at the contact boundary. For the sake of clarity, these two processes are now described in turn, as if they were a polarity; as if one movement could be employed without the presence of the other. However, it is vital to emphasise that this is precisely not what is being suggested: indeed, examination of many failed change initiatives reveals that it is exactly this over-reliance on one movement, without attending to the subtle mixture of the two, that has been responsible for change failure.

Willing the change: self

First, "will" can be described as a movement where we consciously use our self, (and/or our consulting team/group), to intentionally push into, and have an impact upon, others and the situation. We muster energy, resources, strategies, tools, methods, and techniques to design a plan to effect a change in the environment. Accordingly, and relating to OD, this term can be used to describe all forms of intervention where we are aiming to produce a specific, often predetermined impact in the wider field. We know what we want to achieve, by when and are deliberately aiming to produce key outputs.

Most classic "monologic" forms of OD and change management techniques fall into this category: the end point we want has been determined and our change strategy can be conceived of as a linear methodology for getting from A to B as efficiently and effectively as possible. Classic OD change processes including most forms of project management such as prince 2, lean, extreme project management and force field diagrams, GANT charts, SWOT analyses, fishbone diagrams, etc., fall into this category. In all of these methodologies there is a shared emphasis on scoping, planning, executing, controlling, and closing the work to achieve predetermined goals within specific timescales and subject to certain constraints. We probably know the change we want to see and, in terms of the SOS framework (Denham-Vaughan & Chidiac, 2013), discussed in Chapter Four, the self dimension is therefore leading.

Underlying these methodologies however, there are a number of implicit, highly significant embedded change assumptions. For example, that it will be possible to control sufficient variables to achieve the planned change, that others involved will be happy to change once the rational reasons for doing so are explained to them and that it is both possible and desirable to know in advance the particular outcome and product that we wish to achieve in this situation. Within this view/ formulation, deviations from the plan are seen as loss of focus and opposition to the plan is seen as unhelpful "resistance". Generally, therefore, the interventions of change agents are focused on stabilising the situation and overcoming others' resistance, in order to progress the plan as smoothly as possible.

It is when these stabilisation and smoothing strategies are unsuccessful that people end up feeling either forced to comply with an unpopular change initiative, or an increasing sense of chaos as the gap between the plan and experienced reality is seen as increasing.

Case example

When consulting with a senior team within the social care sector, we discovered that over the past two years the team leader had been asked to submit seventeen versions of a local plan describing how his team were rolling out a national plan within their particular geographical area. Although the team had explicitly been asked to take ownership in their patch, and be "creative and innovative" regarding delivery, they had concluded that implicitly, any deviation from "national norms" was unwelcome. At the point of entry this team were disengaged, unmotivated, outwardly passive and, we learnt later, inwardly furious, that their ideas had been overlooked. Our brief as consultants was to get the team "engaged" but no mention was made to us of the seventeen versions of a plan that pre-dated our visit.

Our experience was that we needed to find a way to surface, integrate, and make satisfactory meaning of this team's experience before we could engage them in change processes. The team were unable to reconcile requests for creativity with repeated rejection of their ideas and had fallen into a sense of hopelessness and lack of motivation that now pervaded all their interactions. As such, they were increasingly viewed as "resisting", even though they repeatedly tried to engage.

We worked with the team to examine the national plan looking for implicit "must dos", and then delineated what (small) areas were open for the requisite creativity and innovation locally. In particular, we attempted to re-engage the team on "core business" where they had previously been successful and decrease their attachment to possibilities of radical service change locally. These activities served to reduce the team's confusion between explicit and implicit messages and also realigned them with national priorities that they had previously been focussed on.

It is important to emphasise here that we are not implying that Will based change initiatives are either unhelpful or unsuccessful; often quite the opposite is true. Rather to recognise that they can be high risk in complex and dynamic, "dancing" environments with multiple stakeholders. On the other hand, with relatively stable environments, clear supply chains and respected lines of accountability/command, then they are generally effective and timely ways of proceeding, particularly as "first line" interventions. Even then though, as the example above illustrates, following 'clear' plans and aiming for 'specific outcomes' is still open to misunderstanding and misinterpretation.

Our experience as consultants is that these are the times when we are called in: when, as in our example, classic, will-based, linear approaches have been tried and judged unsuccessful, or alternatively, when it is clear from the outset that the situation is complex, fluid and "wicked" (Grint, 2008). It is in these latter situations that we need to include a more relational, dialogic, and "grace-focussed" approach from the outset.

Gracious responding to the other and situation

To return to relational gestalt theory with change arising at the contact boundary, grace based approaches come in to their own when, far from imposing our will on others and the situation, we can sense the other/situation imposing itself upon us *and we both trust it and wish to inquire into its intent*. These latter points concerning *trust of*, and *desire for inclusion* of, "the other" and "situation" SOS dimensions are vital, and fundamentally affect our presence and ethical stance towards change. Are we committed to a relational and dialogic approach? If so, change becomes far more co-emergent. If not, and attempts at relational work are largely hubris or rhetorical, then the trust of the other risks being broken and possibilities for change in any situation restricted.

In terms of the integral dialectic of will and grace this can be thought of as follows: should we "catch and ride the wave", of opening to genuine otherness arising in the situation (Grace), or resist this "imposition", maintain our course, or strike out in a different direction of our own choosing (will)?

Experiment

You may wish to start an action inquiry concerning your own preferences for planning *vs.* emergence. Pay attention to how much structure *vs.* spontaneity you prefer. In particular, notice your response to situations that cause you to "deviate" from your plan. This inquiry will allow you to begin to develop your own assessment of your "resting state" of will and grace. How much of each element do you lean towards and in what situation? Once you have some clarity concerning your own process begin to notice these preferences in your colleagues. You will also find that whole teams and organisations can also be characterised by their preferences.

One way of considering will and grace is as a change in figure/ground orientation, or flow, from self-other-situation (will), to instead prioritising first situation, then other and then self (grace). As was made clear in Chapter Four, these three variables of the SOS model are, in practice, never considered in isolation. Nonetheless, our conscious intentional capacity is limited to attending to one focus at a time (even when holding multiple foci of interest), so the starting point and directional flow of attentional priorities is vitally important. It is important to note however that, irrespective of the directional flow/movement (will or grace), the ethical attitude towards co-emergence with otherness/dialogue forms the leverage point for change in relational work. Are we really willing to be open and inclusive? And if so, how open and at what cost? These are deep ethical questions that require constant attention throughout any change work.

Within the rest of this chapter, the focus is on these grace-based, relational, and dialogic organisational development approaches but, it is important to repeat that this is not intended to make will-based and grace-based approaches a polarity. It is true that an excess of will can bring disengagement, rigidity, and resistance, but an excess of grace can equally evoke chaos, anarchy, rebellion or disinterest. Accordingly, the key to any change initiative is the integral dialectical tension created by a bespoke mixture of the two forces as appropriate to the specific situation and stakeholders/others who are involved at particular moments in time. In this way, optimal relational gestalt OD can be conceived of as organisational alchemy.

Starting to work with presence and grace: the autonomous criteria of health

Classically, statements were made suggesting that gestalt practitioners were "values-free" and were unattached to specific outcomes when involved in change processes. This simple statement needs some clarification. It is indeed true that more "grace-based" relational gestalt OD practitioners work with an attitude of "creative indifference" to a specific targeted, predetermined outcome, but this is however *wholly different* to them being "indifferent" to outcome. In practice, all relational gestalt OD practitioners are passionately orientated towards the "health" of the organisation, where health is defined by use of the aesthetic and autonomous criteria. These criteria were outlined by Perls, Hefferline, and Goodman, (1951 [1992], pp. 231–232), and were recommended as the sole criteria for determining a "good enough" outcome from a change process. The criteria relate to the quality of the gestalt form/figure as it emerges from a specific field/context at the phase of awareness/mobilisation in the gestalt cycle of experience (see Figure 7.1 previously).

Perls, Hefferline, and Goodman (1951 [1992]) state:

> The figure is specifically psychological: it has specific observable properties of brightness, clarity, unity, fascination, grace, vigour, release, etc., depending on whether we are considering primarily a perceptual, feelingful or motor context. This is of capital

importance (in psychotherapy) for it gives an autonomous criterion of the depth and reality of the experience. (pp. 231–232)

They conclude that it is:

Pointless, therefore, to attempt to deal with any psychological behaviour out of it's socio-cultural, biological and physical context. (p. 231)

As we will see in Chapter Nine, "The art of gestalt interventions", this is vital to the relational gestalt OD practitioner, since it means that theoretically, we judge how to intervene and create change processes by our embodied sense and experience of what is emerging *in the moment*. That is, through our sense of embodied presence, rather than through our alignment to and achievement of predetermined objectives; the latter method being seen as importing "fixed gestalts" that are stable across time, place and person as opposed to a dynamic, "here and now" process of creative adjustment (Perls, et al., 1951 [1994], p. 5).

Of course, in practice however, we have to also hold in mind the necessity for what does emerge to conform to implicit, sometimes explicit, criteria regarding what is appropriate, acceptable, ethical, and desirable, so a degree of "will" is necessarily always presenting and, at a minimum, important for framing the organisational boundaries within which we can operate. Our earlier example illustrated this all too well. Attending to grace does mean however that the *specifics* of both interventions and outcomes are co-emergent and deeply contextual, rather than planned, predetermined and 'importable' from other situations, contexts and cultures. It is this that enables us to work creatively in all organisational situations.

a. **Classic gestalt OD interventions: an excess of "will"?**
   In classic organisational development, gestalt practitioners working in organisations have used the autonomous criteria to raise awareness of specific features in an organisation that they, or others, judged as being ripe for intervention. Often these judgements were directed by the autonomous criteria and meant that practitioners tended to intervene more vigorously where there was a lack of brightness, clarity, unity, fascination, etc.; typically presenting as low

engagement, low motivation, poor performance, poor co-ordination, and lack of commitment to the change process.

Theoretically, this has led to two issues that can be problematic for classic gestalt OD practitioners: first, the autonomous criteria tend to focus on high energy/mobilisation as a "good". Second, and paradoxically, they therefore tend towards acceleration/exaggeration of processes and lean into a more will-based strategic and provocative style (Nevis, 1987). In turn, this has led to a sense that gestalt OD can be quite challenging, creative and experimental: a reputation that has some organisational colleagues quaking in their boots and concerned about potential lack of psychological safety. Keeping this in mind, the criterion of grace can be singled out from the list of autonomous criteria, (above), as having a much needed and different quality, leaning towards quiet receptivity and evocation, instead of bright, vigorous initiation and action.

b. **What is "grace"?**

Traditionally, "grace" has been used to refer to the gifted dimension of life, whether these gifts are seen as coming from god/spirit, of from other aspects of the wider field. In any event, they imply a process where the field/context and specific situation has its own agency and life force, is not static/stable and is certainly not a blank or dead landscape to be written upon. It is our role therefore to be aware of these movements and respond to them, as opposed to resourcing ourselves with energy to Will things to change.

It is enhancement of our embodied recognition, and responsiveness to, these pre-existent movements in the field, that leads us directly to a more relational OD approach. This can be conceived of as leaning in to the "gracious dimension" of the will/grace dialectic, or, similarly, enhancing the grace of our presence as organisational practitioners. Indeed, in previous work (Denham-Vaughan 2014), I have argued therefore for the development of more "relational criteria" for health as opposed to staying with the original list of autonomous criteria. If we look again at what Perls, Hefferline, and Goodman originally wrote in 1951, we read:

> Pointless, therefore, to attempt to deal with any psychological behaviour out of its socio-cultural, biological and physical context.

If we attend more fully to this latter aspect of this sentence, that is, the vital need to prioritise context, the implication is that we start to pay attention to this, rather than the *autonomous* aesthetic sense of the quality of an experience. In other words, we shift our focus from figure more towards ground.

The implications for relational practitioners here are immense: not only do they imply a contextual attentional shift; they support the view of presence articulated by Chidiac and Denham Vaughan in 2007, (and outlined in Chapter Four), as "energetically available and fluidly responsive". In other words, a relational gestalt OD practitioner prioritises responding to the context and specific situational moments as they are unfolding. There is thus explicit attention to "relational fit" and the quality which, in previous work (Denham-Vaughan, 2014), was termed "grace"; a state of being harmonious with and receptive to what is.

Let us consider for a few moments some definitions of grace offered by a range of online dictionaries and which, in 2014, I grouped in to the three categories of aesthetics, ethics, and temporality.

Grace as:

1. Aesthetics:
   a. Seemingly effortless beauty or charm of movement, form, or proportion.
   b. A characteristic or quality pleasing for its charm or refinement.
   c. A sense of fitness or propriety.
2. Ethics:
   a. A disposition to be generous or helpful; goodwill.
   b. Mercy; clemency.
   c. A favour rendered by one who need not do so; indulgence.
3. Temporality:
   a. A temporary immunity or exemption; a reprieve.

Grouping these definitions thus created three dimensions that can support relational gestalt OD practitioners who want to work with increased presence and grace.

First, an attention to the *aesthetics of the co-emergent process*: in other words, how fluid, harmonious, and "beautiful" are the unfolding moments? Do they have a rhythmic, smooth, and harmonious sense of good form, or is there a felt sense of resistance, dullness, absence or indifference? This first inquiry is similar in nature to that of the classic gestalt OD practitioner, where the figure is our focus.

Second, is an attention to the *ethics of co-emergence* itself. Here, the nature of our presence itself takes on an ethical dimension as we try to maintain a rapidly moving creative tension between will and grace: to be both initiating and responding to the situation in every moment. In 2007, Chidiac and Denham-Vaughan described this process as needing the rapidity of attentional shift similar to the speed of a hummingbird's beating wings; the process has to be resonant embodiment and not cognition. Alan Badiou, (2001), calls this degree of attention to an unfolding situation having "fidelity to the event site".

Third, is a sense of having some protected space, where pressure for change, pre-existent plans, and agendas all fall away. Instead, we attend to the timing, flow, rhythm, and varied creative possibilities that are co-emergent in the situation: we can describe this as "being with" and not "aiming".

Development of these three dimensions of grace leads us to an articulation of new "relational criterion of health" for our work, differing from the original "autonomous criterion" proposed by Perls, Hefferline, and Goodman in 1951. Through increasing attention to grace, we become more aware of our impact on the other and the situation as well as knowing our own intentions. We thus acknowledge our relational inter-dependency as well as our independence, recognise our need for relational support as well as for each other's skills and abilities, and privilege and acknowledge our somatic experience.

When working in this way our OD practice will look different; there is more attention to our embodied sense of the environment, and to explicitly sharing awareness with all stakeholders regarding what is co-emerging in the situation. Accordingly, we hold our plans, strategies, agenda, and predetermined outcome as ground, rather than figure, as the process co-emerges. This means opening up a different form of spaciousness and inquiry, particularly in the early phases of scoping and data gathering. In recognition of this, the concept of the liminal space will be introduced next.

The liminal space: an opening to transformational change

The notion of the Liminal Space was formulated in 2010 (Denham-Vaughan) to describe a particular moment in a change process where there is a sense of standing on a threshold. Specifically:

When behind you lies all that is known, you stand on the threshold
of the unknown to which the process of change leads you. This
place, space and/or moment in time is characterized by a willingness to let go of anything familiar and an openness to what is
emerging. (Denham-Vaughan, 2010, p. 35)

These moments in fast-paced organisational life are typically rare,
but introduction of them offers unique possibilities for transformational change. Such spaces are characterised by a genuine openness
to co-emergence and dialogue, combined with an authentic letting
go of predetermined and preconceived agendas and outcomes. As
these processes are described in greater detail in the next chapter, it
is sufficient here to briefly describe the process with reference to the
cycle of experience and the intentional opening of a space for sensing,
resonating, and becoming aware of co-emerging dialogic possibilities *prior* to taking action. This is highly counter cultural, since many
organisations see change processes as opportunities to do something,
sometimes anything, differently. The notion of intentionally pausing
when the field is mobilised, instead of acting, does therefore require
explicit rationale and contracting with all stakeholders to mitigate
feelings of frustration and accusations of time wasting. Instead, opening space for dialogue to emerge is prioritised as an explicit aim of the
intervention

Figure 7.2 shows the opening up of the liminal space between mobilisation and new action and the use of presence to hold the space for
sensing and becoming aware of which co-emerging figures have the
best "relational fit" with the context and should therefore guide new
action. This requires assessment against the dimensions of grace and
the "relational criteria" discussed above.

Figure 7.2 shows how the liminal space is opened up at mobilisation
and held with presence prior to responding. There is an emphasis on the
need to avoid tipping into habitual reactions of the organisation, which
can be generally characterised as either hyper or hypo arousal. More
details are available on these two possibilities in Denham-Vaughan
2010, but briefly hypo-arousal implies that stakeholders might become
disengaged, desensitised, and disaffected with the process, potentially dropping out of the change initiative and falling into "limbo".
At this point, there is no sustained energy for change to gain traction.
Alternatively, some stakeholders, or whole organisations, can become

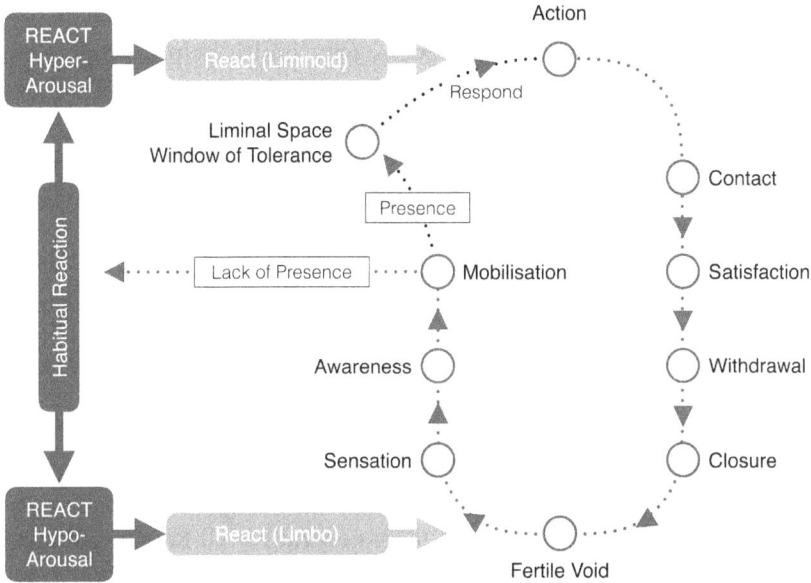

Figure 7-2

Figure 7.2. The presence cycle and the liminal space.

highly hyper-aroused; reactive, agitated, and anxious, with a lot of hares running rather than staying within the change frame. This can be termed a "liminoid" state and it is possible that in this phase emotions will bubble over into conflict, individuals may start "self-medicating" with excess caffeine, alcohol, and other prescribed/non-prescribed substances. In any event, this state also is not sustainable for organisations or individual employees and well-being/resilience often takes a nosedive. Both limbo and liminoid states can be seen in traumatised organisations where there is high resistance to change and a great deal of work needed to re-engage stakeholders in dialogue prior to any chance of a successful change initiative.

The proposal here is that there is an optimal momentum for change and that it is often initially slower/more graceful, than classic OD leads us to believe. In this model, optimal momentum is achieved by explicitly opening up a space for pausing and reflection, (very similar to a mindfulness practice), with the belief that paradoxically, this will ultimately increase the rate at which the organisation arrives at a satisfactory outcome.

For this reason, individuals who wish to facilitate relational gestalt organisational development practices, may find it helpful to develop familiarity with a range of mindfulness strategies, which they can employ to help people temporarily suspend action and move into a more embodied and resonant space. Employment of such strategies has been found to increase resilience amongst practitioners and sustainability across organisations. It is important however to differentiate this mindfulness practice from a more meditative state (see Denham-Vaughan 2014), and more detail about this differentiation comes later in this chapter.

"Theory u" and presencing

While a relational gestalt organisational development approach may be unfamiliar to some, the notions of "presencing" and the incorporation of the concept in "theory u" is generally well known amongst organisational practitioners. Interested readers are directed to Scharmer (2009).

Importantly, what relational organisational gestalt, "theory u" and the practice of both presence and presencing share, is a move from a focus on individual heroic leadership, to the notion of change making as a co-emergent, dialogic and relational process that leans heavily on notions of connectivity, co-dependence, and the process of gestalt formation. In other words, a recognition of the foundational gestalt concept that when individuals come together, the *sustainable* change that can be created is likely to emerge most strongly from their *shared* presence, rather than from the mind of one individual who then shapes a process for others to follow. We would term this a shift in the relational field, implying an improvement and change in both quality of interpersonal relationships, (other dimension), and also the contextual and environmental field, (situational dimension).

"Theory u" is depicted in Figure 7.3 and describes a process of change making that we suggest has much in common with the gestalt process of grace described above.

Note

Where I refer to "self" (or indeed "other" or "situation") I have taken the liberty of employing these terms as they are commonly used in Western culture to describe the relational processes that might more accurately be described as "sense of self" and respectively, "sense of other" or "sense of the situation". I have done this to avoid overly cumbersome language, but realise the risk of "essentialising" relational processes into "things/essences". In this way I have possibly supported an overly Cartesian and modernist worldview still present in mainstream culture but one that, while visible in classical gestalt theoretical discourses, is far more nuanced and dynamic in contemporary relational gestalt discourse.

As can be seen, there is a move from holding a space, (very similar to the liminal space), into a state of presence from which actions then emerge. Interestingly, in "theory u", the "movement to action" is depicted as anti-clockwise, rather than the classic clockwise direction of the cycle of experience outlined in Figure 7.1 earlier in this chapter.

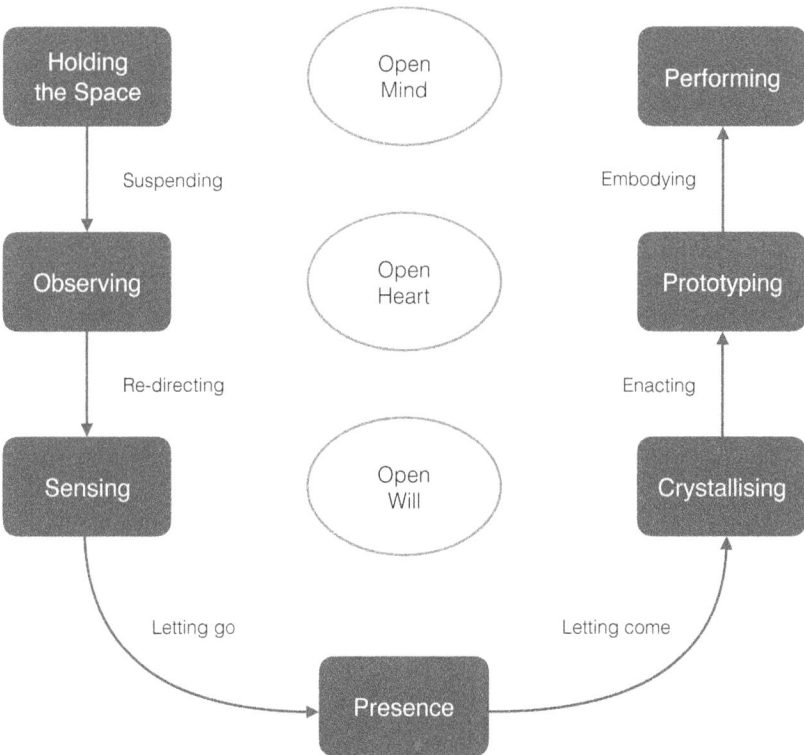

Figure 7.3. "Theory u", redrawn from Scharmer, 2009.

Equally, the state of "presence" is primarily located in "Theory u" at the point in the cycle of experience where gestalt practitioners have classically positioned the "fertile void".

At this point it becomes useful to, differentiate a "meditative use of presence" (where we seek "inside our self" for space), from a "mindful use of presence", (where we seek spaciousness by attending to the "outside world" without judgement or reactivity: a liminal space). In "theory u", the meditative state called "presence" is positioned in the "fertile void" space and the latter mindful state, called holding the space/suspending, between mobilisation and action, in the "liminal space" position (see Edmonds, 2013, for further discussion and clarification). The important point for practice being that in meditation one seeks to decrease mobilisation and attention to external events, while in the liminal space/mindfulness practice, we maintain mobilisation to create multiple possibilities, while suspending action.

Scharmer described the type of presence that is embodied in "theory u" as being a connection to "the deepest source of yourself and will" and in this way is describing a state that is more similar to one of meditation, and an inward focus on embodied physical sensation, thoughts, emotions, hopes, and dreams as opposed to the sort of mobilised presence described in the previous liminal space section, where there is an explicit attention to the wider context.

Of course, in practice this is another dialectical tension; one zone of awareness is figure whilst the other is ground and our attentional biases oscillate. Nonetheless, there is a discipline in holding a particular type of space and in differentiating between the two states. As such, both meditation and mindfulness practices are therefore likely to be helpful for relational OD practitioners working with presence and grace, as they will be required to shift themselves and others between these zones of awareness.

Presence and grace: "theory u" and the gracious spiral dynamic of relational organisational gestalt

At first glance, "theory u" (Figure 7.3) could be described as looking like a variant of the gestalt cycle of experience outlined in Figure 7.1 earlier. Indeed, this similarity between the formulations has led to development of two moving meditations that can be employed in different forms of relational organisational gestalt change practices (Denham-Vaughan,

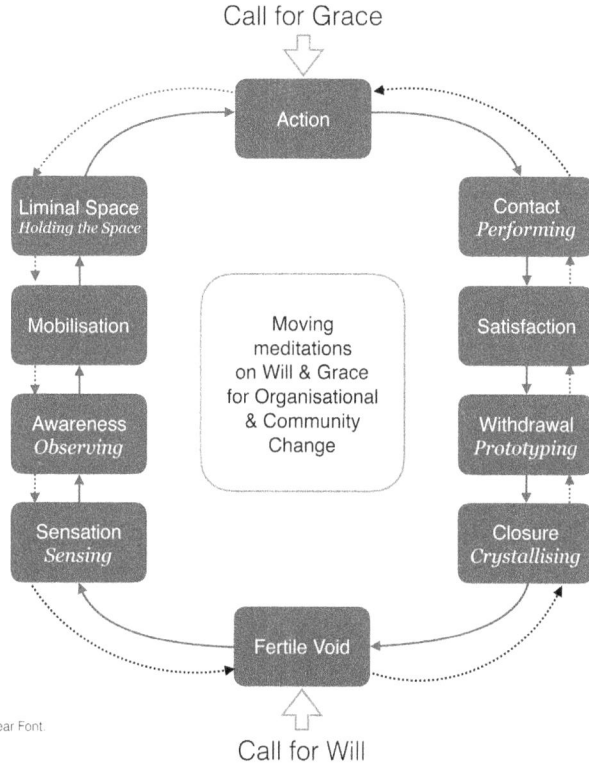

Figure 7.4. Moving meditations on will & grace.

2011). The first form can be described as a "call for will" and the second "a call for grace". Figure 7.4, shows the movement of both around the cycle of experience; will moving clockwise and grace anti-clockwise.

Regarding the movement of "will", with the exception of the introduction of the liminal space, (as a strategy for achieving greater dialogic co-emergence and stakeholder engagement), these are similar processes/diagnostics for change as classic gestalt organisational work and used in similar contexts.

The second movement meditation however, involving a grace based practice, leads us in a different direction; one that looks more like "theory u". This form is designed to be employed in different contextual conditions; those where many change initiatives are already in process, or have been tried and failed and where individuals are starting to feel the sense of fatigue, confusion, and chaos that can be characteristic of contemporary fast moving businesses. At this point, as can be seen from Figure 7.4 the entry point is therefore at the action stage of the cycle, with the first action taken being a *reversal* of the usual clockwise movement in the gestalt cycle towards action/experiment. Instead there is a *reverse* into the liminal space, with the focus on decreasing mobilisation, increasing awareness, enhancement of the sensing function, and a movement towards the fertile void. This is similar to the "theory u" formulation, but the relational organisational gestalt practitioner will also be paying attention to the threefold model of grace, concerning aesthetics, ethics/values and the spaciousness or timing of the change processes. There is therefore, an explicit contracting to decrease momentum, increase embodied sensing and increase the sense of co-emergence as a specific ethical goal that supports the emergence of presence.

To briefly recap, "presence", as stated earlier in Chapter Four, involves alignment of the three dimensions of SOS, and thus expands the field of our "meditation/inner spaciousness" to include awareness of others and the situation. Through this process a sense of an expanded field and shared purpose can therefore emerge (Laloux, 2014). According to Harrington (1996) this expansion creates a much more "enchanted" and dynamic view of the world; a world of "spiritual mystery, emotional colour and ethical significance" (p. 14). Senge et al. (2004) describe this state of presence occurring in the "fertile void" as a key point where "the fire of creation burns and enters the world through us" (p. 240).

Case example

Consulting to a major bank undergoing considerable and rapid change we arrived to meet our sponsoring team of five executives from HR and Rewards departments. A very "ragged" first face-to-face meeting ensued with only two people in the room at the start of the meeting, a great sense of pressure, multiple performance targets that were not being met, team conflicts and disagreement on priorities. We agreed to meet again in two weeks and in the interim, raised our need for clear contracting to ensure we met their agreed priorities: but these were not agreed by the time of our return visit. We determined to use a grace-based initiative in the meeting in the hope of gaining some shared agreement between the team and with ourselves concerning some interim objectives, and, to this end, suggested an "experiment" with each taking a short walk outside for five minutes. On return, we presented our SOS framework very briefly and asked the five people to see if we could enquire into their sense of three different priorities; those of the situation, those for key stakeholders and those of themselves. Once the list was generated we suggested reviewing this together and trying to get a shared "gut sense" of which were the top cards for us to attempt to address when structuring our intervention. Although members of the team did express some frustration at the process of being asked to "resonate" and "score" each of the issues that had been presented, we kept emphasising that if we could reach shared agreement at this point it would bring us into alignment as a team and save time later. We also highlighted that the inquiry enabled us to assess both their stated and "lived" ethical priorities as the business went forward. Although the process of review did take ninety minutes, the team were both surprised and delighted by the depth of discussion that ensued, what they learnt about each other's core values and the resulting contractual clarity that was surfaced, and delivered an agreed way forward.

Summary: organisational structures and forms

This chapter has covered three variations of a relational organisational gestalt OD change process.

First, we reviewed strategies where will is figural and we are aiming to increase energy and initiate action. We have suggested that the classic gestalt cycle of experience (Figure 7.1) and Liminal cycle (Figure 7.2), are both ways of conceptualising these processes in a relationally orientated gestalt organisational practice. Based on the formulation offered in Figure 7.4, we could propose that classic gestalt OD strategies, employing the cycle of experience, may be most effective in organisations where there is an appetite for change, a willingness to raise awareness and energy to experiment.

In some organisations however, there may also be a need for slowing down momentum, particularly where a number of change initiatives have previously been tried or are already in progress. In such situations, people can easily become over stimulated and start to react with habitual patterns of either hypo or hyper-arousal. In this chapter, the concept of the liminal space has been offered as a way of decreasing momentum, and opening up embodied sensitivity to aesthetic co-emergent possibilities for change that can be agreed upon and mulled over together prior to action being taken. As such, the liminal space formulation begins to introduce the notion of grace based change (as characterised by attention to aesthetics, ethical presence, and decreased momentum/temporality), within a classic gestalt OD, will-based change initiative.

A third process was identified which leaned more heavily towards a grace based process and which changed the usual entry point and reversed the sequence of contact. This process, outlined in Figure 7.4, presents itself as the intervention of choice in contexts where there have been multiple change initiatives, the situation is complex, fluid and changing and as such, a dancing landscape is in process. In these situations, timing is often of the essence, with alignment of stakeholders at similar points in the change process being an imperative; this is hard to achieve due to complex interdependencies. For this reason, the grace-based entry point is at "action" (Figure 7.4) with an immediate contract for holding the space and a contracted *decrease* of mobilisation, and increases in dialogue between key stakeholders. This relational/dialogic process, which will be described in detail in the next chapter, opens the way for spaces of collective resonance so that organisational forms can be crystallised/designed and prototyped/experimented with, before being enacted. I acknowledged that this formulation is similar to that offered by Otto Scharmer in "theory u" and offers a highly relational form of gestalt organisational development. It is predicated on a sense of opening to the collective wisdom of others involved in the change process and also the wisdom of the wider field. As such it can be described as an "enchanted form" of relational organisational gestalt. These methods are particularly useful in decentralised, or hybrid organisations, similar to those described by Brafman and Beckstrom, (2006) and Laloux, (2014). As such they present an integral paradigm for use in fast moving, contemporary, diverse, often global organisations and situations.

In the chapters that follow, there will be further discussion on the role of dialogue in mediating such processes and the art of intervening. In combination, the hope is that the initial claims made for relational organisational gestalt to provide a "complex, emergent, relational and multi-dimensional change strategy" (Denham-Vaughan & Chidiac, 2009, p. 253) is now increasingly recognised as a flexible methodology for supporting both pre-planned/pre-formed and bespoke change initiatives.

CHAPTER EIGHT

The practice of dialogue and relational support

> When we surrender to dialogue, the conversation we intend is always different from the conversation that happens.
>
> —*Jacobs*, 2016, p. 148

C alls to action in most contexts resound as bugles signalling the start of scheduled or planned events. Supporting action in organisational settings usually means a clear action plan mobilising people to "do" and get busy with given tasks and responsibilities. As we have seen in the previous chapter, this will-based approach is one way of bringing about change and relational gestalt offers a different attitude characterised by less push but rather an opening of a generative liminal space that attends to needs and allows a natural self-organising flow into action. At the individual or intra-personal level, this process is internal, organic, and often a natural physiological self-regulating function. In other words, with good support, most individuals can act with the environment to have their needs satisfied. In dyads and groups however, the field is more complex and so cohesive emergent action requires a co-generative and supportive space in which needs can surface and coalesce into an impulse towards movement and change. In gestalt, this space is facilitated through dialogue and relational support.

This chapter will therefore begin by exploring the notion of dialogue from a gestalt perspective by outlining key influences on gestalt's dialogic theory and practice before proposing a framework for the practice of dialogue within relational organisational gestalt.

What is dialogue?

In organisational learning terms, dialogue is often looked at as a set of prescriptive behaviours that lead to the creation of knowledge and ideas that are beyond the capabilities of individuals (Rhodes, 2000, p. 218). We can see the importance of this to organisations in that "dialogue projects" are one of the major areas of research at the Sloan School of Management at MIT. The prescriptive approach often given to dialogue misses however the fundamental force behind its generative quality which is principally a relational one.

From a gestalt perspective, the notion of dialogue is not just as a way of communicating shared understanding, knowledge and learning but refers also to a certain quality of relating that supports insight, discovery, growth, and action through contact. Research shows that the key conditions for such innovation and emergence to take place is psychological safety (Edmondson & Lei, 2014). Understandably, individuals will not bring themselves to genuine dialogue in situations or contexts where they fear reprisals, bullying, side-lining or indeed criticism.

Dialogue is both a stance towards others and a set of behaviours that open a safe and supportive haven providing fertile conditions for emergence and newness to flourish. Dialogue is that which both accompanies as well as enables action (Jacobs, 2006; Denham-Vaughan, 2010).

Gestalt draws on phenomenological and hermeneutic dialogue traditions. From a phenomenological perspective, dialogue is understood as a practice given meaning through the consciousness of participants and their making it conscious in conversation with others (Westoby, 2014, p. 70). In other words, it is the sharing of our individual perceptions, thoughts and feelings that contribute to the practice of dialogue. As a hermeneutic practice, the importance of the dialogical exchange is not in what is transmitted between interlocutors, i.e., the content, but rather what participation in that exchange can unexpectedly bring about in the understanding of each speaker and often contrary to their willing and doing (Davey, 2104, p. 35). In a hermeneutic frame, dialogue cannot be planned but emerges in the flow of understanding that is unique and new in each interaction.

* * *

This section will next outline the work of two key thinkers of dialogue: Martin Buber and Mikhail Bakhtin that have, amongst others, informed gestalt theory and practice. What these approaches have in common is that they present relational perspectives on dialogue in that their philosophies privilege the relationship between uncertainty, context-dependence and dynamic emergent change (Stewart, et al., 2004, p. 31).

Martin Buber

Dialogue is a central tenet in gestalt and has in the therapeutic arena been mostly based on the work of the philosopher Martin Buber (1958). Although Buber's approach to dialogue has mostly been looked at within dyadic work configurations such as therapist/client or coach/ coachee, its application to group and organisational settings is valuable and relevant in that it brings a fundamental aspect of otherness and mutuality of relationships.

For Buber, "all real living is meeting" (ibid, p. 25) and by this he means that as human beings we are always in relationship. One of Buber's key contribution to dialogue is his differentiating between different modes of being with others or relational attitudes towards others which he termed "I-thou" and "I-it". The I-thou meeting is relating to other as an "experiencing subject, not an experienced object" (Buber, 1958, p. vii) and so engaging with the other person in a dialogue of equals involving each other's whole being. Lapsing into I-it relating is perceiving only aspects of the other person's being, be it their role or function and so objectifying them in the interaction. I-it is a relationship of detachment, distancing which often denies the uniqueness of the other. This type of instrumental relationship where we see the other person as a means to an end, someone who's useful for that particular task or job is often prevalent in organisations.

In an I-thou encounter, dialogue is about making deep and meaningful contact with another person through listening, understanding, and totally accepting your own, the other's and the newly-created perspective and experience between you. The I-thou stance refers to the capacity to bring all of yourself to the meeting with another while simultaneously remaining open to the impact of the other. It is about respectfully sharing yourself without hiding behind roles, while being genuinely interested in and accepting of others just as they are, without seeing them as means to an end.

Paradoxically, this type of relating is both remarkably simple in concept and hard to offer and experience. It holds boundless possibility as well as risk and uncertainty. In practice, relating involves a rhythmic swaying between both "I-it" and "I-thou" modes of being with another at the emerging contact boundary, and it is exactly this alternating between those two ways of being that is much needed in organisational settings.

Experiment

Take a moment to think of an I-thou moment you have had recently. It could be a transformative conversation or briefer moment with a colleague, client or someone outside of work. Perhaps it was unexpected, with someone you didn't know or with someone you knew well but didn't expect this type of contact. What did it feel like in the moment? How did it leave you feeling after the encounter?

Mikhail Bakhtin

Mikhail Bakhtin, a Russian literary theorist and social thinker views all human social life as intrinsically dialogic and relational. Bakhtin (1986) writes: "Any understanding of live speech, a live utterance, is inherently responsive [...]. Any understanding is imbued with response and necessarily elicits it in one form or another" (p. 68). For Bakhtin, all meaning we make is a co-construction in two respects: first it is produced through dialogic relations to other meanings (whether cultural or contextual) and it emerges through the collaborative activities of the participants in social interaction (Phillips, 2011, p. 28).

His thinking is particularly relevant in the context of organisational life as he addresses the concept of dialogue and power directly. He contrasts between dialogism and monologism where the latter is the dominance of a singular voice often associated with a centralised power system; a single voice speaking the only truth that can exist, without challenge or interplay. Dialogic speech, on the other hand, always involves a multiplicity of speakers and a variety of perspectives; knowledge or truth then becomes something negotiated, contested, and social, rather than something pronounced from on high.

For Bakhtin we are inherently dialogic beings in the sense that meaning—including understanding self and other—is produced dialectically in the tension between different and often contradictory and opposing voices. According to Bakhtin (1981, 1984, 1986) meaning making is the product of two competing tendencies: the *centripetal tendency* towards unity, towards a common and unifying thought or idea and the *centrifugal tendency* towards difference and diversity. We can easily see how organisational life can be understood as a multiplicity of often conflicting voices in which people in conversation are continuously choosing whether to privilege one voice over another, to merge certain voices together or to position voices in ways that lead to consensus or disagreement (Barge & Little, 2002, p. 387). These two tendencies are similar to what Gaffney (2006) calls the "existential dilemma" of groups and the inherent tension in groups to be "a part of" and "apart from".

Experiment

In your next team meeting, attend to the interplay between the centripetal and centrifugal tendencies. Which tendency seems to predominate in the discussion and at what point? Is there a preference for a centripetal position where participants emphasise unity through phrases like "we're together in this" or "we are saying the same thing"; or is there more room for opening up voices that hold differing forms of knowledge and perspective?

It is helpful to view dialogue as a continuum between the singular voice whereby a particular idea or thought is privileged (like that of an expert or leader for example) and at the other end, a polyphony of voices each holding a different meaning or interpretation. In the mechanistic paradigm of organisations, polyphony would be unacceptable and "management" would strive for a centrally agreed voice which sets and guides action. The notion of polyphony is however more in tune with a fluid and living organisation where meaning making emerges from the totality of all influences. Supporting this view, Barge and Little (2002) recognise that conflicting voices can produce a "constructive cacophony", a linking of dissenting voices that leads to the co-generation of innovation (ibid, p. 389).

Tensions between dialogic theories and organisational life

The newcomer to dialogue may at this point be dubious about the application of dialogic ideals in organisations. There are indeed apparent tensions between the ideas of Buber and Bakhtin outlined above and the harsher and less relationally focused reality of organisational life.

A first tension can be framed as holding to the ideal of dialogic principles in situations where pre-set and top-down strategic goals are common and often a necessity. Buber's perspective emphasises process rather than achieving outcomes and Bakhtin's critique of monologisation likewise leads to a democratic opening up for a plurality of voices (Phillips, 2011, p. 96) rather than a focusing of ideas from a few. It is fair to say that the majority of our contact (especially in organisations) is made much more in the spirit of treating the other as an object—which Buber described as "I-it" encounters. Most of our episodes of contact as organisational practitioners, take place at this level of contact as we attend to task, outcome and strategy. Although Buber reified the I-thou meeting over I-it, he also acknowledged the need for I-it as a "technical dialogue" (Buber, 1947, p. 22) which offers up the idea of not only focusing on the interpersonal process in organisational life but also holding the strategic element (White, 2008). Similarly, Barge and Little (2002) write of the need for "dialogical wisdom" as a reflexive awareness of the centripetal and centrifugal voices in conversation. This can be achieved through what they call *blended voices* whereby a balance is achieved between the two tendencies.

There is also a tension between ideals of dialogue that cannot be either reached, or reached for, and the pressures of organisational life to grasp outcome. Indeed, for Buber: "The thou meets me through grace, it is not found in seeking" (1958, p. 11), whilst for Bakhtin there is an unfinalisable aspect of dialogue which means that there can never be agreement on any single truth. These ideals of dialogic practice tend towards understanding and connection (grace) but organisational practice also requires working groups in organisations to reach some mutual agreement to propel joint action (Westoby, 2014, p. 76) (will). In facilitating dialogue, the gestalt practitioner needs to work with this tension as a dialectic, honouring both the unreachable ideals of dialogue as well as the need for closure and action in organisational life. Doing so transparently and in awareness, engages a group to share responsibility for managing this tension.

Stepping into a dialogic space therefore requires us to do so in awareness of the inherent tensions between will and grace, process and task, individual and group, togetherness and differentiation. These polarities are a reflection of the complexity of the dialogic space which cannot be reduced and which the practitioner needs to navigate with trust in co-emergence, and faith that this will lead to more creative and transformative outcomes.

The remainder of this chapter will now introduce a framework for dialogic working which reflects these tensions and captures a relational gestalt perspective of working with dialogue in organisations.

The four quadrants of dialogue: an integrated gestalt framework for organisational dialogue

Building on gestalt theory as well as contributions from Buber and Bakhtin, an integrated framework for dialogue in organisations must contain both an ontological level—that is, how to be with others—as well as methodological level—that is, what the practice of dialogue looks like.

Figure 8.1 shows the framework building on two key dimensions. The first on the horizontal axis builds on Buber's differentiation between I-thou and I-it which can be seen as a contrasting between process and strategy or grace and will. The second dimension on the vertical axis, picks up the tension between unity and diversity, or isolation and confluence, with Bakhtin's centripetal and centrifugal forces.

The framework thus shows a dialogic space of four quadrants encompassing differing types of dialogue styles:

- *Being-with*, which focuses on what Buber refers to as "turning towards the other" where each person's story, perspective, and being is accepted and confirmed.
- *Exploring*, which stays with the individual experiences but invites a more active consideration and focus on specific thoughts, feelings and ideas.
- *Aiming*, which acknowledges the organisational pressures for unity, coherent action, and integration.
- *Dynamic co-emergence* which is the sense of togetherness and unity that cannot be facilitated or anticipated but which emerges from attending responsively to the other quadrants. It is in this space that

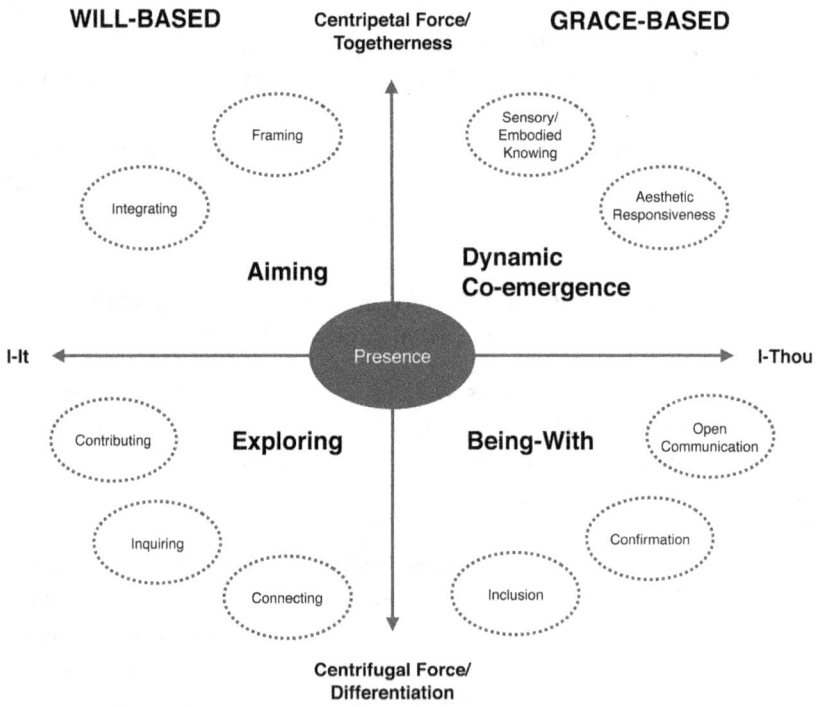

Figure 8-1

Figure 8.1. The four quadrants of dialogue.

we might expect some of our most transformative, innovative and breakthrough moments to emerge.

Being-with

Being-with is the essence of Buber's approach in his description of a relational turn towards other and an invitation to genuine meeting. It is an opening towards an I-thou moment where self and other are reciprocal partners engaged in a "dynamic of elemental togetherness" (Kramer & Gawlick, 2003, p. 24). The focus on this quadrant doesn't typically emerge from an agenda item or set objective to achieve and yet is fundamental to a coachee, group or organisation to function optimally. As seen in case example A later in this chapter, moments of "being-with" often emerge from the existing dynamics in the room and it is up to the facilitator, manager or coach to welcome and open the dialogic space for being-with.

Lynne Jacobs, a gestalt and intersubjective therapist, identified four key "dialogic competencies" (1989) required to enable an I-thou stance. These are presence, inclusion, confirmation, and a commitment to dialogue.

It is worth stating that whilst dialogic competencies are identified, for Buber dialogue is an emergent quality of communication that occurs transiently and often in surprising rather than neat, orderly ways and it cannot be planned or facilitated. These competencies therefore inform a stance rather than a methodology of action in this case. As gestalt practitioners, we can only hold an intention towards an I-thou attitude as the I-thou moment itself cannot be forced or manufactured—we can only be open to the potential for this experience and go with it into the unknown when it does.

Presence

The notion of presence has been covered extensively in previous chapters and central to a gestalt practitioner. For gestalt theorists such as Jacobs (1989) and Yontef (1993), presence is being supported to show our "true self" in all that this entails. This includes being open to how we are impacted by the person we are relating with, whether that feels good or bad. The opposite of presence in this case is "seeming" or pretending.

Inclusion

Inclusion is about standing in someone else's shoes and seeing their perspective without judgment, prejudice or condemnation. It is about understanding the other person's experience without losing a sense of ourselves. In practicing inclusion, we are attempting to understand the world of the other person we are working with in order that they can experience feeling understood. For many, this is often in and of itself a connecting and deeply moving experience. There are a number of ways we can attune to the other and demonstrate inclusion be it cognitively, emotionally or even by resonating at an embodied level. Example of communicating inclusion can include:

- Verbal statements, e.g., "I imagine for you this must be ...", or para-phrasing: "So what you are saying is ..."
- Non-verbal facial expressions, nods, body language, etc.
- Self-disclosure, e.g., "When this happened to me, it was ..."

Inspired by Buber, Bohm (1990) and Isaacs (1999) have introduced similar attributes to inclusion such as "listening', "respecting" and "suspension" which highlight the importance of turning towards the other whilst suspending judgment. Inclusion is an element of dialogue that can be most useful in organisational work. In most meetings we witness people talking, postulating their thoughts, defending their position, telling others what they should be doing, and listening is a seriously under-utilised skill. When many people do listen they are often doing so in order to understand the weaknesses of the other's argument, to advocate their own opinion or to find the space to jump in and talk. When instead we focus on inclusion, our relationships with the person/people we are working with expand and multiple understandings and vast arrays of new possibilities open up.

Confirmation

In confirmation the other is accepted and recognised as being "good enough" as they are right now. It is a stance of acceptance of others without any negative judgment despite failings or struggles. This is not dissimilar to what Carl Rogers (1951), a humanistic psychologist, called "unconditional positive regard" and recognises that we nurture each other's growth and development through acceptance.

Confirmation does not mean ignoring problems or focusing only on the positives or what we find easy. Confirming is recognising and respecting other people's contribution, even when we don't agree with it. This is not easy in organisational contexts where individuals are mostly recognised through their achievements. It demands from us that we separate our appreciation and acceptance for another person from any assessment of their behaviour. Remembering that most people don't set out to do a bad job is helpful in maintaining the attitude of confirmation. This stance holds the wholeness of the other, their unrealised potential and their ability to change and grow as they feel accepted.

Open communication

An essential ingredient of Buberian dialogue is a willingness and courage to be honest with an appropriate level of self-disclosure. Open communication must not be confused with total honesty. It is about being as open as each participant feels supported to be or that the situation can manage. If not used sensitively, clumsy honesty or over disclosure can lead to shame in organisational settings. So, a team coach would for example, refrain from sharing publicly his or her feedback to team members unless this was agreed upon and done in a way which would be supportive to that person or team in that particular context.

Commitment to open communication fits well within the gestalt frame of "use of self" as instrument as it invites practitioners to self-disclose in service of the client. Some of the most impactful and helpful gestalt interventions happen when practitioners share how they are experiencing the person/team they are working with. Similar to Isaacs' (1999) practice of "voicing", commitment to dialogue is about the courage to express what is most needed to move the dialogue forward. Within a dialogic and supportive relationship it is possible to be extremely challenging and share truths that in other contexts might be rejected.

Case example A

During the coffee break of a departmental team meeting, a few people were gathered engaging in casual conversation and commenting on Muslim employees needing to leave on Friday to attend to their religious prayers. As the group gathered to start the session, one man, announced that he was offended by the gossip about Muslims he'd overheard and was considering leaving the meeting. As a facilitator I was aware, in the silence that occurred after his announcement, that here was a significant dialogical moment for this group. Would they respond to the radical invitation of otherness, calling for genuine multicultural celebration of "other" or were they going to retreat? I sat on the edge of my seat aware that despite the need to attend to the urgent task of agreeing operational improvements within the department, here was a moment of dialogical group development in the process—this was a moment where the "being-with" element of dialogue needed to be in focus and worked with.

It would have been too easy to ignore this moment as not being relevant to the work itself and yet, dialogue around this issue was crucial to the overall task. With the group's consent, we allowed time for people to step forward to be inclusive with, and confirming of both the individual who felt offended as well as with the "offenders". This dialogic work can be uncomfortable and slow and yet it is the search for mutual understanding that creates both openness and solidarity in groups.

Exploring & aiming

These two quadrants fall on the I-it side of the dialogic space. They speak primarily to a deliberate intent and behaviour to self-organising around given tasks or set priorities. This is the type of dialogue that at all times keeps in focus the strategic imperatives of the situation or context. Dialogue in this space maintains a focus on the task at hand, how best to explore it amongst participants (*exploring*) and unify around an outcome (*aiming*). The behavioural elements are provided by Lars Marmgren (2014, p. 106), a gestalt organisational practitioner as guidelines for co-operation and emergent self-organisation in groups that would lead to better "thinking together" (ibid). The elements are:

- *Framing*: It is often the case that a group sitting around the same table have different views about what is being talked about. As Marmgren points out, there is often a lack of clarity about why the team is talking about a particular issue or what they are supposed to achieve in their discussion. In some ways this is a type of light contracting that provides boundaries for the ensuing conversation. This framing does not need to be detailed or explicit. A simple statement of inquiry in some cases is enough.

- *Integrating*: Every participant has a responsibility to capture and summarise how he or she has understood what has been said and where the group stands in that process. This needs to be done with reference to the framing made at the beginning of the conversation. Generativity requires the group to learn how to subtly move their attention between the process of individuals and their interrelationship towards the stream of shared meaning that is trying to emerge through the dialogue as people share their contributions.

- *Contributing*: Each participant is responsible for contributing to what is in focus; be it through facts, opinions, fears and hopes. This is not an expectation of knowing but rather a statement of engagement around the given task.

- *Inquiring*: Each participant has a responsibility to enquire into other people's contributions. This could be through probing questions, to clarify or deepen their contribution. In some cases, this also could apply to inquiring into why someone hasn't spoken. In dialogue, participants come with an intention to understand, but also an uncertainty, recognising that any attachment to beliefs or ideas will undermine capacities for dialogue.

- *Connecting*: By connecting to each other's statements, the group members create the conditions for a common gestalt formation and a movement towards unity. Connecting pre-supposes some level of inclusion as participants try to understand what others have said and situate themselves in contrast to that. Participants may feel closer or more distant to each other's ideas, thoughts and feelings and it is that relative positioning that emerges from voicing our response to what others have contributed. This response could be an association, support or even indeed a criticism of what has been said.

Dynamic co-emergence

This quadrant of dialogic relating is characterised by a distinctive shift in energy where a different quality of being in the group or dyad can be felt. There is a unity emerging around relational themes and a common ground that takes shape forming a receptacle for a joined figure. The group or dyad is in flow and newness in terms of perception, options or ideas emerges. The group as well as the facilitator are at their most present; energetically available and fluidly responsive. The facilitator's interventions in this quadrant would typically be few and far between. The group is in the flow of dialogue and the primary consideration would be to respect the co-emergence. Any intervention would be guided by a sensory/embodied knowing and an aesthetic responsiveness to the moment rather than a rational or thought out response.

Unlike some theories of group development such moments do not necessarily require time for the group to reach a "performing" stage, and does not have as a pre-requisite that people get along or have strong personal relationships. It is typically the presence and personal awareness of group members that facilitate such moments.

Rather than "frame" and "integrate" what is known, as is the case in I-it relating, this quadrant relies on a more graceful intuiting of a co-arising moment that unifies and shapes future possibilities. It is more akin to practices such as presencing (Scharmer, 2009) where sensing into the future arises from the present moment. Finally, it is in the dance and balancing of the various quadrants, holding equally the importance of relationship and outcome that emergent and sustainable dialogue leads to supportive action.

Case example B

Busy heads of units have been called to meet monthly, at the request of their head of department, in order to improve coordination and efficiency between units. There is little day to day operational coordination required between units but a clear strategic direction is imperative in order to ensure appropriate funding for the department and positioning within the business overall. Most attendees have very busy schedules and have been struggling to cope with the workload of their individual units. There has in the past been little motivation or attention given to the strategy which has so far been left to the head of department to sort out. Prior to the next meeting, they were advised that the head of department has resigned unexpectedly and it is likely that their units will be merged into another department. The group is quite despondent.

A: Well, I really didn't expect this today (sounding irritated). I came here expecting us to work towards improving things in our areas to make things easier but I'm now left with even more to carry.

B: None of us expected this ... you're not the only one carrying a lot. I'm not sure it is worth my time to keep coming when something like this is dropped on us. What a waste of time this has been.

FACILITATOR: Well, I can understand you being irritated ... what is happening for you all listening to B saying this has been a waste of time? [Inclusion and an invitation for sharing/open communication]

D: I really get it ... I struggle myself and am also not very pleased to hear this as I've had to re-arrange my schedule to be here today. [Inclusion and differentiation]

The facilitator encourages dialogue around elements of "being-with" to share and relate to each other given the new situation. A common theme of feeling demanded of and unappreciated emerges. The group feels more cohesive and supportive of each other's struggles.

C: Well, we've got to know each other and I feel have been making some good improvements [confirming], I really don't want all this to be thrown away and re-structured and feel like doing something. [Contributing]

FACILITATOR: You seem to be agreeing in terms of the impact of this news. I'm wondering what is it you would all want to have happen now? What would be useful? [Aiming: framing intervention]

B: Yes, we have been working well but you [pointing to C] are the newcomer and I've been here before and we keep throwing good work away ... not sure I'm up for it again—sometimes I feel I just need to focus on my unit and not bother about what else happens.

A: We've all been here before. The question is now: is it worth us doing anything to influence the restructure. I'm not sure.

FACILITATOR: There are two options being voiced here: to do nothing and let it all happen, or to try and influence future direction. Where are you all on this? [Integrating and inquiring]

Individuals name their relative position as they explore the option of influencing or not. More energy emerges for the influencing option and actions are discussed [exploring]. The group feels more energised and moving towards a dynamic co-emergence as new solutions and possibilities are tabled.

Summary

This chapter has introduced the four quadrants of dialogue; a frame-work for the practice of dialogue within relational organisational gestalt. It has grappled with the inherent tension in the application of the ideals of dialogic practice in a context which demands outcome and is typically driven by pre-set strategic goals. Supporting action in such organisational contexts is therefore a delicate dance between holding the process for people to connect and understand one another, as well as reaching for coherence and mutual agreement that will propel joint action. Navigating such a dialogic space requires skilful awareness of this tension as practitioners and facilitators balance their attention between aiming, exploring, being-with, as well as staying open to the uncertainty and magic of dynamic co-emergence. The next chapter will cover some aspects of what intervening in such a dialogic space looks like for the gestalt practitioner.

CHAPTER NINE

The art of gestalt interventions

In gestalt, intervening is considered more an art than a science as key choice points are subjective, and respond primarily to an aesthetic of contact in the moment rather than an obvious right or wrong choice. As outlined in Chapter Seven, both the dialectic of will and grace infuse interventions and this chapter will address practical skills and notions that support gestalt practitioners be it coaches, facilitators or managers in this dance of intervening.

The chapter will begin by describing key stages of intervention in the hope of capturing the essence of what skilled practitioners do when in flow. In most forms of art, the artist begins with an arduous learning of skills before gradually, brush and palette become a part of who and how they are. Similarly, a practitioner may at first experience the stages of an intervention as reductive and laborious steps but these with practice and familiarity, will become embedded and embodied in their way of being. The chapter will then outline some key gestalt principles that support the intervening practitioner in balancing challenge and support as well as dealing with uncertainty and shame.

The flow of intervening

Intervening is an act of ethical presence. It therefore emerges from the practitioner's responsiveness to themselves, to others and the situation they find themselves in, as well as from their willingness to be available and in service of what might unfold in the moment. Remembering that effective change takes place at the contact boundary, we could say that within gestalt, intervening is a very intentional act of disturbing the contact boundary. It is therefore a *wilful* action that emerges from both grace and intuition.

At its best, an intervention is an uninterrupted flow of experience in which the practitioner joins their client in a contactful and respectful dance. It is therefore helpful to describe the process and flow of intervening as being situated along the gestalt cycle of experience (CoE) as this also recognises it as a subjective process susceptible and vulnerable to interruptions. Figure 9.1 shows the steps of a gestalt interventions positioned along the CoE.

These steps should not be viewed as a one off sequential events but rather a cycle where the act of intervening repeats until the "unit of work" (Carter, 2004; Rainey Tolbert, 2004) is complete. Carter (2004),

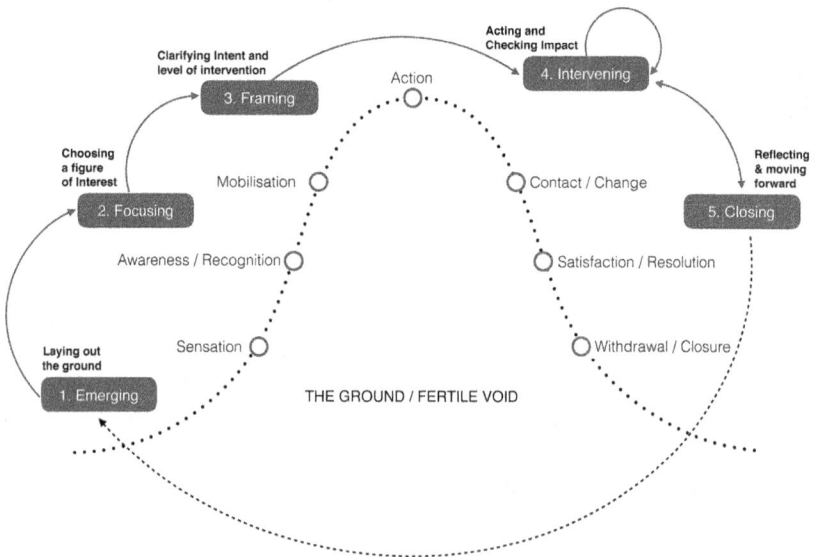

Figure 9.1. The flow of intervention.

a gestalt OD practitioner, writes that a unit of work is a "coherent experience that can be advantageously assimilated. It may be the completion of a task, the resolution of an issue, or a powerful learning experience. A successful Unit of Work creates sustained and meaningful energy" (ibid, 2004, p. 16).

This chapter will address specifically the smallest unit of intervention, that moment in which a practitioner steps forward, says or does something with a deliberate intent of influencing the client in for example a coaching or facilitation role. The cycle of intervening plays out of course over longer timescales such as in implementing a leadership development workshop or transformation programme. The steps are the same but time between each stage affords practitioners the luxury of greater reflection, whilst being responsive in-the-moment is often the most challenging type of intervention.

Example

Working with a group within a large transformation project, the practitioner is facilitating a meeting around improving key processes. One of the more senior managers, "Ben", feels defensive and resistant to changing a particularly problematic and political internal process he has worked hard at making work for his department.

BEN: We always return to this process. We've got it working as best we can. Nothing is ever perfect, and we just all accept it … its good enough.

Following Ben's statement, the practitioner notes the silence in the room and the looks exchanged between participants [emerging]. He decides to focus on heightening awareness of Ben's perception. [Framing]

PRACTITIONER: You sound keen that we leave this process alone. Do you believe that is the position of the majority of managers involved? [Intervening & checking]

BEN: Well yes, I imagine the majority would say the same. [Not looking at others around him]

PRACTITIONER: How would it be to check it out now? [Intervening again]

BEN: … not sure we can do this as many people involved are not here at the moment …

> New figure has emerged, moving away from heightening Ben's awareness of his statement to how to check it out with others ... A new "frame" involving the group as a whole is proposed.

PRACTITIONER: ... well, we could start by asking this group. What is the question you would ask to check this out?

> The practitioner supports Ben to frame the question and listen to the answers of others who now feel more supported by the process to give their opinion.

PRACTITIONER: What are you left with having listened to others? [Inviting reflection and closing]

BEN: well there are points that people raise that we could focus on. But we still need to listen to those that are not here today.

PRACTITIONER: Yes, we seemed to have agreed that work is needed on some key points of the process. We also however need to take an action to check with those people absent. [Practitioner names unfinished aspect of the intervention]

Emerging

All gestalt interventions begin with paying attention to what-is, taking notice of all aspect of the field, including one's own sensations, feelings and thoughts. This is a stage of unfocused awareness and receptive state where meaning or judgement have no place. Some of the questions a practitioner is busy with at this point are:

– What am I most aware of in myself, in others and in the situation at this moment?
– Am I attending equally to content (what is being said and explicitly communicated) and to process (what is being expressed through behaviours, movement, and paralinguistic communication, e.g., laughs, looks, smiles, coughs, etc.)?

Emerging rests primarily on the field theoretical notion in gestalt that we are all interconnected and that our experience is in part shaped by people and events. So, attuning to our emerging experience in the moment holds the potential of picking up valuable data that may be relevant to others as well.

Focusing

One of the biggest challenges for an intervenor is to select between the many pieces of information or data that he or she is aware of at any moment in time. This choice is entirely subjective and an intuiting process based on both experience, and the practitioner's sensitivity to what might be most supportive of both people and task. The choice for the practitioner at this point is to decide amidst all that they are aware of, what feels most relevant to the client now?

Example

During a leadership development retreat, the business unit head is presenting key points of an overall company strategy. She is going through the slides at pace, making little connection with her team of executives. During her presentation, three people seem to be having a conversation, whispering and exchanging meaningful looks and smiles. The mood in the room feels heavy with little energy or motivation. What do I choose to focus on as a practitioner? Is it the disconnected presentation of the leader, the whispering sub-group which feels disruptive or the overall heaviness I am feeling in the team? The heaviness in my chest increases as I notice the rather slumped postures around the room. I feel the need to take a deep breath and move ... what stands out to me most is the energetic quality of the room.

In the example above the practitioner selects, between different figures of interest, to focus on the mood in the room. That is what felt to her most pressing or useful to highlight at that time. In reflecting on this moment of choice, many practitioners recount being guided by a strong desire for change and a sense of creative possibilities that may flow from attending to this particular point. By making use of self, a gestalt practitioner follows one's energetic interest and perception, trusting that this will also be relevant to the client. We could argue easily that another facilitator would have made a different choice and that would have been right for them too. All interventions are co-created and emerge from the uniqueness of both practitioner and client in that particular moment.

Framing

Having relied on graceful and intersubjective co-emergence in the "emerging" and "focusing" stages, "framing" clarifies the intent behind an intervention. It is important to note that "intent" here is not a goal or a determination to get the client to reach a certain desired position; rather it is an invitation or suggestion that must be held lightly and respectfully by following the client's lead rather than assuming an expert position. In "framing", the practitioner attends to shaping their intervention by assessing the client's need and process in the moment and responding to it. The assessment is twofold. First it requires situating the figure of interest (be it a behaviour, statement or action) within the client's overall process and second, deciding at which level of system would the intervention be best directed. Each of these points will be expanded upon next.

Situating the figure of interest

In gestalt, every experience arises from a given ground and follows a certain sequence or self-regulating cycle referred to as the cycle of experience (CoE). Prior to intervening, it is helpful for the practitioner to attempt to situate the behaviour, statement or action within that flow of experience. The usual first step is therefore one of inquiry, to attempt to understand the person or group's phenomenological experience as they navigate the CoE. It is important here not to give in to easy interpretation and keep to the phenomenological skills of bracketing and horizontalisation described in Chapter Five.

Observing, for example, a manager shake their head sternly during a presentation and noticing how unsettling this is to the young recruit who is presenting, offers a multitude of possible framing options. The manager may be unhappy with what is being said, he may be struggling to make meaning of it, he may have remembered at that time he is needed elsewhere, or perhaps he is wondering why the more senior members of that team are not presenting. Or indeed a number of other possibilities may explain his behaviour. Pausing the process on noticing his head shake, an intervenor could inquire: "I notice your head movement and wonder what is going on for you now?" thus exploring where the manager is in terms of his own flow of experience.

Framing is an assessment of "what-is" and requires skilful tracking by the practitioner of the client's process. Tracking as described in Chapter Five is attending to the unfolding movement or process of the client over time by noticing eye contact, posture, movement, facial expression etc. as well as their cognitive beliefs.

One way of framing an intervention could be to inquire and explore the client's process along the Cycle of Experience (CoE)? How is the client (coachee, group or department as a whole) navigating the CoE at this point in time? Are they still at the sensation stage, unclear about a coherent figure? Have they a clear awareness of what needs to be done but are stuck on how to mobilise towards effective action? Or are they perhaps unable to stay with satisfaction, integrating change, and learning? Situating the client along the CoE provides the practitioners with a first point of understanding how intervening might support the next step in the process.

Another framing option would be to assess the level of support (both self-support and inter-personal support) available to the person or group at the time. Is the client well supported through their posture and breathing? Do they appear confident or hesitant, nervous and restless? Inter-personally, how well do people know and trust each other? What are the known and perhaps less visible alliances in the room?

Level of system

Every situation will have an impact on a system at different levels simultaneously. The system's theory lens is useful in framing interventions as it conceptualises the various ways we may encounter a contact boundary. In intervening, it is helpful to identify the following levels of system:

– Self-system
  • Person/world boundary, e.g., "As you speak of this project, you smile".
  • Intrapsychic, e.g., "You are silent, I wonder what is going on for you?"
– Self and other
  • Interpersonal, e.g., "I notice that as you speak quickly, I stop following you".
  • Dyadic, e.g., "When you speak to her, you tend to look away".

– Subgroup—"When you both argue, the group becomes silent".
– Group, e.g., "I notice that as this topic is discussed, there is less energy in the room".

As highlighted by Stevenson (2008) each level of system contains the conflict, problem or situation in its entirety and will influence other levels of system. From a field theoretical perspective, gestalt therefore holds that intervening at any level has the potential to impact the rest of the system.

For wider impact, there is a preference to intervene at the highest level of system possible. This is because from a systems perspective, each level is "nested" in the sense that each higher level contains the next lower level in a nested fashion (Bertallanfy, 1968). This means that change at a higher level always affect the lower levels of system but the reverse is not always true. A good example of this is shown in the fact that often individuals sent out of the work context to get trained, are less likely to bring back what they have learnt to the organisation. Indeed, often individuals sent on training programmes report that the context in which they work makes it difficult for them to put what they're taught into practice (Beer et al., 2016). Intervening at a higher level in this case would be through action learning sets or even team training sessions. Another reason for intervening at the highest level in organisational contexts is to avoid the shame pitfall. Interventions at the self or self-other levels of system are more likely to trigger shame binds arising from individuals feeling personally bad, unacceptable or different (Cavicchia, 2010).

Intervening

In gestalt, awareness leads to change and so at the heart of each intervention is a search for ways of heightening awareness as a precursor to change. Gestalt's primary methodology is therefore awareness which can be facilitated through three main types of interventions: phenomenological, dialogic, and experiential.

– Phenomenological interventions aim through inquiry into the lived experience of an individual or group, to heighten awareness of their process in the moment (more information on phenomenological inquiry can be found in Chapter Five). This is a skilful slowing down of the process to explore the moment by moment experience of an individual or group.

– Dialogic interventions support awareness raising by opening up a safe space and ways of connecting around process and task (more information on dialogue is found in Chapter Eight).

– Experiential interventions provide a safe exploration of individual and group process through doing and acting. This type of intervention is particularly useful as it often supports more sustainable change by offering opportunity to experience aspects of the emerging future. More detail on experimentation will be covered in Chapter Ten.

Deciding which of these interventions to use (and even when to intervene) is a choice point for a practitioner and arises from their presence and attuning to the moment. It is common however that within a unit of work (Rainey Tolbert, 2004), all three types of interventions are used. Indeed, the art of gestalt is in the weaving of these interventions to enable and support awareness and change. Practitioners might for example, begin with inquiring and noticing patterns in their client (phenomenological interventions), then focus on the quality and style of interaction which might further support the inquiry (dialogic intervention), before suggesting an experiment to move the conversation into a wider context or test out assumptions or new findings (experiential intervention).

It is no coincidence that these types of interventions support and echo the key relational gestalt abilities identified in Chapter Three. As shown in Figure 9.2, *sensing* relies primarily on phenomenological inquiry as a way of tracking and heightening awareness, *supporting* emergence depends on the interconnections and heightened contact brought about through dialogue whilst *sustaining* any change is contingent on embedding it by putting it into practice through experimentation.

Practitioners may find they have a natural bias towards a particular type of intervention. For instance, some individuals may tend towards over emphasising the need for dialogue and support rather than phenomenological inquiry and awareness raising, or *vice versa*. It is important for each practitioner to take notice of their challenges and strengths in this area to better expand their range of interventions.

Interventions must be offered lightly with no certainty of outcome or change. In the spirit of a co-emergent process, each intervention is an

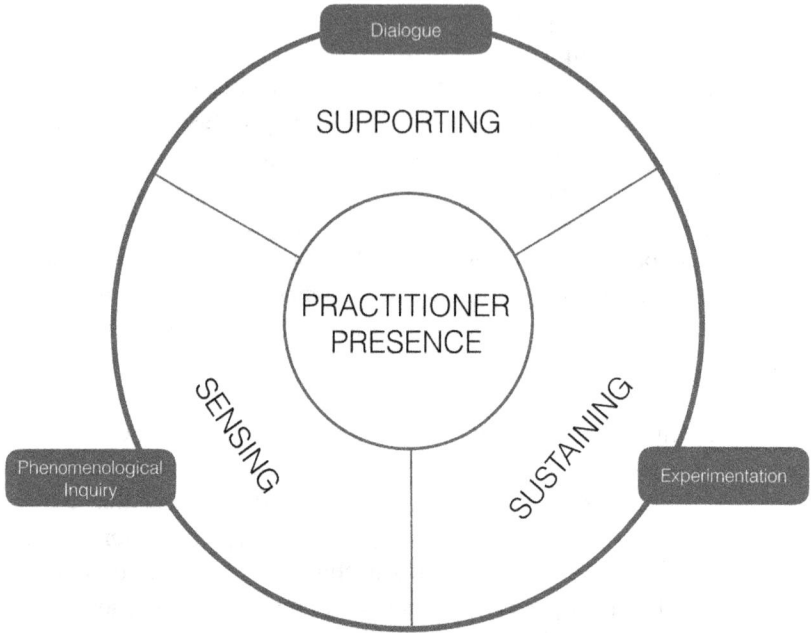

Figure 9.2. Interventions and the relational gestalt abilities.

invitation that the client decides or not to pick up and follow. Checking impact is therefore an essential element of an intervention. How was it received? What has it triggered or invited as a response in the individual client or group? Checking out the impact of an intervention is a fundamental aspect of intervening and maintaining the flow of intervention.

Closing

In the act of intervening, the practitioner steps forward in a particular way; intentionally disturbing the contact boundary in an active manner. New awareness or learning may have happened as a result and it is often helpful to acknowledge this through naming and signalling the end of the intervention. Looking at an intervention as a flow of experience along the gestalt cycle of experience (CoE), "closing" is akin to the resolution/satisfaction stage where learning is anchored, and change and a new status quo is recognised. "Closing" also signals the start of withdrawal into a fertile void and the potential of a new figure to emerge.

It is important to note that closing does not always indicate full resolution. Often, closing an intervention is also noting what remains unfinished or still requires exploration or action. Typically, this could be a next step or an acknowledgment of what hasn't happened.

The stance of a gestalt intervener

What supports the stance of a gestalt practitioner in their moment to moment response to a situation? Along with practitioner presence and responsiveness, there are certain gestalt practice principles that provide both guidance and support to the practitioner at key choice point moments. This section will outline some of these ideas which stem from gestalt theory and practice on how best to enable change in people and organisations.

Leaning into the paradox of change

The paradoxical theory of change is a lynchpin of the gestalt approach and one of the clearest descriptions of an idea originally set out by Fritz Perls, the founder of gestalt. The notion and term originates from an article by Arnold Beisser in 1970 entitled "The paradoxical theory of change". In it he stated that

> Change occurs when one becomes what he is, not when he tries to become what he is not. Change does not take place through a coercive attempt by the individual or by another person to change him, but it does take place if one takes the time and effort to be what he is-to be fully invested in his current positions. By rejecting the role of change agent, we make meaningful and orderly change possible.

Beisser also believed that this view of change applies to social systems and therefore is just as relevant to teams and organisations. Indeed, heightening awareness of the current state, rather than a desired future one, is what often allows sustainable change to take place. This is often counter-cultural in organisations where individuals habitually move rapidly into action assuming their understanding of the issue or problem is shared or the sole truth. For example, "visioning" or "blue-sky" workshops in organisations aimed at creating a compelling vision of the future, habitually begin with imagining a "to-be" state that senior executives aspire towards. Unfortunately, more often than not, those people defining the to-be state have insufficient appreciation of the as-is resources and capabilities for this future state to be accessible. In a gestalt frame, a visioning workshop begins with the recognition of all current aspects of the organisation. By doing so the client gains insight and understanding about as-is attributes and characteristics and begins to see how these might get in the way or support the desired change.

The leaning towards "what is" rather than "what should be" is a hallmark of gestalt practitioners and places the emphasis on fully unpacking all aspects of a current situation to allow for newness and change to emerge. As an intervenor, this means giving full voice to the "what is" of every moment. Often gestalt practitioners are heard to say, "stay with it", meaning there is an energetic quality to the process that invites exploring further a given theme, person or process and heightening awareness. The paradoxical theory of change is an invitation for groups and organisations as well as individuals to remain longer in the sensation-awareness part of the CoE rather than jumping to meaning making.

In practice, this could translate to slowing down a team's process to afford space to all views or at an organisational level, for a senior team to see and acknowledge the reality of employee moral as well as financial or strategic ambitions.

Creative indifference

When intervening, the practitioner is fluid and responsive, and any assumptions are held lightly without personal investment in a fixed objective or outcome. This attitude in gestalt is referred to as a stance of creative indifference. It is a concept originally developed by the philosopher Salomo Friedlaender which has had a significant influence on gestalt theory. Creative indifference holds that every creative act (such as intervening) must emerge out of the fertile void, out of nothingness, unburdened by the familiar or the expected (Frambach, 2003).

Joyce and Sills (2014, p. 40) write of the stance of creative indifference as being similar to the practice of equanimity or mindfulness in

Buddhism. It is therefore a stance of neutrality—rather than one of not caring—where the practitioner stays aware of her tendency to be over-invested in a particular outcome. This does not mean that outcomes and goals cannot be named or agreed or that the practitioner is not whole-heartedly engaged in supporting the client's desired aim. It cannot however be the responsibility of the practitioner (manager, consultant or facilitator) alone to ensure change is happening in a particular direction. By being over-invested in a particular route or way of achieving change, gestalt practitioners lose their neutrality and with it the richness and sustainability of a co-emergent approach. Indeed, Perls writes that:

> By remaining alert in the centre, we can acquire a creative ability of seeing both sides of an occurrence and completing an incomplete half. By avoiding a one-sided outlook we gain a much deeper insight into the structure and function of the organism. (Perls, 1947, p. 3)

Cultivated uncertainty

In working with emergence, the only thing we can be certain of is that we cannot predict what will happen in the next moment. As organisational practitioners we often feel however a legitimate need for certainty at least in our belief that we can help and support our clients. This belief is supportive to both practitioner and client and yet being too certain of the "rightness" of our interventions or correctness of a certain diagnosis or our meaning making can also be abusive to our clients. At what point does the practitioner's perspective become truer than that of the client and not be challenged? Is it right or ethical for a practitioner to hold any view point with certainty given that this would also mean an imposition of power over the client? Staemmler (1997) overcomes this dilemma by supporting practitioners to *cultivate uncertainty* as a fundamental attitude. By this he means inviting practitioners to first stay aware at all times of their uncertainty with regards attribution of meaning and second, using their uncertainty to the advantage of the client. An advantage because cultivating uncertainty is also a stance of hope and positivity and as Staemmler writes: "Cultivating uncertainty means to become optimistic and to expect change to be possible, even if you (yet) cannot discern it" (ibid, p. 47).

Balancing support, and challenge: establishing a safe emergency

The search for awareness inherent to gestalt is not always comfortable. It is demanding and can at times feel overwhelming. Fully recognising, for example, the impact of one's behaviour on others or the extent of dissent within a team or even the toxic effect of a given situation on an organisation is not easy. Awareness can, when unsupported, conjure self-criticism, shame as well as anxiety or even hopelessness. The curse of awareness is that we can't unlearn what we get to know and mining the golden nugget of insight requires safety and good contact.

When intervening to heighten awareness, the gestalt practitioner proceeds therefore with caution. Interventions should be calibrated to ensure they are disturbing enough for newness to emerge, but not so disruptive to leave individuals reeling and ungrounded. The balancing of challenge and support is key to guiding the intervenor's next step. Is the individual client or group able to delve deeper in their reflecting on their process or task? Is there enough support and good contact to counter-balance any criticism, tension or shame?

Traditionally the notion of support has not had much traction in the way organisations manage change. Indeed, the metaphor of the "burning platform" first coined by Daryl Conner (1992) has become a permanent part of the organisational change landscape. Conner (ibid) recounted the experience of a survivor from a catastrophic fire on an oil rig who saved himself by leaping into the icy, turbulent ocean below. As the metaphor goes, leaving the platform (i.e., changing one's way of doing things) will be painful but the alternative is certain incineration. This prevailing view of organisational change required therefore leaders to create "burning platform" conditions to incite people to move to a new status quo. The fact that this often leaves workers cold, helpless, fearful, swimming in a sea of change is not always a consideration.

Rather than the outdated idea of the burning platform, gestalt offers the notion of a "safe emergency" (Perls et al., 1951 [1994], p. 64) where there is enough compelling discomfort but where safety is also an essential component of what supports change. When intervening, the gestalt practitioner invites awareness of the "as is" reality (through inquiry or sharing their phenomenological experience for example), but also ensures enough support or affirmation are present to allow more flexible and responsive creative adjustments (ibid, p. 5) or adaptation to the situation. Dialogic relating typically opens up the space for such support by increasing contact and connection between individuals and between client and practitioner. Perls, Hefferline, & Goodman (1951 [1994]) also refer to the excitement of the "safe emergency" as the balance between mobilising the client's energy within an experiment whilst maintaining a feeling of safety for the client to proceed.

Shame in organisational contexts

Shame in organisational contexts often goes unrecognised and unmentioned. Yet shame is a fundamental organiser of behaviour and action in much of organisational life. This can be seen for example, through the process of goal setting and feedback. Although shame plays a critical role in social self-regulation (Lee, 1995; Tangney, 1995), it also has a negative impact on performance reducing the effectiveness of individuals and teams (Bentley, 2012).

The extent to which people experience and react to shame varies greatly depending on their personal history and current situation. The basic experience connected to shame is of being seen as inappropriate, "less than" and of feeling inadequate or incompetent. Shame proneness may well result from early developmental factors as well as from highly critical and harsh environments.

In gestalt, shame is viewed as a relational and situational phenomenon. This means it arises in relationship and is closely connected to the way people interact (Kaufman, 1989, Lee & Wheeler, 1996). As relational beings, we naturally reach out to others for affirmation and connection. In doing so, we build what Kaufman (1989) calls a "relational bridge" that enables us to trust and be vulnerable with others, and share more of our thoughts and feelings. If our healthy impulse as human beings is to build bridges, shame is the result of broken bridges. The latter will result in a failure of connection, an experience of being dismissed, criticised or even humiliated.

In attending to shame triggers in organisational contexts, we need as practitioner first to heighten our sensitivity to shame cues in order to recognise them. Responses to shame vary widely and can include a desire to hide, run away, withdraw, act defensively or become passively aggressive, angry or even hostile to avoid humiliation—whether real, perceived or anticipated.

These shame cues are reminders to the practitioner that they may need to attend to the re-building of relational bridges either with the coachee in a one-to-one situation or amongst team members in a larger group situation. Dialogic relating which includes support and understanding would be a key aspect of working with shame. The intervenor's dialogic stance (as described in Chapter Eight) includes compassion and acceptance, prioritising connection over task.

Finally, it is important to also view shame at a systemic level as an indicator of what is possible in a given organisational context. An important consideration of an intervenor when faced with shame is to ask if there is enough support in the field for a particular task or desired outcome. Lee (1996) writes "Together shame and support have the potential of enabling contact. Support allows the person to take risks; shame induces the person to pull back when there is no immediate support" (p. 10).

Summary

It is often useful to deconstruct and simplify complex skills in order to better learn them. This chapter therefore attempts to capture the complexity underlying interventions by laying out key stages within the overall flow of intervening: these are emerging, focusing, framing, intervening, and closing. Rather than learning rigid and fixed steps to the dance of intervention, the hope is that this chapter provides enough of the rhythm and feel of the dance for practitioners to create their own steps. Indeed, the act of intervening is subjective, intuitive and arises in the moment as a response to a given situation. At its best, the stance of a gestalt intervenor is guided by the practitioner's presence, use of self and their perceptivity rather than considered cognitive response.

Sustaining

The following two chapters address important elements of gestalt OD work that are key to ensuring that change and growth is sustained. These are experimentation and endings.

The greatest challenge to personal change, or indeed to larger change initiatives, is the lack of sustainability. We often for instance witness in organisations a "hockey stick" phenomenon (Lee, et al., 1997), where the impact of a change initiative is short lived and dependent on leadership attention and focus to drive desired results and behaviours. For change to be meaningful, it needs to be sustained over time which implies a fundamental shift in the habitual ways of being of individuals and organisations.

Organisational learning has often focused on the type of reflective learning which relies on cognitive awareness. However, psychology has shown us that as human beings we learn primarily when introspection/reflection is paired with felt experience. In gestalt, we view sustainability as an assimilation of change which requires a holistic "knowing" (in mind, emotions and body) of what the change means and feels like. Such knowing is often most rapidly accessed in gestalt through experimentation. This section will therefore address the sustaining of change by unpacking in Chapter Ten the creative process of experimentation in gestalt. This will be followed in Chapter Eleven at looking at how unfinished business and poor endings also disrupt enduring change.

Experimentation

What happens in the creative experiment is like artistic expression because it too, has qualities of unusual excitement, discovery and emergency.

—*Polster & Polster*, 1973, p. 237

Gestalt brings together in a coherent and consistent practice the use of active experimentation (Yontef & Friedemann, 2015). This concept refers to trying some new piece of behaviour but it does not mean the use of techniques aimed at reaching pre-set goals. Active experimentation arises from the relational process itself in the present moment. The aim of gestalt experimentation is twofold: first it supports awareness raising by exploring ongoing process, and second, it anchors new learning, ways of being and change through dynamic experiencing in a safe and supportive context.

This chapter will begin by exploring further what is meant by experimentation in gestalt before outlining a useful sequencing to experiments illustrated through examples and case studies.

What is experimentation and what does it serve?

As we have explored previously, heightening awareness in gestalt is a primary method for change as it supports the flow through the cycle of experience (see Chapter Six). Healthy self-regulating is therefore facilitated through awareness because, when we know and understand how we limit ourselves, we open up to choice and change (Perls, 1947). Fritz Perls then later acknowledged that awareness alone could be a slow method of achieving change and so introduced the idea of active experimentation (Perls, 1976) as a way of accelerating learning and growth. As Zinker (1977, p. 124) writes: "Most experiments have one thing in common, they ask the client to express something behaviourally rather than merely cognize".

The notion of experimenting acknowledges that human beings learn better by experiencing, through the trial and error of action research rather than talking about something. This is not a new idea (Lewin, 1926, 1935, 1951; Kolb & Fry, 1975). The meaning of experimenting in gestalt however, transcends the usual definition of just attempting or trying something new and then reflecting on it. Experimenting links to a fundamental way we learn and change through completing a flow of experience (from sensation, awareness, through action to completion or resolution) which sediments learning and change in our personality functioning. Experimentation is a holistic practice which not only supports cognitive knowing but also engages our embodied and emotional awareness. By giving voice and involving the whole of the individual's experience, experimentation lays a solid foundation for more sustainable and viable change.

The oft quoted statistic that success rate of change initiatives is less than thirty per cent (Balogun & Hope Hailey, 2004, Jacobs, et al., 2013) points to the challenge of implementing even very convincing strategic business ideas. The lack of appropriate stakeholder engagement is often a key factor for these failures which seems to demonstrate that cognitive knowing is not a motivating enough incentive for change. Most change approaches frequently try to minimise disruption to "business as usual" and so rely on change teams that are marginal to the day to day operations or, to the people that will actually need to change. Problems then arise at the point of transition from conceptual/small group work to full organisational action. Just understanding the rational for change is not always sufficient for a successful change process. To embrace change, individuals need the affective, embodied, and cognitive understanding of the change ahead and feel safe enough to step forward. Experimentation can create such a context by providing a protected and contained way of exploring and learning what change looks and mostly feels like.

Raising awareness through experimentation

Experimentation always takes place in the present moment and provides vividness to the experience compared to "talking about". Experimentation can emerge in the moment and be as simple as asking a coachee to continue talking about their boss whilst noticing their level of irritation, or inviting members of a leadership team to sit in different places than those they habitually occupy and see how this impacts dialogue in the group. Gestalt experiments range from simple invitations to notice aspects of phenomenological experience, or to discover and work with polarities, through to more complex enactments such as the "empty chair", reversal experiments or hot-housing large scale change. Experiments are live, organic experiences that emerge in the present and are related to the client's exploration or figure of interest. By grading the level of challenge and support, experiments allow for an acting out of often difficult situations in a safe and contained space. Through carefully crafted experiments, individuals and groups can reach new awareness and choices for change.

Example

Coaching a client who is expressing ambivalent feelings towards his new CEO, I ask him to talk to his boss who is 'sitting' in an empty chair placed in front of him. By talking in the present tense, my client is able to access more of his emotional, physical and cognitive process connected to his ambivalence. Then I might ask my client to move into the other chair and pretend to be his boss: "Sit as your boss would. Embody as much of their posture, gestures and tone of voice as possible." By asking my client to "become" the boss, a more vibrant picture of the other person is presented and key ways in which my coachee perceives him emerge. This is a rich ground for us to explore together.

Experimentation is relevant at individual, group or organisational levels. Introducing an experimental approach early on in a change project can clarify what needs attending to as well as provide a refreshing alternative to the more linear organisational model of analysis-diagnosis-options-recommendations, which puts action last. A good example of this is the use of hot-housing in large transformative change. Hot-housing is a method for part of an organisation to be ring-fenced while it experiments with finding better, different, more effective ways of working for a few weeks. The ring-fencing allows the group genuinely to experiment and "try on" new things, behaviours and processes, without having to be careful to avoid mistakes which are an essential part of creativity. Creating this safe, contained and separate environment is a way of letting go of the past and stimulating work groups to behave differently. The hot-housed environment then provides clear awareness of where effort needs to be focused as well as the measured performance improvement that creates the business case for rolling out new ways of working in the rest of the organisation.

Greater sustainability through experimentation

The model of sustainable change initiatives depicted in Figure 10.1 was developed by Gemini Consulting in the 1990s and based on thinking and organisational change ideas from Kotter (1996) and Binney and Williams (1997). What is evident in this model and in most literature around the sustainability of business change is the emphasis placed on "responsible" leaders (Hind, et al., 2009) or hero leaders to determine a clear vision, assess operations, maximise growth and measure outcome as well as attend to power and engagement issues (Doppelt, 2003). This focus on leadership, although essential, still speaks to a top-down change model where leaders alone decide future direction. An emergent approach on the other hands, seeks to engage people at all levels in such a way that change becomes part of who and how they are, precisely because they have actively participated and experienced the process of change itself. Experimentation is therefore a way of co-creating the future by staying experience-near and actively exploring what a future state may look like.

Change programmes have traditionally approached skill and capability transfer from a didactic, course based approach. In such cases, the hoped-for behavioural change is disconnected from the context where

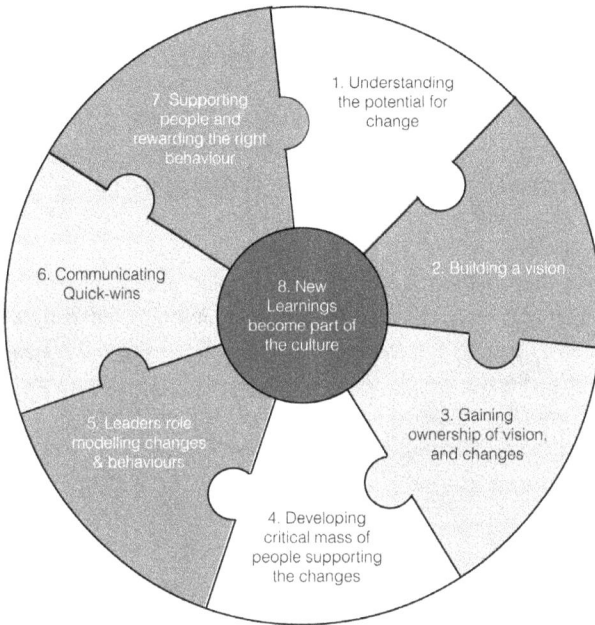

Figure 10.1. Key factors for sustainability change initiatives.

the need for it arose (i.e., the changing organisation). In a gestalt frame, need-fulfilment is what primarily drives new action and behaviour and so, in order to embed change in a sustainable manner, skill and capability transfer has to happen in a timely and choiceful manner as part of the experience of change. In other words, responsibility for learning has to be shared with the emphasis placed on the individual or group to reach for new skills, rather than a push approach to capability building which typically happens at the end of change projects.

Case study

A pull approach to skills and capability building

The focus of a large change project in a retail organisation was to simplify business management procedures in the commercial marketing areas, to support both the introduction of a new IT system and the restructure of key processes. Instead of leaving skill and capability building to the end of the project, the change team identified enabling skills early on. These were selected in cooperation with managers and based on the existing culture and what would most support change in each area. These enabling skills were then made available to team leaders who would call upon (depending on their schedule) specific change capability agents to deliver short (usually 30 minute) trainings during regular meetings or on an ad-hoc basis. These trainings were then followed by team led action learning sessions. The driving question in designing and delivering new skills was "what would support your team to learn and be more effective in the new organisation?"

What was key to the success of the approach was that people felt it was a safe enough environment for experimenting in being different, trying new things out and being upfront about what they didn't know. This contributed to a learning climate which resulted in an increase in energy and good will. These enabling skills were maintained for many years following the change project and became an inherent part of the organisation's culture and way of operating.

The sequencing of an experiment

As was highlighted earlier, experimenting requires a safe environment for individuals to step into and creatively explore new ways of being. Zinker (1977, p. 128) writes that "the making of the experiment is a complex dance, a cooperative journey" *and as* a specific type of intervention, the sequencing of experimentation therefore follows a frame that lends particular attention to aspects of co-creation and support. Figure 10.2 below shows how typical stages of gestalt experimentation (adapted from Zinker, 1977) map onto the flow of intervention outlined in Chapter Nine. The "intervening" stage in experimentation expands

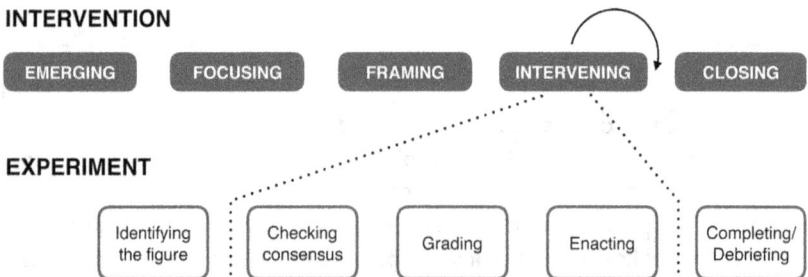

Figure 10.2. Typical sequencing of gestalt experimentation.

to include three steps (checking consensus to experiment, grading and enacting the experiment) that pay particular attention to agreement and grading the experiment so as to provide the appropriate level of both challenge and support.

Identifying the figure

Deciding upon a clear figure on which to experiment is a subjective choice which arises from noticing all aspects of ground, including the practitioner's own experience (emerging), choosing what feels most relevant in this moment (focusing) and being clear about the intent behind the experiment (framing). These steps have been outlined in more detail in Chapter Nine.

Checking consensus to experiment

Suggesting an experiment is already an important departure from the usual way of working in organisations. As Ariely (2010) pointed out, businesses don't experiment as they typically value answers over questions, because answers allow them to take action whilst questions mean staying longer with uncertainty.

The invitation to experiment itself could be as simple as: "Do you want to try something that may be helpful?" The practitioner must however consider if there is enough support for the client (individual, group or organisation) to try something new and risk either failure or worse, embarrassment. It is vital that in suggesting an experiment, the client feels free to refuse the suggestion without feeling pressured. Often it is helpful to explicitly say "It is fine to say no", and pay particular attention to body signals and other signs of reluctance or even adaptation, such as over-hasty agreement (Joyce & Sills, 2014, p. 97). The tracking of the client for consensus is not limited to just the start of the experiment and needs to be an ongoing assessment as the experiment unfolds.

Experimenting requires a good enough working alliance between practitioner and client. This is not typically an intervention a practitioner would lead with when encountering a new coachee or group. When checking agreement, it is often helpful to give the client some rational or cognitive explanation for proposing an experiment. This can increase trust in the practitioner and contribute to feelings of safety in engaging with an activity that may feel odd or unusual. The explanation need not be excessive but could be along the lines "often by trying something different, we can see new choices come up", or "by paying attention to our bodies, we can gain new awareness".

Grading

Once the client has agreed to step into experimenting, the dance of co-creation begins. The opening suggestion must now be shaped by client and practitioner to ensure the experiment sits within a safe emergency; supported enough to take risks and challenging enough to gain new awareness and insight (refer to Chapter Nine for a fuller explanation of safe emergency). The joint pursuit of the optimal point of safe emergency is what is referred to in gestalt as grading.

The practitioner may begin with a loose suggestion of what might be an interesting experiment but grading is the step in which this initial offer is explored, chewed, modified and made right for this client, at this moment in time. If the experiment is well within the comfort zone and range of the client, then it is not likely to provided newness and needs to be graded up. If on the other hand, the experiment is too difficult, or challenging or even shaming, then it will need to be graded down to make sure the client is supported enough to integrate new awareness and learning.

Example

Facilitating a new leadership team around issues of conflict and trust, I suggest that a good starting point in building trust is to get to know each other better (as people not just professional colleagues). The suggestion is well received and so I begin grading the experiment by offering and seeking consensus around a frame to structure the sharing of personal information. My initial thought, given the level of conflict and tension which I've been told about, is to suggest that this sharing happens in smaller groups in order to limit personal attacks and possible shaming. I check with the team and Claire the marketing director says that she would like to hear from everyone and would rather the sharing happened in the larger group. This grades up the experiment and I can see signs and facial expressions denoting that some may find this challenging. Keeping the small group configuration would not challenge Claire enough, but an open discussion in the large group could potentially be too exposing to others. I propose a middle ground by offering a tighter structure around how the sharing process takes place, where people can ask questions for a limited amount of time and must also verbalise what they appreciate in each other's stories. I also make it clear that I will be facilitating the process "in order to make sure we keep to time". My suggestion grades the experiment down a notch and introduces a little more safety compared to an open or unmoderated discussion. I then purposefully seek agreement from each team member, checking for signs of consensus, encouraging each one "to check and see if this works for you" and asking if there are any other suggestions to improve on the process. As a facilitator, I am attentive to signs of reluctance and to individuals that might need more support in the experimenting itself.

The level of risk is determined by checking with the client throughout the process of experimenting. At times, experiments may need to start off with small achievable steps and rise in difficulty over time as trust in the facilitator and within the team increases. In the example above, if the facilitator had sensed greater reluctance from other team members, then perhaps she would have insisted on the initial suggestion and provided Claire with a greater challenge in her smaller group. The options for grading can only emerge in the moment and need to be supportive of both individuals and task.

Finally, in grading, it is essential that the practitioner take account of their own limits and sense of support and not suggest or go along with an experiment that is outside their own zone of comfort. To hold the safety of the creative space, the practitioner needs to be well supported in themselves.

Enacting the experiment

In the enacting of the experiment, a practitioner is alongside, monitoring levels of support and challenge and responding to the unfolding experiment. What happens next cannot be predicted or anticipated. The practitioner will support and guide, making use of their own feelings, and their noticing of the client's process as well as their imagination and creativity. For example, a coach who has invited their coachee to verbalise their anger towards a colleague imagining him sitting in an empty chair may notice in themselves a desire to shout or move their hands. Trusting that this may also be relevant to their client, the coach may suggest to their coachee that they raise their voice or move their torso forward and see if new awareness emerges.

In every experiment there is an element of uncertainty and the practitioner needs the flexibility to let go of, or down-grade an experiment or suggestion that is either looking ineffective in mobilising the client's energy or invoking anxiety or shame. This close tracking of the client's energetic shifts and responding to them is a key part of being alongside clients in experiments. This has been referred to as "riding pillion" (Denham-Vaughan, personal communication) to describe the embodied tracking and moving with our clients that is required of us in experimenting. It is an embodied relational dialogue guided by an aesthetic receptivity rather than a considered cognitive response in the moment. At times, this dialogue may move us to heighten the energy, to push or confront and at others, it may lead us to slow down, withdraw and wait.

As Kepner (2003, p. 9) writes, "as gestalt practitioners, our goal is to create the conditions and situations where something not previously accessible in experience is made available to ongoing contact and therefore to growth and development". He goes on to say, "The particular techniques we use are not important in and of themselves, only in how they serve the task of generating an experiential field that may make more available for the client's experience the domain and process we are interested in supporting" (ibid, p. 9).

This firmly sets experimentation as emerging in the moment and unique to the moment. There are however some categories of experiments that may be useful for coaches and other organisational practitioners to consider and familiarise themselves with.

- *Polarity or two-chair work*, which heightens awareness of two conflicting or contradictory voices in a tension or conflict situation (either within a person or group).
- *Empty chair*, which invites a client to address an imaginary other in the room or enact a situation they want to explore in the present.
- *Amplification or moderation* of a particular behaviour; this can be done by asking the client to exaggerate a particular behaviour, e.g., "Can you clench your fist even more as you speak of your colleague". Suggest the client exaggerate the opposite behaviour, for instance invite a team that habitually waits for the leader to give their opinion to volunteer their thoughts first. Or alternatively, a practitioner may

invite a group to slow down their communication flow as a way of unpacking and noticing the way they dialogue.

- *Directed awareness or focussing*; which asks clients to focus on a particular aspect of their experience in the moment, which could be how they walk, or move or their feelings and embodied sensations as they speak of a particular topic or address a particular person. This could also be used at the level of a group for instance by calling attention to levels of energy in the room, how loud or not people have become, etc.

- *Metaphors* are also good ways of engaging people in organisations to articulate less cognitive aspects of their experience. What metaphor would best fit this situation or issue? For example, a senior team was able to express the frustration of inter-personal issues and lack of clarity in their job roles by describing themselves as "an eleven-year-old football team, all chasing the same ball".

Case study one

Ann, a senior director of a public service organisation, states in her coaching aims that she would like to explore her lack of self-confidence. As her coach, I am curious about this given her strong assured manner and the fact that she is well recognised as a successful leader in developing an important part of the organisation in the last few years. When I share my curiosity, Ann reflects then on her background as a nurse and how this included no management experience and how self-conscious she feels still about that. As we explore her sense of herself as a nurse versus a manager, a strong polarisation of those two instances of herself emerge. I become curious and invite Ann to experiment with embodying those two states more fully.

As Ann experiments with describing and embodying these two parts of herself, she becomes aware of how much easier and more comfortable it is to "be" her nurse self. She looks more at ease, smiling, confident and feels "knowing", "effective" and "doing real work". Her body looks energetic, hands expressive as she tells me what it was like to be a nurse. It also holds for her a sense of fitting in, a knowing of the professional community to which she belongs and also the boundaries of what she knows she could do and what is outside of her capabilities.

Conversely, as her manager self, Ann speaks of feeling "stiff", "held back" and "overly cautious". The metaphor that emerges to describe herself in that place is a cliff, high up which looks out over things but where her footing is unsteady. Her upper body is more rigid, her arms more straight by her side as if she is holding herself back.

Intrigued by how distinct those two polarities seem, I then invite Ann to stand up and take position as her nurse self at one end of the room and place her manager self at the other. Standing alongside her, I ask her to take a few steps towards her manager self. She stands for a moment, looks up and then again down towards her feet and says "my feet don't want to move". Her eyes tear up as she becomes aware of how difficult it is for her to own the polarity of her manager self, to recognise that she could belong or deserves to be there. This feels like a moment of strong awareness for Ann and we slowly return to our seats, deconstructing the experiment, and reflecting on what meaning emerged for her in that. She speaks of how lonely and isolated being a manager has been in recent years as the organisation grew and became more "formal". She speaks of how in the early years, she was still the nurse that "made things happen" as the team was small and operations required her to be more hands-on and part of a team. The recent growth meant more formal events and more expectations of her as a manager and leader. This she feels she struggles with, and leaves her feeling out of her depth. At the end of the session, I ask Ann to reflect on the new insights gained during our meeting and become more aware of the times where she feels "out of her depth" or less able, and notice how the context is impacting her in those moments.

Case study two

Working with a senior team on the initial stages of a restructure following a merger, it was clear people were reluctant to let go of aspects of their previous organisation which they valued and identify what needed to change. When the team engages in discussion around this point, the conversation often gets stuck on particular issues and how to fix them.

Wanting to access a less cognitive and verbal experience of how they perceived their organisation, I propose they experiment by each finding a metaphor that best captures their previous organisation. This first suggestion is received willingly and they each name their metaphor often receiving knowing smiles and nods as different members offer their image, for example: a dancing bear, or a "nice" but stuck robot, or giant entangled tentacles. Noticing the raised interest in the room, I then grade the experiment up and ask if they are willing to also embody their metaphors, give them movement, voice or sound that would add another dimension to describing key aspects they want to convey. I model an example and carefully check if everyone agrees to this. The energy in the room is good and the team members then "met" each other as their metaphors in different configurations. I pause the process often to check observations and comments about the experiment and also what they are taking away as key values that feel important to them in the new organisation. Debriefing was rich as people speak of getting to know each other better and that a sense of joint values was emerging for the new organisation. Following the meeting, the team is able to agree on key organisation design criteria for the new structure.

Debriefing

In experimenting we come to new awareness even when the experiment doesn't unfold in an expected or familiar way. There is information and useful awareness in that too. From that perspective, experiments never fail and allowing for ample time for debriefing and review is usually time well spent.

The debriefing stage needs to be led by the client rather than assumed learnings or insights imposed by the coach or facilitator. As Zinker writes: "never assume that your client, having completed an experience, learned from it what you did" (1977, p. 146). Experiments often also hold embodied and emotional content and so, integration of learning may take time and not be immediately available to a cognitive meaning-making part of the brain. Insights and awareness might crystallise at later stages and be brought back into the work.

Summary

This chapter outlined a key aspect of gestalt organisational work which focuses on experimenting as a way of raising awareness, gaining insight and trying out new ways of being. Experiments are carefully shaped experiences, enacted in the moment and which contain a suitable and balanced level of challenge and support. Experiments can offer powerful learning experiences in organisations as they harness the power of creativity by encouraging trial and error and risk-taking in a safe space, thus shifting habitual patterns of behaviours and understanding.

CHAPTER ELEVEN

Endings and unfinished business

Every beginning has an end and every end has a new beginning.

—*Kalwar*, 2010

In every beginning is an end. Yet, in most organisational cultures, endings are often either avoided, left unacknowledged or positioned as a celebration of a future state. Attending to endings is counter-cultural for most organisations still steeped in a mechanistic paradigm and where completion of an activity or task primarily signals availability and readiness for a new assignment. With many organisations it is far easier to keep starting new projects rather than reduce or stop them. Projects of course often do typically conclude with celebratory drinks or meal indicating the end of the contractual engagement but little attention is usually given to the separation process itself.

In gestalt, endings are an important aspect of our overall experience and need as much attention as beginnings. The gestalt cycle of experience highlights in its recurring pattern that the quality of disengaging from one activity will have an impact on the next cycle and figure. As emotional beings, the way we end is a key aspect of our forward journey and of the sustainability of the work itself.

This chapter will address the importance of ending in OD work as well as cover various types of endings from the planned to the unexpected or undesirable and how this impacts organisational work. The gestalt notion of unfinished business will be explored as a guiding frame to ending interventions.

Why attend to endings in OD work?

Similarly, to William Bridges (1991) who writes of organisational transitions and the need for endings before beginnings, gestalt theory tells us that ending well sets the tone for new beginnings. Indeed, the cycle of experience stresses the importance of the closure and withdrawal stages as key moments of integration and assimilation of change and learning. By attending to endings and closure, we are at our most present to experience the "fertile void", a space of creativity, responsiveness and openness to new awareness and needs. Any unfinished business that hasn't been recognised or acknowledged will necessarily impinge on what comes next, on the formation of a new figure of interest.

Unfinished business

Unfinished business is a term commonly used in gestalt. Perls (1976) saw it as resulting from interruptions to the cycle of experience where individuals struggled to be fully in the here-and-now and kept wanting to return to an event that had interrupted them having their needs met. Applying this to organisational life, we can see how for example, a manager who did not have his idea heard or recognised in a satisfying way in the initial stages of a project might still cling to it, returning to the same point in a bid to satisfy this need or even worse, perhaps finding other less appropriate or relevant ways of having his voice heard. Unfinished business results typically from experiences in the past which have not been met with a satisfying resolution. Putting aside these incomplete gestalts is something we do regularly in our lives as interruptions, compromises, and normal life demands it. However, some more significant experiences although set aside, seem to return to our attention and leave us with a sense of discomfort or frustration. If significant enough, these events permeate our lives and become both figure and ground (Melnick & Roos, 2007). A possible sign of unfinished business in a team process for example, could be noticing the team "going around in circles" and "cycling" around the same issue or point with no resolution or progress. This stuckness could be attributed to unaware behaviours triggered by historical experiences (what happened back then) rather than conduct that is responsive to the present moment situation.

Example

The CEO of a small construction company had been in role for the last two years and taken the organisation to new markets, heightening operational productivity and profitability. Wanting to make further improvements to the business, he recruits consultants to look at his strategic options and explore opportunities for the business. During a review meeting, the consultants put forward amidst many options the idea of a merger which the CEO strongly rejected with little discussion or consideration. His team expressed surprised at the quick elimination of the option but the strength of his rejection signalled that, unusually given his openness, this was not a decision to be questioned.

As a coach to the team, the awkwardness around his reaction suggested to me that exploring this would be best done on a one to one basis. On exploring the issue, it quickly transpired that he had stepped down from a previous job following a difficult and contentious merger situation. Unfinished business from his past was interfering with his decision making today and the idea of a merger triggered a fixed response resulting from his past experience.

Gestalt holds that unresolved issues in the past will impact how we engage with and view the present moment. The end of an activity or action is an important moment to surface any unfinished business and open a space for possible resolution. Whether a coaching relationship, a group workshop or a large change project, time must be given to pause and reflect on what went well, what was unfinished and what was learned in terms of task as well as process and relationships.

Attending to unfinished business does not mean necessarily resolving all issues or even achieving satisfaction. It is important however to name what needs remain open or unsatisfied, recognise limitations and distinguish between what is possible given resources and time versus what is desirable. Even when issues are not resolved or needs met satisfactorily, a fair process is fundamental to the way we achieve closure. As Kim and Mauborgne (1997) write about fair process, "All of us, whatever our role in [an organisation], want to be valued as human beings [...]. We want others to respect our intelligence. We want our ideas to be taken seriously. And we want to understand the rationale behind specific decisions" (ibid, p. 69).

An iterative cycle of ending and re-engagement

Attention to the ending process is necessary because often too many OD projects linger unproductively or end abruptly without adequate follow up (Van Eron & Burke, 1995, p. 395). The word "end" often conjures the idea of a final point or moment in time when that 'end' takes place. This can feel too binary and reductionist for what is viewed in gestalt as an ongoing and cyclical process of review. With every completed cycle, with every activity or intervention, there is an end, a withdrawal of kind to reflect on the activity, learn, process and integrate as a helpful catalyst for the next figure to emerge.

Working in an emergent paradigm where each next step is a necessary co-creation between client and practitioner, attending to the latter parts of the cycle of experience is a necessary pre-condition of the ongoing work. Endings are needed points of the process through which both client and practitioner can decide on the path ahead and renew their engagement (or not).

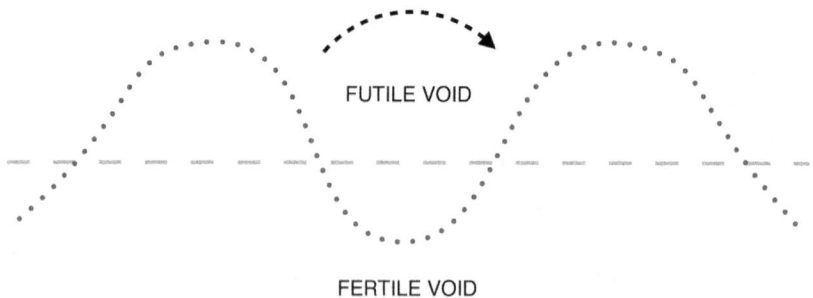

FUTILE VOID

FERTILE VOID

Figure 11.1. Wave hopping and the fertile void (Bentley & Congram, 1996 [2014]).

In not attending to closure and ending phases of the cycle, individuals and teams are more likely to leap from action to action and enter what Bentley and Congram (1996 [2014]) call the "futile void" in contrast to the fertile void of a healthy cycle. The wave hopping (depicted in Figure 11.1), in effect bypasses id functioning (below the horizontal line) and so the next action is less connected to what is most needed or relevant in the moment.

Honouring the emotional engagement

As we have seen in previous chapters, gestalt OD work emphasises the importance of the use of self of the practitioner within a relational context. The working alliance is of primary importance for gestalt practitioners as they co-create a safe container for the work. This relational way of working fosters and depends on a genuine emotional engagement rather than a transactional obligation. For example, working as a consultant alongside a manager in her new role on a transformation project, supporting her to step up to challenging situations is emotionally engaging for both the practitioner and client. There is a sense of togetherness that develops through living the highs and lows of organisational life and journeying together. A client once disclosed years later upon meeting him that what was most helpful during the consulting engagement was those Friday evening calls we had whilst he was driving home, that allowed him to process the week and feel supported in difficult times. The presence of the practitioner is therefore often both catalytic and supportive to clients and so, attending to the "absence" of the practitioner feels equally important as a way of acknowledging and honouring the changing situation (e.g., the end of the work engagement) and its impact on the relationship. This would free the client and practitioner to consider, if appropriate, new beginnings and a different relationship.

The way in which we each as human beings manage endings is particular to us and our lived experience. We each have established relational patterns—often called attachment styles—that determine our preferences in how we end with others, both in our intimate lives and professional engagements. It is helpful for us all to recognise and be aware of these habitual patterns and how they might play out in our work.

Experiential exercise

What is your habitual way of approaching endings?

Take a few moments to consider ending experiences in your own life. This may include moving to a new job, finishing a significant project or even the end of a personal relationship. Is there a way you typically end relationships? Do you leave quickly and not look back, do you perhaps emotionally leave early and feel disconnected from the actual ending. Conversely, do you hang on and avoid endings by saying "I will see you soon" and attempt to maintain the same level of contact despite ending?

How are these relational patterns reflected in your work as an organisational practitioner?

Types of ending

Most OD engagements are by definition temporary relationships which end with the completion of a particular project or assignment. Although endings are often assumed to happen in a planned and organised approach—once the work has been completed—quite often, endings happen in an unpredicted way. It is helpful therefore to distinguish between different types of endings: *expected, chosen* and *forced.*

The "expected" ending is where the engagement runs its course and the agreed upon task comes to an end. This is the typical planned ending which is anticipated in time and outcome and worked towards. A "chosen" ending on the other hand, is when one or both parties make a decision to terminate the engagement. The work may not have completed but an ending is chosen nonetheless. This could be because of a lack of fit between coach and coachee for example, or simply due to new priorities emerging for the client.

It is important not to view a chosen ending as a failure of engagement or poor contracting but an essential part of a co-emergent approach where each intervention and review triggers a possible ending. Indeed, in relatively stable work environments, expected endings may be the norm whilst in more dynamic and complex contexts, the mechanistic and predictable assumptions underlying this type of ending makes less sense. In an emergent OD frame, endings are chosen in the sense that outcomes are less predictable and naturally trigger review points that could result in either a re-contracting or ending.

Finally, a "forced" ending is typically when an unforeseen event in the field of either the client or practitioner forces the end of the engagement. An example of this could be a takeover or merger which makes leadership development work obsolete, or even a personal event which means the practitioner or key client are unable to complete the work.

Example: chosen ending

I was asked to join the coaching team on a large team-coaching transformational project in an NHS Hospital Trust. The project had begun six months ago and this top down intervention was aimed at improving performance targets across the various departments as well as encourage a more open and collaborative culture. Multi-disciplinary teams were therefore brought together in each department for focused team coaching sessions.

One of the team I was assigned to was invited to participate in the project early on but hadn't got their logistics organised yet. I spoke to three of the key players prior to the first team coaching session and agreed that up to fifteen key staff were to be selected from the various functional areas (e.g., consultants, doctors, nurses, midwives, technicians, therapists) relevant to the department. On the agreed day for the first session, around forty people show up to what—I later found out—was their departmental training session. A team coaching session was not possible given that number of people so another session was organised with only key individuals. The energy in the room at the start of session two was heavy with a few people at check-in voicing their displeasure of "having to attend" the session and not seeing any benefit in the initiative. Although many issues and team challenges were voiced, there was no common agreement or motivation to engage with each other. Some toxic interpersonal dynamics were present between two individuals which made it unsafe for people to be open. As a practitioner, all I could do is notice and feedback what was happening in the room and keep looking for any ground of engagement or joint motivation. The harder I worked at looking for a common figure, the more resistance I encountered. It felt like I was trying to do the work for them and despite them! This was not a good starting position for a team coaching intervention. I named their lack of readiness to engage with a team coaching intervention and despite organisational pressures we decided not to go ahead. As a practitioner, choosing to end felt like the more ethical position.

Ending considerations

Although endings may come about in different ways allowing more or less time to plan and consider ending tasks, it is nevertheless useful to outline some key ending considerations for OD practitioners. In much OD literature, the ending or separation phase is primarily about assessing the project or change and putting in place whatever is needed to transition to a new state. Cummings and Worley (2009) for example, describe the final stage of traditional change projects as "evaluating and institutionalizing change" (ibid, p. 31) which stems from a behaviourist mindset and focuses on reinforcing (sic) change through feedback, rewards, and training (ibid, p. 31). Ending and separation tasks and considerations are however more than just about reinforcing change. In the freedom we have to choose and influence an ending is an implicit commitment. Having the autonomy to separate renders "staying with" a choiceful and motivating act and can signal the commitment of both practitioner and client.

Agreeing a separation process

It is not desirable for endings to happen through drift or lack of momentum. An important part of initial contracting includes an agreement around a separation process. In an emergent paradigm, this type of contracting would ideally be iterative and comprise a process of frequent reviews. It is important for the commitment to iterative contracting to be respected by both parties even when the engagement feels like it is going well and there is apparent agreement on the way forward. The example below is not unusual and highlights the dangers of drifting without an agreed separation process.

Example

A coach was working with the CEO of a medium size public sector organisation for about a year. The initial contract was to include a review every six sessions. At the first review point, time was made to look at the work done, progress achieved and what was still needed. The work was going well with both coach and coachee pleased with the flow and growth being achieved. When the coach raised the topic of a review before the twelfth and eighteenth session, the coachee waived it off saying she

---

was keen to continue. Rather than making the space for a more relational exploration of the work and working alliance, reviews were seen as a contractual milestone and gradually became less figural resulting in the work starting to drift with no clear review or ending process. After a summer away, the client cancelled two sessions due to conflicting commitments. She then sent an email to her coach saying she would like to pause the coaching sessions for a few months due to work pressures. The coaching never resumed leaving both client and practitioner with no ending process or way of processing potential unfinished business.

Many people have set patterns for ending and a tendency to avoid endings is not unusual. Setting a clear process for separating supports both parties to recognise and name when the time is right for separating and initiate an open conversation around that. Rothwell and Sulilvan (2005) quote the example of an OD consultant who established ground rules for separating which involved both parties committing to a day session off site whenever either party was considering an ending. This allowed for appropriate time to process the engagement, work through the issues and if needed, agree a separation process that was amenable to all.

Knowing when to end

As organisations are continuously facing change, OD work to improve effectiveness and efficiency is usually ongoing. Knowing when to separate from a client is a key skill for OD practitioners as lingering excessively when the engagement is no longer benefiting the client, or indeed exiting too rapidly are both unhelpful and at times unethical.

Knowing when to end is complex and the following questions may be helpful to practitioners in exploring this dilemma:

- Is my presence both supportive and challenging to the client? If not, have I possibly slipped into a polarised role (either over-supportive or over-challenging)?
- Am I over-invested in a particular outcome or direction? If yes, have I lost my creative indifference and is it time to move on?
- Have I "gone native" and become part of the organisational issue/problem? If yes, is my presence still motivating change?

- Do I feel motivation and progress in the work? does the client?
- Can I envision the organisation after I leave? Am I working towards that point? If not, why not?

These questions don't necessarily signal a need to end but help frame the question of whether separating might be more beneficial to the client and the work. Of course, ending an engagement too early is equally ethically questionable as this also means leaving the client in a poor position to manage a change process that was co-created. Bearing the hard times with our clients is also part of the OD practitioner's role.

Celebrate achievements and acknowledge what was unfinished

When the end is in the sight, whether expected, chosen or forced, addressing all implications of the ending is a shared responsibility for client and practitioner.

Ending an OD engagement must be linked back to the contracting phase. This is true for managers as well as internal and external consultants. Have the initial objectives (modified through iterative reviews) or contracted obligations been met? What was not attended to or remains still unfinished, both in the work and the relationship? Whether an expected or chosen ending, it is ethical to make space in the ending process to review how the client will continue what was started and what is needed for that aspect of sustainability.

An assessment of the work is important but not the sole task of ending. Celebrating the joint effort and work that has been achieved is a significant aspect of closure. Often difficult or challenging work engagements are made possible through supportive team environments or helpful professional relationships. The ups and downs of organisational life are made smoother through these relationships which are worth honouring and remembering. Kahneman et al. (1993) write about the peak end rule which states that the way an experience ends determines the happiness we ascribe to it. Positive psychology has also shown us that forming favourable narratives of our lives (and working lives) is a key aspect of wellbeing.

Finally, as the relationship is a primary vehicle for a successful engagement, it might also be appropriate to discuss how the relationship between client and practitioner can be re-established following separation. What feels right or appropriate for both parties?

Managing your own unfinished business

In the case of forced endings or chosen endings that have not been properly communicated, the external practitioner may find themselves "out in the cold" with little access to the client. A previously responsive client may seem more distant, not answering calls or emails with their usual speed. Whether the work has been completed or not, this freezing out, which can happen as a result of shifting priorities will naturally result in feelings of unfinished business. The lack of relational connection also often opens the space for projections on both sides with the practitioner wondering if they have inadvertently offended their client whilst the client struggles with shifting priorities and not knowing how to update or have that 'difficult' conversation with the practitioner.

It is often helpful to find other ways of re-engaging with the client system to find out what might be happening or had happened. This could take time and happen at a much later stage (or not at all) and it is useful therefore for the practitioner to seek supervisory help in processing their own sense of loss and unfinished business. As Melnick and Roos (2007, p. 104) write: "If we prematurely 'move on' without honoring the learning embedded in the loss, an important opportunity for growth and development has been lost. On the other hand, if we linger too long, and if the loss is constantly figural, unduly influencing and distorting the present and future, then possibilities for newness and creativity are also diminished."

The trap of idealisation and dependence

As OD consultants, we often get into this work because we love to help and/or be needed. This might also however inadvertently foster a type of dependency on the part of the client. In that sense, being successful as an OD practitioner can be both blessing and curse. Success may encourage projections onto practitioners of being super effective or efficient and dis-empower the client organisation who then believes they are not able to manage or work without the help of that practitioner.

A primary ethical objective of OD practitioners is to make themselves redundant and leave the organisation with the capabilities needed to continue functioning without them. Issues of dependency and hubris or arrogance on the part of the practitioner may however contribute to poor endings. Unfortunately, this is rarely considered in the design or delivery of an OD project and capability transfer is not always attended to early enough, if at all. Naming this early in the engagement process is an important and ethical consideration.

It is helpful therefore for the practitioner to recognise the trap of idealisation and dependence early and work towards challenging projections. Endings must be clear and unambiguous as possible. Often, practitioners feel they need to linger "just in case" or be available for a "quick" call or chat. Typically, the practitioner finds themselves doing unpaid work or conversely, the client feels they are still paying for the practitioner's time after the contracted services have ended. The lack of clear boundaries can result in messy and unhelpful situations for both practitioner and client.

Summary

This chapter has covered the importance of ending and closure processes in gestalt OD work. Irrespective of the many types of endings whether planned or not, working with an end in mind is an essential element of emergent working and contributes to the sustainability of the work overall. Key considerations of ending have been outlined which also recognise that the task of ending and separating requires particular attention and competencies—both emotional and rationale—which are worth developing as OD practitioners.

PART III

APPLYING GESTALT TO ORGANISATIONAL SETTINGS

This last part of the book offers case studies and examples of using gestalt to support different types of OD interventions. Before starting with illustrations of work, the first chapter addresses key challenges and questions that new comers to gestalt in organisations ask when they start to introduce this approach into their work. As an emergent approach, contracting and framing the work is crucial and often challenging to clients who are used to procuring change or OD work with anticipated, predictable or precise outcomes.

The following chapters then present four different applications of gestalt in organisations. First, a transcript of a gestalt co-coaching session provides an insight into the experience of both coach and coachee. Second, work with a family business conveys the importance of creating a safe container to explore unaware id processes. The third case study draws on work with a leadership team in a public-sector organisation in the midst of transformation. Finally, the last case study covers a merger situation in the pharmaceutical industry.

What these cases have in common is that they highlight how gestalt has supported both the work and the practitioner. As most consultants, coaches, managers or organisational practitioners know, working in organisations is complex and includes both effective and messy parts. This is why these cases hopefully don't just read as simply stories of successful work but also reflect the ups and downs of genuine OD work.

CHAPTER TWELVE

Practice considerations in introducing a gestalt approach

With emergence and responsiveness at its heart, the practice of gestalt has at times more of a kinship to art rather than a science. As such, it understandably sets certain challenges to the organisational practitioner given the predominance of outcome-driven and mechanistic thinking prevalent in most organisations. This chapter is designed to support practitioners to introduce gestalt into their work. It will therefore address some of the concerns and queries that newcomers to gestalt raise as they begin to apply the approach to their practice. Common questions therefore mostly centre on the challenge of facing a mechanistic mindset and the "how to" of introducing gestalt to those contexts. This chapter speaks directly to the budding gestalt practitioner and so focuses on those entry stages and initial contracting conversations as these often frame the ensuing work.

Be clear about the benefits of a gestalt approach

In approaching OD work from a gestalt perspective, a practitioner must be clear about the benefits that such an approach will provide a given project or situation. When introducing the idea of gestalt to your organisation, the first challenge is often to get enough trust for the client to invest time, energy and resources in what might feel like an unfamiliar approach.

As outlined in Chapter Three, a gestalt approach to OD or change is most useful in conditions where linear planned solutions are not evident but where a relational and behavioural component is essential to a successful outcome. Gestalt fosters the right conditions for emergence and so uncertainty is an intrinsic part of where most interventions start. Table 12.1 below lists some of the key benefits of gestalt and may provide a good starting point to a conversation with a client.

It is worth noting however that many gestalt practitioners do not lead with these benefits but rather demonstrate the approach in the way they are, in their use-of-self. Unlike some other OD approaches, gestalt is not a methodology or technique but more of a stance and way of being which informs and shapes interventions. Often clients may not be aware that a practitioner is informed by gestalt and would perhaps comment on the practitioner's presence and how they inquire into issues or facilitate better conversations.

Table 12.1. Some of the benefits of a gestalt approach.

1.	It focuses on heightening awareness and so makes explicit what is often implicit.
2.	Change happens in the here and now, as well as later.
3.	It focuses on the interpersonal and intersubjective dimensions in working with individuals, teams, and organisations to improve communication and relationships which leads to improved productivity and employee morale.
4.	It is a co-emergent and customised process rather than a pre-packaged service.
5.	It is highly participative where client and practitioner together shape the next step.
6.	As a relational and dialogic approach, it supports better conversations between individuals and within teams leading to shared figures of interest and co-ordinated action.
7.	It is experiential and creative so that change often happens in the moment.

Awareness of pre-entry

Entering a system is always a hazardous act. This is when as a practitioner, you are more likely to cross boundaries that you may be unaware of or make (often erroneous!) assumptions about a new client based on previous experiences. It is also easy to assume that entering a system happens at that moment when the first conversation or face-to-face meeting with the client takes place. Whilst this is undoubtedly an important instant of connection, there is much "pre-entry" contact which would have usually occurred before that point such as the referral process, email exchanges or even a procurement process.

From a gestalt field theoretical perspective, it is helpful to hold the context of this pre-entry stage in awareness and recognise that it would unavoidably configure that first meeting. For example, a practitioner who gets recommended for a piece of work through a common contact or colleague will need to navigate expectations already in place before he/she has even met the client organisation. Surfacing these implicit expectations can often be an important aspect of the work and of building a working alliance. Similarly, for internal managers or consultants, awareness of the ground of the politics already at play before the engagement has even started is an essential component of the pre-entry stage.

Building working alliances

As outlined in previous chapters, gestalt practice is relational in the sense that it stresses the importance of relationship as a vehicle and container for change to happen. Establishing a working alliance is therefore an essential building block for the work of a gestalt practitioner. This involves the development of an "active partnership, a bond of trust between you and your client in which you share a mutual understanding of your work together and its goals" (Joyce & Sills, 2014, p. 43). This step can be complex when engaging with a large system or organisation where the client is often not the individual procuring the piece of work. On large OD projects, it is common for instance to have joint consultant and client teams where individuals from within the organisation are seconded onto the project for a duration of time. This serves both the purpose of heightening client engagement, facilitating co-emergence as well as transferring capabilities to the client organisation. For gestalt practitioners, change can only be supported in relationship and so, attending to and nurturing these working alliances is a key aspect of any organisational engagement. Relationship and task go hand in hand, with time and effort being given to both.

Demonstrate gestalt practice

With use of self as a primary tool, gestalt practice is chiefly a way of being as well as a set of assumptions about what leads to healthier individuals, teams and organisations. As such the most effective way of introducing gestalt is to demonstrate it in the way you conduct your initial meetings and negotiations.

As a gestalt practitioner, you are for example less likely at this first meeting to want to unpack or deconstruct the root cause of the presenting problem but rather to inquire phenomenologically to understand the likely underpinning dynamics that have led to the issue. In doing so, the gestalt practitioner would for instance explore the whole SOS (self, other, and situation) perspective, asking:

- What are the conditions/contexts that may have contributed to this situation? (situation)
- Who is impacted by the presenting issue? How is this manifest? (other)
- How does this affect you, your job, position, relationships? (self)

These initial conversations then become less about "briefing" the manager or consultant but more about genuine dialogue. Rather than a one-way information flow, the meeting brings new insights or perceptions that flow from the questions you ask them and which they might not have considered. New awareness and therefore change is already happening. By conducting your initial meetings in this way, you are demonstrating your way of working.

Iterative contracting

During initial discussions, a practitioner is often met with the client's view of what needs to be done. Client expectations and desired outcome from an OD engagement are usually based on what is factual, visible, and needs prioritised attention (e.g., a process that is not performing well or a team that is not producing the expected results). As portrayed in the wave model (outlined in Chapter Three), these issues are often the visible signs or symptoms (ego functioning level) which result from id or personality function issues at a deeper and less in awareness level. Tackling the "broken" process through—for example—a process re-engineering intervention would yield result in the short term but, alone would rarely be sustainable. So, the tension at the entry stage of a project is to arrive at a contracting agreement that holds both the client's needs in the moment and the possibility to explore what is less in awareness and intervene at that level.

One of the greatest challenges to OD work today is that it is procured by leaders who talk about a changing culture and empowered workforce but are often resistant and reluctant to let go of the power to decide, control and shape the future. Being an ethical OD consultant (internal or external) may at times mean challenging the basis of the problem or issue we are called to help with. Unfortunately, often consultants are called in to legitimise a manager's effort to sell an idea internally or conversely to take the blame for unpopular decisions or cutbacks. Rather than colluding with the status quo, OD practitioners need to also name the lack of leadership and what is needed to make the organisation more effective. This isn't about selling on more work, but about providing an honest and authentic presence to the client.

In a gestalt frame, it is therefore useful to think of the contracting stage as an iterative process that can be re-visited and remains fluid to respond to the emergent needs of the organisation or project. This view of "contract" and level of changeability requires trust and transparency between parties which takes time to establish. It also demands of the practitioner to, as Staemmler (1997) writes, cultivate uncertainty and be optimistic, expecting change to be possible even if it cannot yet be discerned. An explicit naming of this iterative contracting also supports co-emergence rather than fixed and predetermined outcomes. To support this type of work, regular review and reflection meetings must be an inherent part of the ongoing work.

Opening space for co-emergence … neither leading nor following

Gestalt principles hold that awareness leads to change. Heightening client awareness is thus the primary activity of a gestalt practitioner who journeys alongside in that process; neither anticipating nor falling behind the client. It is not therefore helpful to speak of a diagnosis phase for example as the word diagnosis itself implies a medical model which does not sit well with gestalt's field relational and co-created stance. Co-diagnosis or co-emergence fits better with a gestalt collaborative approach where consultant and client come together to explore a given situation not necessarily from a starting point of assuming a problem but with a stance of inquiry and curiosity. In introducing gestalt as an approach, a practitioner is therefore likely to emphasise the collaborative inquiry and partnership rather than present as an expert that imposes a diagnostic frame, carries out the diagnostic exercise and then feeds back to the client group/organisation. Approaches where data are collected and analysed behind closed doors and the outcome then shared (or worse imposed!) on the organisation lose the opportunity for the sensing phase to act as a catalyst for change.

How much and what to share with clients?

The "co" of co-emergence signals a mutuality where both practitioner and client need to step forward and make use of themselves, sharing insights, thoughts as well as feelings and perceptions. The power and weakness of a phenomenological method is that all data is meaningful. Often as gestalt practitioners, we need to sit with uncertainty and not-knowing as a useful stance to model to the organisation, thus allowing for newness and a different type of knowing to crystallise. In those moments, it is useful to recognise when and what to share. To be discriminate and not assume that all phenomenological observations are meaningful or more valid than those of my client's. Again, a practitioner sharing their subjective noticing is an intervention in itself and should be done with care of context and of the level of support of the listener. In my early consulting days, I recall for example moments when highly observant and intuitive consultants were thrown out from client meetings after sharing their perceptions of the organisation. Although these consultants may have been accurate in their observations, they didn't calibrate and attend enough to the client's level of support in hearing the feedback in that way and at that moment. A co-emergent process implies of course, that we won't always get this right as we can't anticipate our client's reactions and so, presence and responsiveness to what emerges is key. As practitioners we also need to attend to our own blind spots, biases and preferences. The role of supervision in this case cannot be over-stated.

Summary

This chapter has stemmed from the frequently asked questions posed by practitioners new to the gestalt approach. The hope is that the ideas presented here on how to introduce gestalt will support you in both presenting this—perhaps counter-cultural—approach in your organisational work and provide you with some tips and guidance around initial entry conversations.

CHAPTER THIRTEEN

Relational gestalt coaching: a transcript of dialogue at work*

Sally Denham-Vaughan and Marie-Anne Chidiac

In the mid to late 1990s links were starting to be made between "emotionally intelligent leaders" and business performance (Opengart, 2005; Goleman, 2000). Not only are leaders expected to cope with growing complexity and stress, but an awareness of one's own style, prejudices and personal impact are now common leadership requirements in increasingly global and multicultural organisations.

Many coaching techniques try to emulate the fast moving, action-oriented surroundings of businesses, but in this confluence we think

* This chapter by Sally Denham-Vaughan and Marie-Anne Chidiac appears in an extended format under the title "Dialogue goes to work: Relational organisational gestalt", in Hycner, R. & Jacobs, L. (Eds). *Relational Approaches in Gestalt Therapy*, Cambridge: Gestalt Press, 2009.

Permission from Lynne Jacobs co-editor of the book *Relational Approaches in Gestalt Therapy* to re-publish in Chapter Thirteen a re-written chapter previously entitled "Dialogue goes to work: relational organisational gestalt", from Hycner, R. & Jacobs, L. (Eds). *Relational Approaches in Gestalt Therapy*. Cambridge: Gestalt Press, 2009.

Permission from Deborah Ullman, President of Gestalt Press to publish in Chapter Thirteen, the rewritten chapter previously entitled "Dialogue goes to work: relational organizational gestalt", from Hycner, R. & Jacobs, L. (Eds). *Relational Approaches in Gestalt Therapy*, Cambridge: Gestalt Press, 2009.

they lose sight of the power of relationships and strategies of dialogue, to maximise potential. Our experience is that optimal personal growth via coaching is facilitated by our authentic presence and relationship with our clients. Relational coaching thus requires both backbone and heart (O'Neil, 2000), both rigour and relationship. The business world is ready for coaching that emphasises the need for integrating and developing qualities of both "will and grace"; where "will" can be defined as "directed action" and ability to initiate, and "grace" as a quality of "receptivity" and responsiveness (see Denham-Vaughan, 2005, for a full discussion).

In particular, we believe it is important to move away from coaching based on the deficit (acquisitional) model. Historically, coaching contracts overstress the need for upfront objectives and demonstrable outcomes; the starting point frequently being what is "wrong" with an individual and/or what needs fixing, and with a gathering of feedback to garner relevant data.

In contrast, the radically relational (Staemmler, 2016) ROG coaching model illustrated in this chapter includes the use of a complex, field-oriented approach, where issues emerging for the coachee are viewed as a function of the current relational context with the coach. The dyadic meeting thereby offers a window to aspects of relational style that could be relevant at work, both in assisting individual performance, and also—through the new relational experience in the dyad—a window to additional relational skills that can be offered to a team. For example, specific elements of relational support that enable a firmer sense of self and mobilise creative potential can be identified, practised and transferred to the working situation.

ROG coaching rests of the assumption that "what needs to happen" will emerge as a product of the contact made between coach and coachee. It is not a context where the coachee needs to arrive with a clear, pre-formed "agenda for change" or where the coach sets targets or goals. The most important dimension is considered to be the emergent relational aspect; the evolution of what "we" are going to address together. It is however, the coaches' responsibility and task to take the lead in establishing the relational supports within which this occurs. The coach initiates attempts to understand the coachee's experience and desires. Successful exploration requires a mutual co-regulatory and reciprocal process that is a feature of quality dialogic relational gestalt work. Elements of this process will now be explained in more detail.

A relational gestalt coaching framework

ROG coaching aims to develop the coachee's relational competencies by exploring his or her relational needs and then examining how these are met, (or not), with other people. We emphasise, both theoretically and practically, how different ways of being emerge as a function of changing environments, be these physical or relational. In other words, we explore the minute ways in which the self I am here-and-now with you is directly, immediately and constantly affected by who and how you are with me and vice versa. In our contracting process, there is thus an explicit focus on the coaching relationship as the major educational vehicle and context for learning and development.

The following four key dimensions capture aspects of the uniqueness of ROG Coaching.

The working alliance

We have found that in order to create sufficient psychological safety (see Chapter Eight) for relevant personal, often profound issues to emerge it is vital that the coach attends closely to the coachee's experience of the coaching relationship.

For instance, finding the right balance between challenge and support is crucial, particularly when the coachee is shame prone, or if they work in extremely shaming organisational environments. Too little support from the coach can result in the coachee withdrawing and "hiding" (moderating contact described in Chapter Six); while an "overdose of niceness" can lead to avoidance of looking at the coachee's contribution to difficult situations. In summary, it is important to create relational conditions where the coachee's issues can emerge, rather than be hunted down or lost in a wash of overprotectiveness.

Since the coaching situation necessarily involves an exploration of work performance, with either an overt or covert expectation of "improvement", there is often potential for shame. This "evaluative" component, combined with possible exposure of previously hidden and/or unknown developmental relational issues requires considerable skill from the coach. Kets de Vries (2005) refers to this process as establishing the "clinical orientation" or utilising the clinical paradigm, and states this is vital if coaching is to be beneficial.

Dialogic dimension

Building on gestalt theory as well as contributions from Buber (1958) and Bakhtin (1981), Chapter Eight of this book outlined a framework for dialogue in organisations which mapped the dialogic space onto four dialogue styles:

- Being-with, which focuses on what Buber refers to as "turning towards the other" where each person's story, perspective and being is accepted and confirmed.
- Exploring, which stays with the individual experiences but invites a more active consideration and focus on specific thoughts, feelings, and ideas.
- Aiming, which acknowledges the organisational pressures for unity, coherent action, and integration.
- Dynamic co-emergence which is the sense of togetherness and unity that cannot be facilitated or anticipated but which emerges from attending responsively to the other quadrants.

It is within this latter quadrant that the coach aims to spend the majority of their time, and that yields the most noticeable results in the workplace.

Developmental dimension

The use of the words "radically relational" within this chapter when referring to ROG coaching incorporates additional features to traditional dialogic gestalt, (which is, of course, also "relational"). We used this term to refer specifically to the model outlined fully in Hycner and Jacobs (1995), which features use of Kohut's (1984), "self-object" transferences, together with a methodology originating in contemporary Intersubjectivity theory (see Stolorow, Brandchaft, & Atwood, 1987). Intersubjectivists examine the minutiae of relational patterns emerging in the here and now between therapist/coach and client/coachee. In particular, the "intersubjective" domain is highlighted as revealing interpersonal patterns which can be explored and transformed by the coach's skills of "affect attunement"; understanding and embodied and affective responsiveness to the coachee.

These psychodynamic theories add a developmental dimension to the exploration of the here and now dialogue. They enable the coach to view the habitual relational patterns that emerge during a coaching process as reflective of archaic relational "lacks", or "needed" relationships by the coachee but potentially also by the coach, so supervision is vital. These often present as powerful unfulfilled longings within current relationships. Within an organisational environment, it is our experience that knowledge of, and ability to work with, these self-object transferences is at least as important as an appreciation of classic transference responses created by "repeated" relational situations. We actually see more individuals struggling with the absence of key relational supports they need from their leaders/colleagues in order to function optimally, than we do instances of positively damaging behaviours. Hence, the focus on "what is missing or longed for" can be crucial. In practice, we find it helps to identify these Kohutian self-object needs and transferences as they emerge, not only in the content of the material, but especially within the coaching dyad.

Although we use this clinical paradigm, we are not seeing emergence of these self-object needs as developmental deficits that need to be clinically addressed, but as evidence of healthy, ongoing longings for mirroring, idealisation, and twinship, which support psychic stability, containment and growth. For example, a positive idealised relationship with a leader can create a sense of identify and containment during a change process. Leaders should therefore be able to both recognise their own needs for idealisation and encourage and tolerate those needs when they are present in others. Similarly, needs for twinship and a sense of belonging, of being part of something, can reinforce self-worth, self-esteem and bring a sense of intimacy and sharing. Within an organisation, this can give a clear sense of an individual's contribution to the whole, and positively reinforce performance. Likewise, being accurately mirrored can give a real sense of competency and self-worth; of being seen as an important individual. We believe that increasing awareness of this developmental dimension provides us with the lens through which to focus on growing edges for coachees and sometimes for coaches.

The field/contextual dimension

A key difference between relational gestalt psychotherapy and ROG coaching is that the latter process is primarily an aspect of an organisational process rather than a private individual initiative. As such, the ethical imperative is not only to the client, but also to the organisation. On occasions, this can lead to conflicted feelings in the coach, which require thorough examination and exploration in supervision. It is vital however that the coach holds this organisational focus, and also has a good understanding of the situational demands of the work system and the inherent challenges it poses to the coachee.

Context and background

The coaching transcript that we have provided here offers a window into ROG as it is practised in a coaching context. It is important to note that the transcript is also a "live experiment" aimed at developing, explicating and articulating relational organisational gestalt coaching principles. As such, it is taken from a series of coaching sessions that were undertaken to support and develop practice. Sessions have taken place over approximately the last six months, and have generally lasted between twenty-thirty minutes, occurring at approximately four-week intervals. Sessions have generally taken place face-to-face, but due to travelling commitments, have occasionally been done over the phone.

The transcript has been organised in this way in order to provide a direct insight into not only the thinking of the coach, but also the coachee. Previous work, (Chidiac & Denham-Vaughan, 2007) concerning the use of presence and "fit" between individuals, concluded that in a genuinely horizontal and dialogic relationship, the client has presence as well as the therapist/coach. This means that the coachee's insights, opinions, and changes throughout the session are as important as the coach's, and that both individuals contribute to the "dynamic co-emergence" (see Chapter Eight) of the session.

In what follows, there is the unique opportunity to read the individual formulations of coach and coachee concerning what is going on in the session. These formulations were evolved in isolation from the dyadic partner. Each point of punctuation for commentary also includes theoretical linkage to exemplify the theoretical teaching points that we have already articulated.

Introduction to the transcript

Coachee. At our previous coaching session I had dared to tell my coach a very brief dream image I had experienced about six weeks earlier.

I had mentioned the image before, but had not told her the content. Last session had therefore felt like taking a huge risk in admitting I had dreamt about standing with her and a work colleague. It had emerged that I had been left with a very good and strong feeling from the dream. She had been very nonchalant about me dreaming about her, which had helped me, even saying it was a pretty common event in a coaching relationship. On the basis of that, although I still felt confused, I had decided to take things a bit further.

Coach. During our last session, the coachee brought the figure of a dream in which I figured. Although it was clear the dream held a lot of significance for her, I felt that she was hesitant in exploring it fully with me. I had felt tested and was left with imagining she had needed to see if I could handle her dream and her pushing me away. I felt curious to see if the dream would re-emerge in this session, as it seems to hold connotations of defiance and aggression, while also validating our connection.

Theoretical linkage. With the coachee "taking a huge risk" in admitting to the dream and the coach feeling tested, the previous session seems to have been one in which a foundation was being set for more challenging work to be done. This is an important aspect of building the working alliance, (dimension 1), in coaching and ideally should be made more explicit and named.

Here, we also noted the importance of the calmness of the coach while hearing the dream, and "normalising" dreaming about her, which had regulated the coachee. More intense and focused responses on the part of the coach around the dream may have been too shaming and resulted in the meeting taking on the flavour of a therapy session. This can often be unhelpful and lead to the coachee feeling humiliated and over-exposed.

COACHEE: So ... I feel in a very different place from when I met you last time because I was feeling quite strong and robust then and I feel a bit more ... maybe vulnerable. I don't know, but less defended. [Pause] I would like to start by saying what I was left with.

COACH: I'd like to hear that.

COACHEE: It's different. There was this whole thing that I felt embarrassed and awkward about, feeling like a toddler, feeling that somehow I wanted to run off and do things, and yet I wanted somebody also to hold some limits. I thought, "I'm sure this relates to why I don't do certain things at work", "why I don't actually end up running things".

I have run things, but I have sort of made this commitment, "no
more!"

COACH: Because if you run things then what?

COACHEE: I'd be on my own!

COACH: So there won't be that connection?

COACHEE: And nobody will hold me. I won't feel held. And that's the bit that
I think. I just feel I've had too much time in my life holding myself,
you know, and other people. So I feel a lot of conflict about "well,
if I take these next steps up, then it feels like, I am back to holding
myself and making my decisions and holding everybody else". It is
actually a better position for me to be the second person down in
something, even if I don't feel a lot of respect for the person at the
top and feel that I should be doing it. That's a lot of conflict and tension ...

COACH: Yes, huge tension.

COACHEE: Oh, I can't believe I said this ... I've got to breathe in a bit. I can't
believe I got that out.

Coachee. I could not believe that I had said these statements to my coach.
I was having a huge rush of adrenaline, rather as if I had just been surf-
ing, hit a big wave and needed to come up for air. She was still looking pretty cool, which was important to me keeping going. I was really
uncomfortable, as although I knew this is what all my issues are about
at work, I still hadn't expected to end up talking about it.

Coach. I experienced the coachee as very present and authentic in
putting forward what was going on for her [dimension 2]. I was aware
of how important and also shaming it was to have described her process so honestly. Although she seemed to have a strong response, I felt
confident in the coachee's self-support and wondered about her feeling even more infantilised or "like a toddler" if I dwelled on, or bla-
tantly avoided, the shame process. I therefore decided to "stay with"
even though I felt anxious and was wondering if she felt too ashamed,
whether I would be deflected or pushed away as in our previous session. I felt on delicate ground to get the balance right in order for us to
work on what she was bringing.

Theoretical linkage. The coachee seems to have experienced great
mobilisation and has a very embodied response. In working with this,
the physical and vocal calmness of the coach is very important. The
coachee is highly aware of nonverbal ways of relating, and these tend
to be far more important and figural than content issues. The process
is suggestive of a longing for an "idealised other". This is potentially

a self-object transference that may suggest a problematic archaic issue occurring at work. The relational work gives a very useful diagnostic insight into this. It is hard to see how this would emerge in acquisitional coaching. Throughout this section of transcript, the coach trusts the presence of the coachee and their ability to engage in dialogue when there is sufficient relational support. Each coachee will need different types and styles of support and it is the responsibility of the coach to moderate their relational style to facilitate the meeting. This process is established through the formation of the working alliance; dimension (1) in ROG.

COACH: How is it to have got it out?

COACHEE: I don't feel proud of that, you see. I don't feel proud of it.

COACH: That you need somehow to be held?

COACHEE: Blughch! You've said it now, that's revolting. I feel patronised and sort of infantilised and er … blugh. I don't like that.

COACH: Wow, I've really said it now. And I notice your reaction and I'm thinking of the times in my life where I couldn't have done a lot of things within organisations unless I knew there was someone behind me. And your reaction is how disgusting that you might even need that. "How revolting?"

COACHEE: Absolutely. I do feel that. I feel that … I feel ashamed of that … I feel I really don't like you mentioning it. I really don't like that.

COACH: Because you have to do everything on your own?

COACHEE: It's just better; it's just better for me.

COACH: How?

COACHEE: I don't know, that's the conflict you see. I just hit this point of conflict that I used to do everything on my own and that's why I was successful. To me they go together. However, I felt lonely, envied, erm … lonely is the word that keeps coming out. I don't know what I want to try and say. Because it's like—be more successful, that means I'm going to do it on my own.

COACH: That sounds so clear, the absolute certainty that there is no way that you actually can be successful without absolutely doing it on your own.

COACHEE: Yes.

Coachee. I am right at my limit of walking out/ending the session. I imagine she didn't realise how much I disliked all this, but I had a sense that I'd rather have been anywhere else. I imagined there would have been negative consequences to me leaving and I could still see that all this was probably important, but I wasn't enjoying the session. I was impressed again by the fact that she stayed calm and just kept right on going.

Coach. I felt like I was skating on thin ice. On one hand, I was intensely aware of how uncomfortable the session was for the coachee and on the other was worried if she would experience me as having backed away if I didn't stay with what was most figural. I tried to normalise the feelings she was talking about by sharing some of my own process [inclusion and open communication—dimension 2]. This was still too much and so in my last intervention backed away from what felt like an early developmental need to be held and supported to how this manifested and impacted her in the workplace.

Theoretical linkage. Both coachee and coach are trusting the process, working as authentically as they can mutually support. There seems to be enormous shame now that the archaic longings have been stimulated and surfaced. Coaching can be potentially less shaming than therapy as the transparent coaching agenda is "performance improvement". This is more acceptable to narcissistically wounded, yet successful individuals, who are commonly encountered near the top of organisations. The systemic dimension (4), is always concerned to bring the figure back to the context of the organisation and the coachee's performance within it. This is an ethical issue in ROG and in this case, also supports the coachee to feel more "acceptable," or at least less "psychopathologised" and shamed.

COACH: How did you learn that?

COACHEE: Hmmm [pause]. It's like I manage my team, you know. I know they're behind me and I know that actually they give me a whole lot of support and my deputy is incredibly supportive of me. It's people above me or equal to me that are my problem.

COACH: Let's just check this. You can get support, you can almost ... be held by someone as long as they report to you.

COACHEE: Up to a point. I would always expect that come the crunch, I would look after them more. But if they were fine and I wasn't, then yes, I would feel I could get support from them. But when it came to the crunch, I'd feel it was my job to lead them, and I would.

COACH: And that feels lonely.

COACHEE: Yes, that's the bit that somehow feels, I would like to have equals ... you know I told you about the dream ... I think that's about having equals … about having partners and I feel uncomfortable with that … mistrustful with that … like I'm going to be disappointed in that. I said this thing to you, as well about the image, there is this thing about these people are "other". Not aggressive quite, but stronger … I don't know.

COACH: How? Less pushy, less supportive?

COACHEE: No, standing up, being counted. Yes, standing up and being counted. I feel they probably would and I wouldn't. I'd take the easy way out.

COACH: So the others in your dream … would actually take it on?

COACHEE: Yes, they'd take it on and do it. And I wouldn't. But I am not so sure you see, that makes it very black and white. I am not so sure. Because that is one side of the story and then there is the other part of the story, that is … Uurggh, I don't know. I know I feel I am going into areas that I don't know about so well. No, no, I don't want to, not for today.

Coachee. I'd enjoyed getting back to talking about work and then found myself talking about the dream again. The session felt out of my control, which I am not very used to. I kept being surprised. I wasn't really sure what she was doing because it didn't look like much; and yet I found myself back to saying some quite revealing stuff.

Coach. Looking at the coachee's process in the workplace seemed less shaming and she looked more grounded. I was pleasantly surprised at how quickly the dream re-emerges and felt appreciative of the coachee's presence. She clearly tells me that some parts of the dream are too difficult (shaming?) to go into today. I feel respectful of this and yet wondered at the importance of staying with what felt like an important relational figure. I decide to share some of my sense of the dream and tried to convey some of the support I took away from her previous description.

Theoretical linkage. Still dealing with Kohut's notion of the "idealising transference", the need that people have to relax and sink into the competence of admired figures and caregivers. The competence of the coach raises this longing. Although most of the time, it is the coachee who leads the figure, the dialogic dynamic co-emergence of coaching also means that how the coach experiences the meeting in the dyad may potentially hold a new awareness for the coachee. Methodologically, this involves a use of inclusion to build a mutually reciprocal regulatory system, with each party sharing awareness as it emerges.

COACH: OK, not for today. Can I tell you what I remember from our conversation previously about the three in the dream? Somehow although the three were alone they also all stood together.

COACHEE: Yes, it was like the Three Musketeers.

COACH: In a way, you were saying that the other two would stand on their own ... would go it alone, and yet they are not. There was stability in the three.

COACHEE: Yes. I don't know. It's a real dilemma. It is that issue of feeling I back off things because I don't want to lead them on my own. And by "on my own", I mean with a far less competent team. My Team at work I have chosen, I chose and recruited everybody.

COACH: My guess is you feel you have groomed them so they would be in support of you.

COACHEE: I feel very embarrassed, very wobbly about that.

COACH: Because you need it?

COACHEE: It reminds me when I was talking with a colleague about X and ... [pause] and she said "well, you have chosen him very carefully" and I felt very embarrassed about that but it would be ... [pause] that friendship has not happened by chance. That would be to do with competence and trustworthiness.

COACH: Yes.

COACHEE: You look as if that's obvious?

COACH: It feels so obvious, I think every person who goes into a new job, you know, the leader, brings in his or her own team. It's like "why wouldn't you choose them?" Somehow there is a "should" there.

COACHEE: There's a "I should be more generous" to people who are less "able", but I think I have had enough of being generous.

COACH: Oh yes, so the "you feel you should be more generous" means that you should have the relationship with someone less able? It feels heavy.

COACHEE: It is heavy; its very hard work trying to get people to perform competently at things actually they are just not very good at.

COACH: I'm curious that that's what you need to do, that's what you need to carry with you.

COACHEE: I think that this is the bit of my story that I carry with me. I regulate other people in order that they function well.

COACH: [Sigh] I feel sad.

COACHEE: I feel sad ... and angry actually. Angry and a bit pissed off with it. Because I feel I'm carrying dead weights.

COACH: I get a sense of the dead weights pulling down the possibility of new and exciting stuff. I wonder, how can you have that without having all the dead weight?

Coachee. The same thing happens again. I get to my limit and say stop, she stops and then just carries straight on … and I let that happen seemingly quite happily. This is all new territory for me; therapy did not have this effect of me opening up so quickly as I always felt the therapist had an agenda of infantalising me and wanting me to show more emotions. I am really surprised that here I am talking about emotions quite happily. That may sound paradoxical, but it felt very genuine and real to me … much more so than some of the scenes in therapy where I would eventually cry/rage a lot just to get her off my back!

Coach. I am pleased that we both felt supported to stay with the overall figure despite a few difficult, shame filled moments. Her early introject around needing to be more generous with those less able felt at odds to me within an organisational setting and I wonder if somehow naming this in the context of her work facilitated her making the connection with an archaic way of being in the world. As she gets in touch with what must be a very familiar pattern of "having to" regulate others, I experience the heaviness of her struggle and feel saddened by it.

Theoretical linkage. Here we see the healing power of the idealising self-object transference being very lightly held by the coach, but used to great effect. The coachee is experimenting with whole new ways of being that involve getting support without feeling totally shamed and/ or inauthentic. This has great potential to make a real difference at work by increasing the coachee's willingness to both lead *and* get support. There is clear evidence of raising material from "id" self-functions into a much clearer figure that the ego aspect of self can get hold of and make choices about. The coachee links the figure of the dream back to the organisational context. This illustrates that the systemic dimension (4), is always present in the phenomenal field and that linkages to developmental patterns and figures happen spontaneously, without having to directly explore the past "content" issues. In fact, interventions that do focus on these issues (such as, "tell me about your family of origin", etc.), subtly cross a boundary between coaching and psychotherapy and are generally inappropriate within a coaching context. If the coachee raises such material, it is usually helpful for the coach to confirm the effect such information may have in terms of a "legacy" affecting the present work situation, rather than enquiring into the content of the historical narrative.

Conclusion

This brief commented transcript has hopefully shown the power and richness of a relational gestalt approach to coaching. These are some of the key learning points that emerge from the chapter:

- The coaching "goal" can be brought into sessions by the coachee *or* emerge as the coachee and coach work together; contracting is iterative and ongoing.
- Both coach and coachee can be cognitively, emotionally, and physically affected by and learn from the process.
- As the process is radically relational there is sometimes some uncertainty regarding exactly what statements or issues sit with who: this uncertainty reduces the risk of shame and shame defending/ avoidance in the coachee but requires the coach to sit with a high degree of uncertainty and vulnerability. Supervision is vitally important with this form of coaching.
- There is a high level of awareness raising of habitual relational patterns that can implicitly emerge at work. This opens the door for clarity, action, increased choice and improved performance.

CHAPTER FOURTEEN

Gestalt work with a family business*

Nicky Burton

Introduction

In this chapter, work with a family business looking at succession planning is explored. Although the main work initially centred on exploring the governance options for the business, it expanded to include a gestalt led piece which focused on clarifying the extent to which the family members wanted to be involved in the running and support of the business. Such succession conversations are in all contexts difficult and uncertain and never more so than when entangled in family dynamics. I wish to convey in this chapter how the use of a gestalt emergent, dialogic and phenomenological approach supported

---

* This chapter is based on an article by Burton, N., Chidiac, M-A., Harris, N., & Norton, A. (2011) "Gestalt organisational work with a family business: A story of awareness, emergence and co-creation", *British Gestalt Journal, Vol. 21 (1)*. The article was re-shaped by Nicky Burton for this book.
Permission from Christine Stevens the editor of the *British Gestalt Journal* to re-publish in Chapter Fourteen, a previously published article entitled "Gestalt work with a family business" which was re-shaped and updated by Nicky Burton.
Permission from Nicky Burton to include in Chapter Fourteen a previously published article in the *British Gestalt Journal*.

the heightening of awareness of implicit and out of awareness dynamics within a family and business.

Background

Family businesses are generators of significant employment and wealth and form more than ninety per cent of the world's companies (Economist, 2015). Boston Consulting Group defines family businesses as those where a family owns a significant share and influences important decisions and has experienced a transition between one generation and another, or is planning an intergenerational transfer. Using this criterion, thirty-three per cent of US companies and forty per cent of French and German companies earning over $1 billon per annum are family businesses. In Asia and Brazil, family businesses are even more prevalent. Family businesses are renowned for their strong sense of ownership and for taking a long-term perspective. However, one of the greatest challenges for family businesses is succession. As few as one third of family businesses successfully survive transitions between generations (Economist, 2004) giving life to old sayings such as "peasant shoes to peasant shoes in three generations" in China and "shirt sleeves to shirt sleeves in three generations" in USA.

The family in this case study operates a highly successful international business in over twenty countries, providing products and services across several business sectors from telecoms to agriculture. The founding generation (G1) are now all deceased. The second generation of six brothers (G2) all hold leadership positions in the business. They have all encouraged their children (G3) to work outside the family business to gain broad experience and to use the resources of the family to fulfil their potential. The fourteen G3 children are in their twenties upwards; five work within the family business.

Contracting with G2

My initial contact as an external consultant working with family businesses was with the G2 brothers, five of whom were approaching retirement whilst the sixth and youngest brother would continue to run the business. The brothers wished to create an orderly succession plan and robust governance structures to enable the family business to thrive in the long term. Equally figural was their desire for the six branches of the family to remain connected and not divided by succession and governance plans.

The G2 brothers initially contracted around a structural piece of work to explore organisational and governance options for the family going forward. Like with any organisational design work, the future structure needed to be shaped by existing values and wants. As a result, several workshops were held to work with the G2 levels and it quickly became apparent that the brothers needed to have a more accurate understanding of the views and plans of G3 including the extent to which they wanted to be involved in running, as well as owning, the family business.

In family businesses, intergenerational planning is particularly challenging. As family and business systems overlap, family members may hold simultaneously multiple roles for example, parent, business partner and CEO with associated implicit and explicit family and business expectations. Operational and strategic decisions need therefore to be addressed within the context of family relationships as well as business realities. It was clear that as parents the G2 brothers wanted their children to be happy, fulfilled, financially independent and connected with the larger family. As parents and businessmen, they desired the business to remain with the family with family members owning and preferably involved in running the business. They also were aware of the need to appoint capable people to key roles to grow the business and were keen to identify ways to bring their children into the business and give them relevant experiences in preparation for stepping into senior roles, if they so wished.

During these initial workshops, I was struck by the unity of aims and perspective expressed by all five brothers. With such a clear apparent figure, shouldn't the implementation be straightforward? Yet, the brothers felt stuck in moving forward into action which alerted me to a moderation to contact. Exploring the id function within that G2 team, I wondered about the polarity of their expressed position, in other words where was there less unity? In what ways might they be less aligned and where there may be different needs, especially as one brother was not retiring and would continue to run the business. By heightening awareness of differences, we surfaced the needs of the brother who would continue to run the business to have good leadership support around him and the sense of loss for him, and his brothers, around this transition. Conflicting emotions began to emerge. These centred around the importance of appointing professional managers or developing family members and the tension between wanting their children to be fulfilled whilst also wanting them to take up leadership of the business. What the group also began to share were more judgmental parental views about some of the personal and career choices that their children had made.

The degree of emotion around this transition, and some of their children's choices, which only gradually emerged, was such that none of the brothers felt able to have conversations with their children about their futures. Indeed, one of the brothers recounted his sense of failure and disappointment about a similar conversation with his son and his reluctance to risk their relationship further. As we explored G2's aims and emotions—their sense of feeling stuck became more evidently linked to having to balance business decisions and close relationships. They were taking too much responsibility for deciding the "right" course of action for their children. It felt therefore important to provide G3 with an opportunity to discuss their current thoughts about their future as well as explore the possibility of working (or not) in the family business. In line with gestalt's theory of change (Beisser, 1970), moving forward with the business meant paradoxically meeting G3 where they were!

As consultants, we proposed an extension to our initial contract with G2 to include a separate but connected piece of work with four aims:

– To brief G3 about G2's intentions and forthcoming transition;
– To help them reflect on their own plans for the future;
– To facilitate conversations between G3 and G2 for those individuals wanting to be more involved in the family business and finally;
– To strengthen relationships within G3.

We discussed with G2 that we would also need to contract with G3, agreeing how to work together in order to create the sort of space and relationships where G3 felt able to explore their future plans. Whilst G2 understood this, we had lengthy conversations about boundaries and confidentiality, coming to an agreement that as consultants our role was to facilitate G3 to explore and have conversations with G2, not to assess and report back on G3 to G2. Paying attention to these different layers of contracting with G2 and G3 enabled us to manage boundaries between the two generations which enabled both trust and a holding container for our work with the G3 group.

Contracting with G3

My first impressions of G3 were of an energetic, noisy, affectionate group of young men and women from many different countries and diverse experiences keen to get to know their cousins in other branches of the family. Some seemed to know each other well whilst others remained more cautious and distant as if on the edge of the group. Thinking of my own family, I wondered about the emotional undercurrents and relationship tensions between different family branches and what was going on for those physically in the middle of the group as well as those physically on the outside of the group.

I had a sense of the considerable respect G3 had for G2 as their parents spoke to their assembled children about their plans and hopes for the business. There were many questions showing an enormous appetite amongst G3 to learn more about their family business. I also sensed their lack of exposure to the depth, range, opportunities and challenges facing their family business. Whilst they had benefitted from family wealth in their upbringing, few were directly connected with the source of that wealth.

Several clear figures began to emerge. The group was interested in having time to think about their life choices; in understanding the family business—its history, its future possibilities, in key business concepts like profit and loss, in philanthropy and to how use their wealth for the greater good; in getting to know each other better. There seemed to be considerable shared enthusiasm for this agenda. As we began to explore what might happen next, I noticed energy levels changing and slowing. Some spoke about tension between wanting to be more connected to their wider family and the family business whilst being reluctant to take time away from their own careers and families. Others shared feelings of ambivalence and shame about being more involved, comparing their own careers critically with their parents' business success; others felt unready and unwilling to take on leadership responsibilities in the family business. A few still were keen to get involved. From initial shared enthusiasm, a range of feelings emerged, from excitement to uncertainty and shame. After much discussion, the fourteen cousins agreed that they would like to meet again and spend time getting to know each other and exploring just what each of them was interested in doing with their life whether as part of the family business or not. A date was set for four months' time.

The safe container: building a facilitator team

I set about creating a facilitator team to meet a number of conditions: a team able to work at the level of awareness, relationship and dialogue and committed to work from wherever our clients were starting. Above all, I wanted to form a team that would be able to create a safe space for G3 to build relationships and develop the trust in each other necessary to explore their future options. On reflection, I wonder if in my selection I wanted to mirror the client system in selecting team members who had not worked before as a team but who also each brought something different as well as the potential to enjoy working together and support each other.

Three of us (Neil, Marie Anne, & Nicky) have trained as gestalt therapists with Neil specialising in family therapy. Marie Anne, Andy, and Nicky have corporate backgrounds covering a wide range of disciplines and are experienced OD consultants and coaches. Whilst I was the common connection, Neil, Marie Anne, and Andy didn't know each other and so a priority was for everyone to meet, get to know each other and how we like to work to be at our best. Issues of co-facilitation and support were figural and during our first meeting, we focused on what we could offer each other and the client and how we could work together and support each other. The intensity of our first meeting and commitment to making this work seemed to set the scene for what we wanted to create for our clients.

Designing the intervention

The two criteria that primarily informed the design of the workshop were first the facilitating the exploration of personal needs and wants in relation to the family business, and second creating an environment that supported good quality of contact amongst all participants. With these in mind, the workshop design could be viewed in terms of the cycle of experience (see Figure 14.1) where exploration of id functioning (between sensation and awareness) leads to a clearer figure of interest around which to mobilise. Our hope was that G3 individuals would experience a quality of dialogue that would penetrate beneath their habitual thinking, creating new awareness and insights, energising exploration of fresh possibilities or commitment to existing paths. We also somehow needed to create a safe enough environment for this

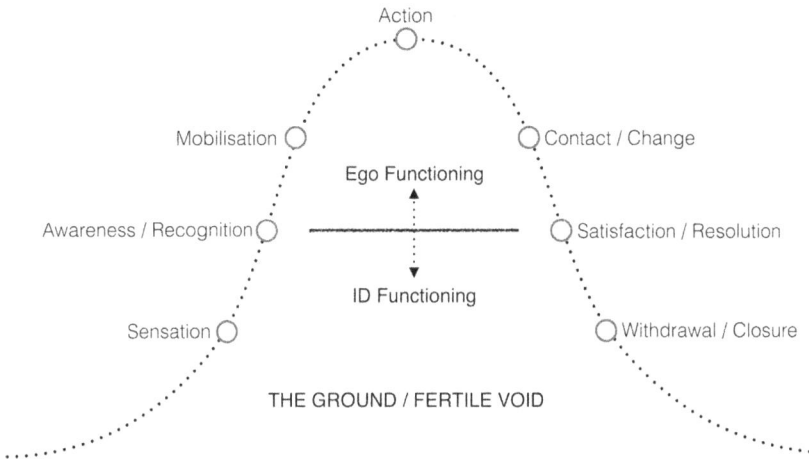

Figure 14.1. Exploration of id functioning.

exploration of id functioning at the individual level and enough sharing within the larger group to develop both trust and deeper connection between the G3 group members.

Our final design therefore emphasised opportunities for dialogue and experimentation through a sequence of large and small group conversations. We chose to create safe and holding groups in which participants could explore what they wanted to do with their lives and the extent of their involvement with the family business. As facilitators, we would encourage participants to explore phenomenologically each other's process and help balance both challenge and support amongst G3 members. By supporting good dialogue to take place between family members, we were keen to encourage not only increased individual awareness but also an emergent awareness of the family as a whole.

The workshop structure provided a space to hold the group and whatever conversations, emotions and tensions might emerge. Our planning of the event was at a high level, holding that the detail would be shaped by emergent figures as individual and group work unfolded. The dialectic of emergent and planned characterises organisational gestalt work, creating tension, and excitement: the tension of working with uncertainty and the exciting freedom of allowing the most pressing and often most useful figure to emerge. Working as part of team of co-facilitators amplifies these feelings as potentially conflicting figures, adding another layer of complexity.

Developing a working alliance

With the exception of myself, the other facilitators had not met the group before the actual workshop. However, we had met them through our discussions as well as through detailed biographies from previous interviews which provided a sense of each family member and some of the family dynamics. Although this may have configured for us as a team of facilitators the field of possibilities (in terms of who could or would step up to the challenge of leading the family business), we were also aware of holding this information lightly and allowing for new or contradicting data to emerge.

One question we discussed at length was how to work with known tensions within the G3 group either at the inter-personal/generational level or between branches of the family. Acknowledging and working through some of these tensions may improve long-term relationships (a desirable outcome for G2), but may also be time consuming and possibly feel unsafe. The word "family" often implies a cohesive unit that may struggle with infighting but unite strongly in the face of external threats. Based on my initial meeting with the G2 group, there wasn't a conflict which felt pressing and needing to be addressed before the workshop. With relatively little time to facilitate a demanding process aimed at supporting each other, establishing a rapid working alliance with all family members was essential. Similarly, to clinical work, most organisational interventions require a swift establishing of a working alliance as businesses are reluctant to fund longer, more expensive workshops. We agreed that given the limited time we had with the G3 group (two and a half days), we would initially focus on building a strong working alliance and stay responsive to any tensions or conflict that may emerge in the moment.

Building a working alliance requires us to be both present and available for contact. Presence defined as "energetic availability and fluid responsiveness" (Chidiac & Denham-Vaughan, 2007) captures the duality of attending both to our own process and that of others in authentic meeting. In an organisational group context that often means stepping forward and signalling availability for contact rather than waiting to be approached. Another aspect of being present is about modelling authentic contact and being responsive to other. The first few workshop sessions therefore provided the participants with the "tone" of the workshop, with our presence as a team of facilitators calling forth their own presence as participants. We did this by discussing and modelling aspects of good dialogue and issues of risk and vulnerability. We also made it clear that we would be operating as a cohesive team of facilitators and would be sharing information between us throughout the workshop. We were not "participant-leaders" (Ronnall, 2008, p. 226). The boundary of us, (facilitators), and them (participants) was clear and supportive to the overall group process. The relaxed dynamics of our facilitator team at the early stages as well as the clear leadership of professional and ethical responsibilities provided a sense of safety and containment, preparing the way for more intimate work in smaller groups.

What happened: dialogue and experimentation

The first group conversation involved all of the G3 group meeting with the younger generation of another family business. The conversation was framed as an experiment: an opportunity to ask questions and learn about others' experiences and choices and to prepare for similar conversations with each other. We paid attention to grading the experiment to be safe yet challenging and mid-way, the facilitator team conducted a process review. Was the group getting what it needed? What was hindering them? What might they do differently? We coached the group in phenomenological inquiry as a way of exploring experience, feelings, aspirations, and meaning making more directly and the differences between discussion and dialogue, before a second round of conversation. Operating at multiple levels, we were developing skills for dialogue with each other whilst also widening perspectives and possibilities through the experience of another younger generation in a family business. The experiment was a rehearsal for the small group work they would experience over the next two days.

The workshop continued with a sequence of structured and facilitated small group conversations that created shared, safe ground from which individuals could work with whatever figures emerged for them. Our role was to support the small group to help whoever was working to be self-reflective. The listening and understanding of siblings and cousins was essential to promoting dialogue that deepened relationships from I-it to I-thou (Buber, 1958), creating an intimacy that enabled individuals to talk movingly about their hopes, frustrations, and relationships. As facilitators of these conversations, we moved between groups to avoid dependency, checking in with each other to keep abreast of the progress of the dialogue in each group. An additional benefit was to let G3 experience our different styles.

As the workshop purpose was to explore the needs and wants of individuals, most conversations focused on the sensation/awareness part of the cycle of experience against the background of their involvement in the family business. The last conversation however focused individuals on identifying personal actions to mobilise them towards their future direction. Individuals shared briefly their actions in the large group as part of reconnecting the small groups with each other and to identify collective themes for a future learning agenda for discussion with G2. With considerable energy, each person committed to discuss their thinking about their future direction with a member of G2, not necessarily their parents, within the next few months and certainly before the next G2/G3 family meeting.

Endings

The difference in the energy and feel of the group at the end of the third day was palpable. There was a clear appreciation for each other and of their differences as members of the same family. They had for the first time connected with each other in a way that was both meaningful and enlivening. The workshop had enabled the third generation of this family business to begin a productive process of personal reflection about future direction as well as supported a deeper sense of connection between them. The energy in the group had shifted from a detached curiosity in the first meeting to a more involved, enthusiastic and supportive feel.

As an intervention, the workshop had met G3 expectations of meeting, connecting, and exploring their connection with the family business. From the G2 perspective, expectations and hope of greater involvement in the family business was not to be. Whilst interested in learning more about their family business, few beyond those already working in the business engaged in the possibility of running the business. Each of G3 left the workshop with a personal plan, in a position to have an initial conversation with G2 about their future hopes and aspirations. However, geographical dispersal and the lack of engagement with the opportunity of running the business coupled with the shadow of unspoken and embedded expectations in parent—child relationships, meant there was insufficient environmental and self-support to begin these conversations. The exception was those already working in the business, who felt sufficiently mobilised and supported to act on their development plans and talk to G2. Although this might not have been the desired outcome for the five G2 brothers, it nonetheless allowed them to move forward more resolutely with planning the transition and recruit a general manager from outside the family.

As a facilitator team, we reflected on our experiences with the group and working with each other. We were aware of our complementary strengths and our openness with each other: Nicky's focus on the direction and flow of the workshop, Andy's pragmatism, Marie Anne's attention to our teamwork and transferences and Neil's confident process reviews and insights into family dynamics with G3 and how we were able to support and challenge each other to work well as a facilitator team throughout the workshop. Having enjoyed our work together, we met after the workshop to explore possibilities of a family business practice together. Perhaps in parallel process with G3, our enthusiasm failed to mobilise into concrete actions and the energy of our pre-existing individual practices called to us more strongly.

Final reflections: a shift in the client's personality function

In Chapter Three, we saw how the gestalt theory of self (captured in a wave metaphor) provides us with a lens through which to view the dynamic nature of organisations and the interplay of internal and external dynamics and influences. In the wave analogy, sedimented ways of being are often linked to prevailing narrative and culture (sea bed and personality function). The actual body of the wave (ego function) represents what the organisation says and does, its visible structures, patterns and influences. Less visible internal dynamics and unrecognised influences are represented by the seawater or id function). Heightening awareness of the aspects of the overall field especially those less visible aspects can be a useful component of an intervention and allow for loosening of some of these ingrained structures.

This family business' deeply sedimented narrative and culture was of an entrepreneurial family succeeding in some of the most challenging and unpredictable markets in the world, bringing employment to a turbulent region and handing opportunity and responsibility on through successive generations. The narrative encompasses not only to their own family but a wider family including all employees, articulated in colourful stories of overcoming obstacles and continuing to employ and pay people even during periods of downturn or difficulty. This narrative fuelled G2's desire to give G3 every opportunity to participate in the family business as owner managers rather than just as owners in order to sustain the family narrative and business culture. To this end, G2 was keen to fund any G3 seedling business ideas with a view to developing new ideas and business opportunities within rather than outside the family business. For the few entrepreneurs in G3, this generous possibility did not match their unarticulated but emerging desire for independence from their parents and the family business to prove that they could succeed on their own terms (id function). For others in G3, unclear about their future career path, the workshop served to raise awareness of sensations, feelings and possibilities that might lead to mobilisation in their own careers and as family business owners, rather than managers, in time.

In terms of ego function, G2's parenting had distanced their children from active involvement in the family business yet, approaching the transition from G2 to G3, they wanted to engage their children with the idea of being active owner managers in the family business. This shift was reflected in the sense of distance and variable energy levels in G3 about the family business. G3's active engagement in the workshop, in personal reflection and connection with cousins, contrasted with their lack of mobilisation to talk with G2 also reflects this shift and gap. G2's sense of frustration, acted out initially by seeking to pressurise the consultants to provide post workshop confidential feedback and assessments, led to the uncomfortable realisation that G3 did not feel the same way about the family business. G2 realised that whilst they could count on G3 to be active, concerned owners, they could no longer sustain the family narrative of handing the business on through the generations to owner managers. Instead, they would need to update their narrative and develop resourcing and governance plans to bring in and find ways of working with professional managers to lead the business forwards through successive generations.

CHAPTER FIFTEEN

Bringing gestalt to cyber security*

Maggie Marriott

Introduction

The twenty-first century is often described as the "information age" and certainly the UK government is encouraging all of its departments to share information and make as many services as possible available to the public online. This has transformed how, in the UK, we tax our cars or submit our tax returns and as a consequence it has also put more of our personal information at risk of cyber theft. Protecting this information is key to the stability of the UK economy and is a mammoth task.

Cyber security is therefore a term that encompasses the protection of information systems from theft or damage and is a major focus of investment by the UK government. This case study describes how

* This chapter is based on an article by Maggie Marriott "Bringing gestalt to cyber security: a case study" (2016) *British Gestalt Journal*, *Vol. 25 (2)*. The article was also the winner of the 2015 Student Essay Prize.
Permission from Maggie Marriott to include Chapter Fifteen a previously published article in the *British Gestalt Journal*.
Permission from Christine Stevens the editor of the *British Gestalt Journal* to re-publish in Chapter Fifteen, a previously published article entitled "Bringing gestalt to cyber security: A case study" written by Maggie Marriott.

gestalt concepts of dialogue, field theory and phenomenology were used to help the board of a government department identify how they needed to transform to respond to the growing threats to the cyber security of the UK.

Context and background

The client organisation was a large and mature government department that historically had a very low public profile. The people in the organisation were leaders in their field and the culture of the organisation was very reminiscent of academia—constant questioning, research, reflection, and the right for everyone to have an opinion. The system had worked very effectively for most of the hundred years of its existence but the pace and nature of the outside world had changed considerably leading to a risk that their work was not keeping pace with the cyber security needs of the government. There had already been five failed transformation attempts in the last five years and having worked with parts of the organisation in the past, I was asked to support the board with the sixth attempt.

With awareness of this narrative of failed attempts, I reflected back to the board director in our initial meetings that a lot of time and money had been spent and minimal change had happened, so maybe it was time to take a fresh approach. Rather than launch into another transformation methodology, I was particularly aware of the need to meet people where they were because "one must stand in one place in order to have firm footing to move and that it is difficult or impossible to move without that footing" (Beisser, 1972). A co-diagnosis needed to underlie the next intervention. Indeed, gestalt theory encourages us to take a unified field approach (Parlett, 1997) which involves finding out how the current field is organised, including "what the 'currently active gestalts' and projects are; the divisions and styles of boundary making; the figural concerns of individual, group, or community, as well as the stable (or continuously regenerated) features that endure" (ibid, p. 23).

In his most recent book Malcolm Parlett (2015) explains "that people are basically different all the time, and vary according to the total situation which they are currently experiencing—as well as, in part, constructing" (pp. 66–67), so it is wise to take account of the whole situation. I explained to the director that such an approach would enable us to understand and then effectively tackle the root cause of the issues rather than the symptoms. I was also clear that it would take time to understand the field through sensing and raising awareness before mobilising to action.

Sensing into the field

When I first entered the organisation my phenomenological sense was of people in immense pain who did not dare to look at the source of that pain, as if they were all shielding their eyes from the truth and keeping themselves as busy as possible. I was noticing people talking only about the immediate issues, listening without hearing and holding a lot of tension in their bodies. Deflection and retroflection were evident moderations to contact within the main board team members.

To work effectively with the board, it was clear that I needed to create a more supportive and holding environment to start addressing some of these key moderations to contact and enable dialogue. My first proposed intervention was therefore to facilitate a two-day residential offsite away from the normal working environment to create a safe and supportive environment.

I did not yet know how I was going to use the event but knew that what was most needed would emerge. In preparation for the offsite residential, I talked formally and informally face-to-face to as many people as I could about their work and how they felt, how the organisation was run, who did what, why and when, to help me identify which patterns became figural, because "[L]ives and collective systems intertwine and need to be considered together as a unified field" (Parlett, 1997, p. 1, original italics). The figures I noticed are explained in Table 15.1 below.

Whilst I was sensing and identifying potential figures for attention there was a major change in the field with the arrival of a new senior leader. He was given responsibility for the existing board directors, including my client.

A new leader

The new leader was curious about my work and why it was necessary. I knew that at our first meeting I needed to be fully present and to have "energetic availability and fluid responsiveness" (Chidiac & Denham-Vaughan, 2007). The conversation was initially stilted; there was little eye contact and a lot of leg twitching by the leader. I began

Table 15.1. A description of the organisation through a gestalt lens.

The organisation was a closed system	A closed organisation "places great value on its organization charts, division of labor, superior-subordinate relations, policies, processes, controls, and stability, rather than customers, suppliers, markets, technologies, or community" (NTL Institute, 2014, pp. 285–286).
And stagnant in complexity theory terms	The axes in complex systems (Waldrop, 1992) range from rigid stability to chaotic turbulence; this organisation was closer to the rigid stability end of the spectrum making the system resistant to change.
People knew the reality of the situation but nobody was voicing it, the corporate script did not match reality	The organisation's view of itself was of being highly valued and highly functioning but all knew this to be untrue. Beisser's paradoxical theory of change suggests the organisation was trying to be what it was not which was inhibiting their desire for change and "that change occurs when one becomes what he is, not when he tries to become what he is not" (Beisser, 1972). I have found the model of "Immunity to Change" (Kegan & Laskow Lahey, 2009) a helpful approach to understanding resistance and the "multiple forces [...] many of which pull in different directions" (Nevis, 1987, p. 147).
Each person had a slightly different perspective of the problem	The nature of the work and that each person was an "expert" led to fragmentation "in which the people involved see themselves as more separate than united, and in which information and knowledge are chaotic and scattered" (Conklin, 2006, p. 3).
And related to each other as I-it	Most relationships were I-it rather than I-thou (Buber, 1957) as when "we approach the people and things as if they were objects or functions whose existence is for us to affect, control or manipulate" (Sills, 2012, p. 23).
The problem space was a "wicked problem"	The environment the organisation was working within was one of severe economic constraint and increasing technical and political complexity. It could be described as "wicked" where problems "are never solved. At best they are only re-solved—over and over again" (Rittel & Webber, 1973, p. 160).

by explaining my research and thoughts for the offsite event, making sure I pitched at the same level of energetic intensity I was sensing from him. I then sat back and asked him how well this resonated with his own perspectives since joining and what his needs were. Slowly the eye contact increased and his body relaxed as he too sat back in his chair and the depth of the conversation grew.

By the end of the conversation he agreed to keep sponsoring the project and we discussed other ways I could support him to build relationships in the organisation. My impressions of him were best captured by a metaphor of a new child arriving at school as the head boy; he doesn't know the written or unwritten rules, and has no friends or allies who could teach him. The other pupils all know each other well and know how to work the system; they don't need this new boy, are suspicious of him and close him out. This was a challenging position for the new leader and a significant new dynamic in the top team. The offsite was more needed than ever.

The two-day offsite: safety, experimentation, and dialogue

Prior to the offsite I captured elements of my sensing activities in the form of both quantitative and qualitative data which included for example, the huge number of meetings the board attended, what news stories they shared on the intranet and people's perceptions of how the organisation was being run. Although several figures of interest emerged for me, it was important to allow space for co-emergence and so the offsite would focus on inquiring and heightening their awareness of how they ran the organisation and, the quality of dialogue and contact in the team.

The board members had a clear predisposition to begin at the action stage of the gestalt cycle of experience so heightening awareness through an inquiry process gave them the sense of an action focused event that could only be answered through contact and dialogue. What follows is a brief summary of my approach to the offsite process.

Building a space that felt both safe and challenging was key. I therefore developed a question-based agenda that enabled me to meet the needs of the attendees for structure whilst allowing me total flexibility to seek answers to the questions in the moment. I used the Disney creativity strategy technique developed by Robert Dilts (1994) because of its simplicity to use and its natural fit for the four corners of the room.

I set up three corners of the room as "dreamer", "realist" and "critic" along with quantitative information to befit each. In the fourth corner I built a "campfire" encircled by chairs and named it the "neutral corner". Knowing that sitting around a campfire tends to have a comforting and soothing impact on people I felt this would promote a relaxed atmosphere for interaction and dialogue and this is where I asked them to begin.

The attendees had little or no opportunity to hear directly from the public about the value of their work. In fact, it is likely most UK citizens are totally unaware of the difference their work makes every day. I found myself wanting to reconnect their work with the emotional impact it has. From my gestalt training, I knew that I was part of the field and so I began by telling them how important it was to my family and me that the organisation was as good as it could be. I was relying on them to do their best work to help keep my daughters safe. I then explained that my co-facilitators and I would reflect and bring to their awareness what was happening, as well as our phenomenological response, when we thought it would be useful, something which caused a few raised eyebrows at first.

I asked them to leave their roles out of the circle and to tell each other stories about experiences from their working life with the aim of providing opportunities for I-thou (Buber, 1957) moments of relating. After what felt like an initially uncomfortable way of being for the group, I took them back into their comfort zone of analysing the data around the room, encouraging them to discuss whatever became figural. On return to the campfire there was muttering between people, many crossed arms and furrowed brows which led me to think people were "holding back" rather than openly discussing their concerns. At this point, I brought out a blow-up elephant and asked if there was an "elephant in the room", with the hope of giving the group the opportunity to make issues figural. It brought great laughter and did lead to a discussion of key issues such as the unrealistic quantity and diversity of the demands made of them; the lack of coherence of their work; and the unsupportive behaviour of some key stakeholders. As the two days progressed the discussions grew in depth and quality and the group started to put the elephant in the middle of the circle themselves suggesting their growing awareness and acceptance of what had previously been unspoken. By the end of day two, my role as facilitator was minimal and the power of the group was strong. They spent the majority of the time in the awareness phase, sometimes moving to mobilising and then back to awareness. It was only in the last hour of the two days that they spoke unanimously of their commitment to a new a direction and their full support for the new leader.

The results

As a result of the offsite work a paper outlining the need for major transformational change was quickly put to the full board and accepted. A summary of the transformation agenda with a gestalt lens is below.

Table 15.2. A description of the future state organisation through a gestalt lens.

The organisation needed to become an open system	An organisation where "[E]mphasis is given to external stakeholders" and where change becomes easier because "the organisation has a comprehensive picture of its dynamic environment and its internal structures are limber" (NTL Institute, 2014, p. 286).
And move towards the "edge of chaos" (Waldrop, 1992)	A number of agile and disruptive projects were proposed that would begin to shift the balance towards the edge of chaos and acceptance that a "rhythm of awareness-energy-action-closure built around smaller units or incremental changes is much more manageable" (Nevis, 2001, p. 204).
Where everyone knew the reality of the organisation's situation	The board accepted the reality of where they were and were willing to admit and build from it; they had accepted Beisser's paradoxical theory of change.
And needed to relate to each other as I-thou	They wanted to build healthy relationships with employees, customers and suppliers, an I-thou relationship with a "genuine meeting of person to person" (Sills, 2012, p. 23).
And that the problem space was "wicked"	It was accepted they were working in a world of "wicked problems" where "diverse values are held by different groups of individuals—that what satisfies one may be abhorrent to another, that what comprises problem-solution for one is problem-generation for another" (Rittel & Webber, 1973, p. 169), and they could only succeed through collaboration.

The board now meet and regularly have healthy dialogue and the transformation was announced across Whitehall. The organisation's engagement model is now focused on customer needs and ongoing communication, both face-to-face and online with the creation of blogs and a Twitter feed that would have been unthinkable just six months earlier.

Conclusion

I hope this case study has shown how taking a gestalt approach of meeting people where they are and encouraging others to do the same can be deeply effective. The outcome of the offsite could not have been planned or anticipated and relied on a co-emergence in the moment. As a gestalt facilitator, I needed to be fully present, manage my uncertainty, and trust the process would unfold with the right level of safety, support and challenge.

I believe that the powerful combination of dialogue, field theory and phenomenology played a large part in my client's decision to transform their way of leading and working and ensuring the vitality of their department and the protection of UK citizens' information for years to come.

Acknowledgment

Thanks to Ms Gerrie Hughes and Dr. Marie-Anne Chidiac for their support and encouragement in the production of this piece.

CHAPTER SIXTEEN

Supporting a merger in the pharmaceutical industry

Introduction

Businesses often use mergers and acquisitions (M&A's) as strategies to strengthen and maintain their market position. M&A is considered as a relatively fast and efficient way to expand into new markets or acquire new technologies. What may seem straightforward from a financial or market share perspective is however by no means assured in implementation. Indeed, a majority of M&A's fall short of their stated objectives and desired financial gains and studies have shown that typically seventy to ninety per cent of acquisitions are failures (Martin, 2016). Although some failures can be explained and justified by financial and market factors, many can be traced back to "softer issues" such as culture, communication, and the selection of the "right" management team.

This case study focuses on work undertaken for the integrated systems (IS) function within a large recently merged pharmaceutical organisation. The merger brought together two large pharmaceutical organisations based in the UK and Europe respectively. The combined IS function included 350 staff worldwide spread mostly over three main locations.

This chapter will describe a consulting engagement that lasted around nine months to support the IS function to complete its integration activities. Although the focus here will be place on change and OD interventions informed by gestalt theory and practice, the project also included other approaches (e.g. project management, business case and financial analysis, strategic planning) to support the client meet their desired operational and financial outcomes.

Situation & context

This project began in the post-merger phase at a point when the high-level structure of the new organisation was announced and so new appointments were made only at the very top levels of business units and some key functions. As is usual in merger situations the case for the integration of the two businesses was strong but there was little detail or plan for the implementation of the very ambitious synergy targets specified for each part of the business.

In the IS function, the new CIO had not yet been appointed and both the IS heads of the merging organisations were meeting and working

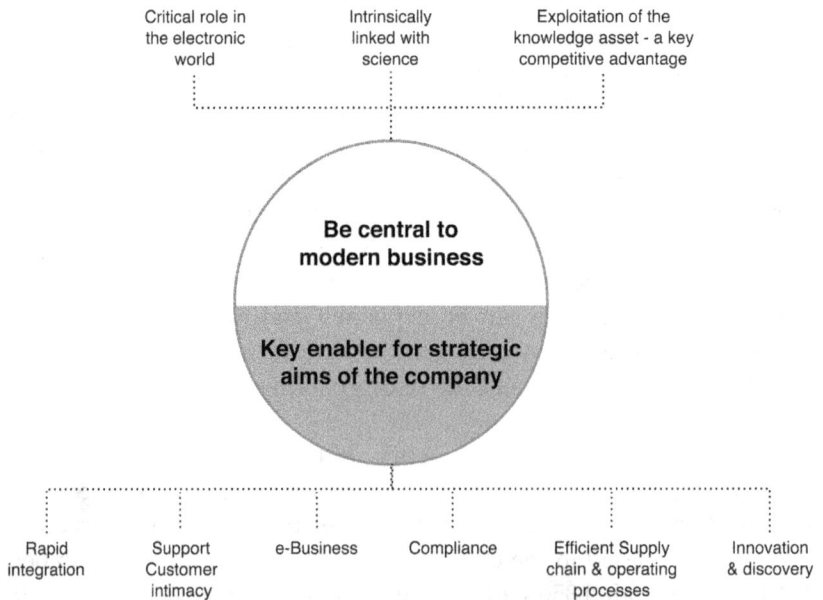

Critical role in the electronic world

Intrinsically linked with science

Exploitation of the knowledge asset - a key competitive advantage

Be central to modern business

Key enabler for strategic aims of the company

Rapid integration

Support Customer intimacy

e-Business

Compliance

Efficient Supply chain & operating processes

Innovation & discovery

Figure 16.1. The business expectations of the IS function.

together to support the transition. The starting point of the project was driven by the need to support the merger activities and the integration task teams. Both IS leaders sat on an integration leadership team (ILT) that managed the process. As shown in Figure 16.1, the expectations of the business from the IS function were high and the expected financial synergies were equally challenging.

Initial contracting

The consulting team of which I was a member was introduced to the organisation by Tom the UK Head of IS to support key integration priorities. Tom had in a previous job worked with the project lead and knew that our approach was based on both solid transformation experience and a humanistic frame which took account both of people and task.

With the pressures of the merger, the project was initially proposed to address the following key integration priorities within the function.

1. To achieve systems integration without unduly impacting business performance.
2. To complete the appointment process.
3. To establish the operating/budgeting processes for IS.
4. To sign up and deliver the synergies.
5. To agree a strategic programme for each area.
6. To capture the people.

Although point six addressed the people element, it was clear that what was most imperative in those initial contracting meeting was how to achieve the savings and synergies. The project objectives were initially to provide a focal point for IS integration activities, project manage integration teams to meet business milestones, and manage any escalation processes.

Understandably, the client's main focus was to have operational support at a time of intense flux and uncertainty. Although integration tasks teams were already in place, there was a concern that these were not delivering rapidly enough and not being responsive a collaborative new way forward. A project management office was to be set up and key processes and procedures put in place to address the very really challenge of integrating diverse systems within a complex new organisation.

Tom was aware that our humanistic and gestalt approach to organisational improvement meant we attended to both the explicit business challenge and the implicit, out of awareness people dynamics. The initial contracting conversations included a clear discussion of the people and cultural issues that often meant that mergers and integrations failed and the need to attend to these aspects alongside the operational and financial focus. With limitations on budget and a cultural piece or work being led by another consultancy at the wider organisational level, Tom and his European counterpart Frederic agreed to limited OD interventions to assess the impact of the work on IS staff in the various locations.

Although the client understood that attending to people issues and culture would enable the function to operate more effectively going forward, there was still an ambivalent response and a prioritising of the immediate task: the message was clear that change and OD interventions would be "low priority and must not interfere with the integration work". Using the wave model (Figure 16.2) as a guiding framework, what was most visible and pressing to the client at this point was the concern to meet the business demands around integration. Although both Tom and Frederic were clearly frustrated by the lack of responsiveness and inability of the task teams to deliver, this was not for them currently a focus for the work. As a consultant team we needed to respond to the client's most pressing issue and presenting problem (the face of the wave) and provide enough holding and psychological safety before exploring the sea depth or seabed (id and personality functions).

Wave as Ego
Above the surface, visible, what we say we do – the resulting action

Sea Waters as Id
Less visible, unacknowledged dynamics, connected to local currents and flows

Seabed as Personality
Sedimented but changing slowly with time – the culture and narrative

Figure 16.2. The wave model.

First impressions

I was first struck by the similarities in culture between the two merging organisations. In both companies, I met people who were friendly, analytical, and quite academic in their pursuits and interests, as well as generally cautious and reluctant in facing changes that were afoot. Although positive and hardworking, the metaphor that best captured the people I met in my first visit to the impressive buildings of the new organisation was that of an ostrich which although busy and productive, would rather not lift her head and look around in case her known, familiar environment would be changed. The use of English as the main language in the project did not at first appear to be a hurdle to communication as everyone was very fluent. Other cultural differences although visible seemed less of an issue as staff in all locations were used to interact with others across national boundaries.

Cracks in the leadership front

When meeting both IS leaders, their commitment to their staff and organisation was evident. They were both working hard at making the transition work despite the personal uncertainty surrounding their situation; clearly only one of them would be appointed CIO to the new organisation. Tom was the younger, aspiring leader who had only joined the organisation about five years ago whilst his European counterpart was closer to retirement having been part of his organisation for over twenty-five years. Rumours seemed rife—even amongst the team of consultants-which person would get the top job; experience or youth? This implicit competitiveness felt very figural despite both leaders being courteous and professional in every aspect.

It was interesting to note during initial contracting discussions, the ambivalence of both IS leaders in engaging their staff in OD activities which might unpack id function dynamics. It was as if they were both holding themselves and the organisation tightly, waiting for the decision on the CIO job. From a gestalt perspective, we could look at this as a desensitised organisation, one in which there is not, at this moment, enough support and safety to explore feelings and emotions.

Parallel process

The group of ten consultants of which I was a part, and which were brought together to respond to this project came from two different organisations. It is interesting to reflect that in many ways, the sub-grouping within the consultant team was echoing the divide in the merged organisation. It was clear that to provide a holding and safe context for the client, we also needed to work and dialogue within the consulting team. This parallel process was identified quite early on and we therefore initiated bi-monthly sessions to address our process and build relationship and trust within the team. We worked on sharing perspectives and differences and in doing so, named possible parallel processes or issues of identification with either part of the client organisation. It was very supportive for us to attend in this way to the impact and influence of the context and situation in which we were working in as a consulting team. This enabled us to be more aware of our behaviours and interactions with each other. The SOS model (situation, other, and self) covered in Chapter Four was a supportive framework for us to use and recognise the interlinking of these three dimensions.

Sensing

With a cautious remit to look at id functions within the organisation, we put in place two simple and low-key interventions: drop-in rooms and calibration groups.

Drop-in rooms

In each site, a project room was allocated to the integration team. The rooms were situated in locations that were both visible and easily accessible to staff. The room was always staffed and signs were put up to invite individuals to stop at any time of the day for conversations or information about the project. The most basic and often underrated "sensing" activity is to talk to people in a free-flow of open ended conversation. People were invited during these conversations to leave a comment on a board if they wished, or write feedback or ask a question of the leadership team anonymously (or not).

Calibration groups

A calibration group consisted of six to eight members of staff, selected randomly across all grades and roles that would initially meet once fortnightly as implementation progresses, to openly discuss their thoughts, ideas and feelings around the integration.

The group sessions were short (around thirty to forty-five minutes) and allowed for open discussion around a range of issues to do with the merger activities but will also be steered with a range of questions/ issues which the integration project team are interested in feedback on.

These groups were established in each location and facilitated to ensure that anonymous output was generated from each session so that appropriate actions can be taken in response to the feedback.

* * *

These two simple activities provided the project with live, immediate feedback on the organisation's id function—what was happening in the sea depth below the wave. Output from these conversations was then fed back to the integration leadership team alongside the regular reporting on operational and integration tasks. What rapidly emerged from these sensing activities is the vulnerability of the European staff to feeling "taken over" by the UK organisation and that despite some enthusiasm for being part of a more international and larger company, the IS staff in general felt that their contributions were not valued within the wider organisation. This was summarised by the comment "we just do the grunt work and people only notice us when things go wrong". It was fascinating to see the ripple effect of individual conversations and how these seemingly innocuous comments would filter through the organisation and affect change.

Supporting

At long last after three months into the project, Tom's appointment as the new CIO was announced. The news brought both relief and also some disgruntled voices from European staff. The urgent task was now to appoint the IS leadership team in order to avoid greater uncertainty at the level below the CIO. Despite strong coaching, Frederic was not willing to make a quick exit and so his lingering presence further fuelled the discontented voices. This was a difficult moment in the project and was experienced through frustrating interactions and lack of progress on some integration tasks. As a project team, we needed to keep dialogue open and compassion for those people that were feeling disappointed with the process. Holding that space within the project team helped model this behaviour to the client and also supported us to not polarise, become impatient or punitive.

Tom's appointment opened the possibility for another contracting iteration with more openness to OD interventions and activities. The benefits of the sensing activities were recognised and budget was released to enable greater engagement of staff around cultural and integration issues. Integration activities were ongoing and on-track and synergies were being identified. From an OD perspective, the new status quo needed to be supported. This was achieved through the following activities:

– Maintaining sensing activities.
– Coaching and supporting the new IS Leadership team, starting with an offsite event.
– Dialogue events which were held at key locations which addressed both cultural and site issues linked to the merger.

Sensing activities

The output from these were still regularly fed back to the Leadership team and in doing so triggered an impetus to share more the emerging

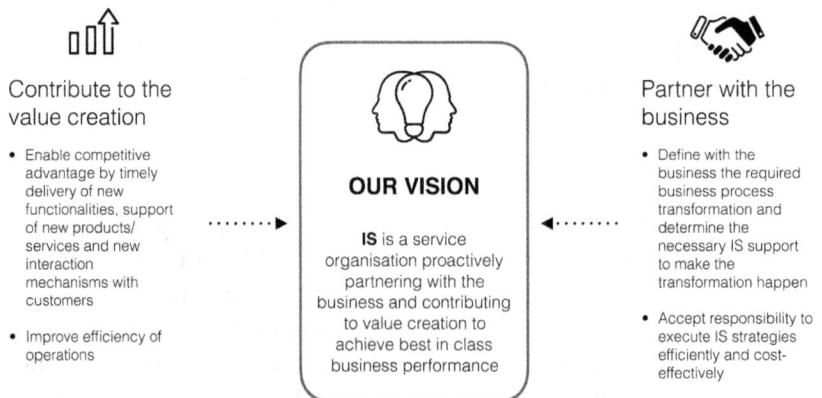

Contribute to the value creation

• Enable competitive advantage by timely delivery of new functionalities, support of new products/ services and new interaction mechanisms with customers

• Improve efficiency of operations

OUR VISION

IS is a service organisation proactively partnering with the business and contributing to value creation to achieve best in class business performance

Partner with the business

• Define with the business the required business process transformation and determine the necessary IS support to make the transformation happen

• Accept responsibility to execute IS strategies efficiently and cost-effectively

Figure 16.3. The IS vision.

IS strategy through a series of conversational meetings at different sites. The IS vision shown in Figure 16.3 responded well to the staff concerns in being marginalised or not valued within the business and more effort and visibility was given to collaborative projects with the business units.

Coaching the new IS leadership team

Soon after they were appointed, the new IS leadership team met for a two-day facilitated event to address the team's priorities as well as their dynamics in working together. Although most members had met, they had not worked alongside each other or in this new team configuration. It was important to start by acknowledging the history and narrative of each member as well as allow enough space to explore the inevitable sub-groupings that existed within the new team. Attending in this way to the personality function of the team strengthened the team dynamics and allowed out of awareness behaviour to be articulated and responded to. An example of this was provided during the offsite when a British person used humour and light banter in commenting on an ongoing discussion in the group. A Swiss member of the group responded that he found the comment disrespectful and that it made him less willing to discuss the topic further. Team members were starting to voice and share how differences in their culture and ways of being were impacting their interactions in the moment. Although brief, this moment during the offsite captured the growing sense of safety in the team that allowed for more meaningful dialogue.

The event was followed by monthly coaching sessions alongside individual coaching of some members of the team by external coaches. The team coaching centred on building greater dialogue skills and the need for resilience and mutual support in a period of change. Gradually, over time the language and tone in the top team changed from being more individualistic and task focused to a more collaborative and supportive attitude. Also, being able to openly acknowledge the emotions and difficulties of transitions allowed them to better support their direct reports in that process.

Dialogue events

The thinking behind these events was to open a safe space in which issues of culture, difference, and integration could be voiced and discussed. Each event was attended by two members of the leadership team (one member from each legacy organisation) and were facilitated jointly by a consultant and an internal member of staff.

The events began with focusing on the merger as an ongoing transition and built on the ideas of William Bridges (2009) who writes of needing to attend to endings before beginnings. This allowed people to acknowledge their legacy organisations, recognising both the loss and gain of the new organisation. By attending explicitly to cultural aspects (national and organisational), the events explored the personality function of the merged organisation bringing into awareness perhaps the more entrenched aspects in each culture. Although open to the positive influence of these dialogue events, the new CIO was also wary of what might emerge in these sessions. Supporting him and the leadership team in being open to the emergent nature of these sessions was an important part of preparing these meetings and debriefing them.

Gradually dialogue events became even less structured and the space used for updates and dialogue. It was fascinating to watch a less formal or agenda-driven meeting develop in the IS function. Dialogue events have, in some locations, since become regular happenings which take place early in the day and valued by both staff and leaders.

Sustaining

Eight months into the project, the tasks of integration working teams were completing with ongoing work transitioning into business as usual. Some of what had started as transition activities around the merger gradually became business as usual for the new organisation. As far as the consulting team was concerned, the project was coming to a close and sustaining the new organisation's processes and behaviours meant leading these from within.

As a result of the project work, the IS board created a new position which they called the "head of internal communication & change" and appointed a key member of staff who had supported the change effort during integration activities. As the consulting team gradually disbanded, my final role was to support this member of staff. I found it helpful to recognise in these last stages of the project that my stance needed to shift from a co-created collaborative role to a supportive/ coaching position. This change was discussed and negotiated and allowed her to gain greater ownership of her new role. This step of journeying alongside the client, letting them lead and experiment is an important one for embedding learning and skills in the organisation. Although I had experience of capability building on other projects, gestalt theory allowed me to view this step not as a didactic exercise but as an experiment through which the client experiences the new behaviour and assimilates the change.

It was a pleasure to see that one of her first initiatives was to create a network of change facilitators for the IS function. In what ended up being a nine months assignment, the change to the culture of the IS function was most visible in the fact that change and people issues were central to the leadership agenda.

Reflections and lessons learnt

For a project that was initially focused on coordination and project management, the impact on the culture of the organisation was noticeable. The IS function went from being highly analytical, task orientated to a department where the leadership team was more open, willing to engage in dialogue and more sensitive to cultural and people issues. This case study not only illustrates the working of the wave metaphor in an organisation but is also a good learning about the balance between responding to the client's most pressing need (the task or what is not working) and holding a holistic view that process and narrative inform the task and need to be addressed for a sustainable solution. Attending to the unnamed dynamics (id function) and culture (personality function) of the legacy organisations in the merger provided a greater impetus for change and newness. A gestalt approach to change therefore invites the change practitioner to look beyond the task requested by the client and view the organisation holistically.

What I have also consistently witnessed in my organisational work is the correlation between successful organisational change and the quality of leadership. So, alongside belief in an emergent bottom-up approach to change, I hold the importance of the leadership role to bring about this type of change. Emergence does not imply a leaderless organisation—quite the opposite. Effective change relies on leaders who can facilitate the emergence of new ideas and listen unthreatened to "what is". Needing to support Tom's anxiety that the open dialogue events would result in a "moaning session" was an essential component of my role as a relational gestalt practitioner. Support to all aspects and parts of the field cannot be underestimated. In gestalt, support is that which accompanies (Denham-Vaughan, 2010) and being present, meeting clients where they are as well as modelling trust in the unfolding of a situation are essential skills of a gestalt practitioner.

REFERENCES

Agassi, J. B. (Ed.) (1999). *Martin Buber On Psychology and Psychotherapy: Essays, Letters, and Dialogue.* Syracuse, NY: Syracuse University Press.

Alvesson, M. (2002). *Understanding Organizational Culture.* London: Sage Publications.

Ariely, D. (2010). Why businesses don't experiment. *Harvard Business Review, 88*: 34.

Badiou, A. (2001). *Ethics: An Essay on the Understanding of Evil.* London, UK: Verso.

Bakhtin, M. M. (1981). *The Dialogic Imagination.* C. Emerson & M. Holquist (Trans.). Austin, TX: University of Texas Press.

Bakhtin, M. M. (1984). *Problems of Dostoevsky's Poetics.* C. Emerson & M. Holquist (Trans.). Austin, TX: University of Texas Press.

Bakhtin, M. M. (1986). *Speech Genres and Other Late Essays.* C. Emerson & M. Holquist (Eds.). Vern W. McGee (Trans.). Austin, TX: University of Texas Press.

Balogun, J. & Hope Hailey, V. (2004). *Exploring Strategic Change (2nd ed.).* London: Prentice Hall.

Barber, P. (2012). *A Reflective Guide to Facilitating Change in Groups and Teams—A Gestalt Approach to Mindfulness.* Oxford: Libri Press.

Barge, K. & Little, M. (2002). Dialogical wisdom, communicative practice and organizational life. *Communication Theory, 12(4):* 375–397.

Barlow, A. (1981). Gestalt therapy and gestalt psychology: Gestalt-antecedent influence or historical accident. *The Gestalt Journal, 4(2)*. Available online at: www.gestalt.org/barlow.htm [Accessed 30th March 2017].

Beer, M., Finnstrom, M., & Schrader, D. (2016). Why leadership training fails—and what to do about it. *Harvard Business Review, October 2016*: 50–57.

Beisser, A. (1972). The paradoxical theory of change. In: J. Fagan & I. L. Shepherd (Eds.), *Gestalt Therapy Now: Theory, Techniques, Applications*. Palo Alto, CA: Science and Behavior Books.

Bentley, T. (2000). *Facilitation*. The Space Between Publishing.

Bentley, T. (2012). Shame in organisations. *Gestalt Review, 16(1)*: 88–109.

Bentley, T. & Congram, S. (1996 [2014]). *Gestalt a Philosophy for Change*. Available online at: www.suecongram.co.uk/03_Downloads/papers/Gestalt_Philosophy.pdf.

Bertalanffy, L. von (1968). *General System theory: Foundations, Development, Applications*. New York: George Braziller.

Binney, G. & Williams, C. (1997). *Leading into the Future: Changing the Way People Change Organisations*. London: Nicholas Brealey Publishing.

Bion, W. R. (1967). Notes on Memory and Desire. *Psychoanalytic Forum, 2*: 272–273.

Bluckert, P. (2015). *Gestalt Coaching: Right Here, Right Now*. NY: Open University Press.

Bohm, D. (1990). *On Dialogue*. Cambridge, MT: Pegasus Communications.

Boring, E. G. (1930). A new ambiguous figure. *American Journal of Psychology, 42*: 444.

Brafman, O. & Beckstrom, R. (2006). *The Starfish and the Spider: The Unstoppable Power of Leaderless Organisations*. NYC, NY, USA: Portfolio Publications.

Bridges, W. (2009). *Managing Transitions: Making the Most of Change (3rd ed)*. London: Nicholas Brealey Publishing

Buber, M. (1947 [2002]). *Between Man and Man (2nd ed)*. London and New York: Routledge Classics.

Buber, M. (1958). *I and Thou*. R. G. Smith (Trans.). New York: Charles Scribner and Sons, 1923.

Burns, B. (2006). Kurt Lewin and the planned change approach to change: A reappraisal. In: J. Gallos (Ed.), *Organizational Development*. San Francisco: Jossey-Bass Publishing, pp. 133–157.

Bushe, G. R. (2013). Dialogic OD: A theory of practice. *OD Practitioner, Special Issue: Advances in Dialogic OD, 45(1)*: 11–17.

Callahan, J. F. (2014). *Relational Gestalt Practice: Key Concepts*. The Gestalt Legacy Project.

Carter, J. D. (2004). Carter's cube and a gestalt/OSD toolbox: A square, a circle, a triangle, and a line. *OD Practitioner, 36(4)*: 11–17.

Cavicchia, S. (2010). Shame in the coaching relationship: reflections on organisational vulnerability. *Journal of Management Development, 29(10)*: 877–890.

Chidiac, M-A. (2013). An organisational change approach based on gestalt psychotherapy theory and practice. *Journal of Organizational Change Management, 26(2)*: 458–474.

Chidiac, M-A. (2013). Creating a coaching culture: relational field coaching. *Development and Learning in Organizations, 27(3):* 11–13.

Chidiac, M-A. (2017). Gestalt as a relational approach to organisational development. *British Gestalt Journal, 26(1)*: 48–56.

Chidiac, M-A. & Denham-Vaughan, S. (2007). The process of presence: Energetic availability and fluid responsiveness. *British Gestalt Journal, 16 (1):* 9–19.

Chidiac, M-A. & Denham-Vaughan, S. (2009). An organisational self: Applying the concept of self to groups and organisations. *British Gestalt Journal, 18 (1)*: 42–49.

Clark, M., Denham-Vaughan, S., & Chidiac, M-A. (2014). A relational perspective on public sector leadership and management. *The International Journal of Leadership in Public Services, 10(1)*: 4–16.

Congram, S. & Mayes, R. (2015). *Engendering Balance: A Fresh Approach to Leadership.* Engendering Balance Publishing.

Conklin, J. (2006). Dialogue mapping: Building shared understanding of wicked problems. Chichester, West Sussex: John Wiley & Sons.

Conner, D. (1992). *Managing at the Speed of Change.* New York: Random House.

Critchley, B. (1997). A gestalt approach to organisational consulting. In: J. E. Neumann, K. Kellner, & A. Dawson-Shepherd (Eds.), *Developing Organisational Consultancy.* Brighton: Routledge, pp. 127–139.

Critchley, B., King, K., & Higgins, J. (2007). *Organisational Consulting: A Relational Perspective.* London: Middlesex University Press.

Cropanzano, R., James K., & Konovsky, M. A. (1993). Dispositional affectivity as a predictor of work attitudes and job performance. *Journal of Organizational Behavior, 14*: 595–606.

Csikszentmihalyi, M. (1990). *Flow: The Psychology of Optimal Experience.* New York: Harper and Row.

Cummings, T. G. & Worley, C. G. (2009). *Organization Development and Change (9th ed).* Cincinnati, OH: South-Western College Publishing.

Davey, N. (2014). Just send me word: The promise of dialogue. *Journal of Dialogue Studies, 2(1)*: 35–46.

Denham-Vaughan, S. (2005). Will and grace. *British Gestalt Journal, 14(1):* 5–14.

Denham-Vaughan, S. (2010). The liminal space and twelve action practices for gracious living. *British Gestalt Journal. 19(2):* 34–45.

Denham-Vaughan, S. (2011). The liminal space and Theory U, paper presentation, ROOTS Conference, November, Bommersvik, Sweden.

Denham-Vaughan, S. (2014). Present at the Edge: Leading Large Scale Change. Invited keynote speaker: GANZ, (Gestalt Australia and New Zealand), Conference, Brisbane, Australia, September.

Denham-Vaughan, S. & Chidiac, M-A. (2009). Dialogue goes to work: Relational organisational gestalt. In: R. Hycner & L. Jacobs (Eds.). *Relational Approaches in Gestalt Therapy.* Santa Cruz, CA: Gestalt Press, Routledge, Taylor and Francis, pp. 249–296.

Denham-Vaughan, S. & Chidiac, M-A. (2013). SOS: A relational orientation towards social inclusion. *Mental Health and Social Inclusion, 17(2):* 100–107.

Denham-Vaughan, S., & Chidiac, M-A. (2016). The aesthetics of health and well-being in organisational life: Key relational supports. Paper presented at EAGT/AAGT Conference, Taormina, Italy, September 2016.

Denham-Vaughan, S. & Gawlinski, M. (2012). Field-relational coaching for gestalt beginners: The PAIR model. *British Gestalt Journal, 21(1):* 11–21.

Dilts, R. (1994). Strategies of genius: Volume 1. Capitola, CA: Meta Publications.

Doppelt, R. (2003). The seven sustainability blunders. *The Systems Thinker, 14(5):* 1–7.

Edmonds, V. (2013). In dialogue with Sally Denham-Vaughan. *Gestalt Journal of Australia and New Zealand, 10(1):* 7–23.

Edmondson, A. C., & Lei, Z. (2014). Psychological safety: The history, renaissance, and future of an interpersonal construct. *Annual Review of Organizational Psychology and Organizational Behavior, 1(1):* 23–43.

Einstein, A. (1950). On the Generalized Theory of Gravitation. *Scientific American, 182(4).*

Elsner, R., & Farrands, B. (2012). *Leadership Transitions: How Business Leaders Take Charge in New Roles.* London: Kogan Page.

Fairfield, M. (2004). Gestalt groups revisited: A phenomenological approach. *Gestalt Review, 8(3):* 336–357.

Fairfield, M. (2013). The relational movement. *British Gestalt Journal, 22(1):* 22–35.

Frambach, L. (2003). The weighty world of nothingness: Salomo Friedlaender's creative indifference. In: M. Spagnuolo Lobb, & N. Amendt-Lyon (Eds.). *Creative License: The Art of Gestalt Therapy.* New York: Springer-Verlag Wien, pp. 113–128.

Francis, T. & Parlett, M. (Eds.) (2016). *Contact and Context: New Directions in Gestalt Coaching*. Santa Cruz, CA: Gestalt Press.

Friedman, M. S. (1955). *Martin Buber: The Life of Dialogue*. London: Routledge & Kegan Paul.

Gaffney, S. (2006). Gestalt with groups—A developmental perspective. *Gestalt Journal of Australia and New Zealand, 2 (2)*: 6–28.

Gaffney, S. (2013). *Groups, Teams and Groupwork Revisited*. Queensland, Australia: Ravenwood Press.

Ginger, S. (2007). *Gestalt Therapy: The Art of Contact*. London: Karnac.

Goleman, D. (2000). *Working with Emotional Intelligence*. New York: Bantam.

Govindarajan, V. & Trimble, C. (2011). The CEO's role in business model reinvention. *Harvard Business Review, Jan–Feb, 89 (1–2)*: 108–114.

Grint, K. (2008). Wicked problems and clumsy solutions: The role of leadership. *Clinical Leader, I (2)*: 54–68.

Hanafin, J. (2004). Rules of thumb for awareness agents: With a tip o' the hat to herb Shepard. *OD Practitioner, 36 (4)*: 24–28.

Harrington, A. (1999). *Reenchanted Science: Holism in German Culture from Wilhelm II to Hitler*. Bognor Regis: Princeton University Press.

Heerey, E. A. & Crossley, H. (2013). Predictive and reactive mechanisms in smile reciprocity. *Psychological Science. 24(8)*: 1446–1455.

Hind, P., Wilson, A., & Lenssen, G. (2009). Developing leaders for sustainable business. *Corporate Governance, 9(1)*: 7–20.

Husserl, E. (1931). *Ideas: General Introduction to Pure Phenomenology, vol 1*. New York: MacMillan.

Hutchins, G. (2012). Business needs to learn to see separate challenges as part of the whole. *The Guardian*. Available online at: www.theguardian.com/sustainable-business/business-work-more-like-nature [Accessed 30th March 2017].

Hycner, R., & Jacobs, L. (1995). *The Healing Relationship in Gestalt Therapy. A Dialogic/Self Psychology Approach*. Highland, New York: Gestalt Journal Press.

Isaacs, W. (1999). *Dialogue and the Art of Thinking Together*. New York: Doubleday.

Jacobs, G., van Witteloostuijn, A., & Christe-Zeyse, J. (2013). A theoretical framework of organizational change. *Journal of Organizational Change Management, 26 (5)*: 772–792.

Jacobs, L. (1989). Dialogue in gestalt theory and therapy. *The Gestalt Journal, 12(1)*: 25–67.

Jacobs, L. (2000). Respectful dialogues. *British Gestalt Journal Vol. 9(2)*: 105–111.

Jacobs, L. (2006). That which enables: Support as complex and contextually emergent. *British Gestalt Journal. 15 (2)*: 10–19.

Jacobs, L. (2016). Dialogue and double consciousness: Lessons in power and humility. *Gestalt Review, 20 (2):* 147–161.

Jaruzelski, B., & Dehoff, K. (2010). How the top innovators keep winning. *Strategy & Business magazine, Booz & Co, 61:* 1–14.

Joyce, P., & Sills, C. (2014). *Skills in Gestalt Counselling and Psychotherapy (3rd ed.).* London: Sage.

Kahneman, D. (2011). *Thinking, Fast and Slow.* New York: Farrar, Strauss, Giroux.

Kahneman, D., Fredrickson, B., Schreiber, C., & Redelmeier, D. (1993). When more pain is preferred to less: Adding a better end. *Psychological Science,* 4(6): 401–405.

Kalwar, S. (2010). *Quote Me Everyday.* Morrisville-Nc: Lulu.com.

Kaufman, G. (1989). *The Psychology of Shame—Theory and Treatment of Shame-Based Syndromes.* NY: Springer.

Kauffman, S. A. (1993). *The Origins of Order Self-Organization and Selection in Evolution.* New York: Oxford University Press.

Kegan, R. & Laskow Lahey, L. (2009). Immunity to change: How to overcome it and unlock the potential in yourself and your organization. Boston: Harvard Business Press.

Kepner, J. (2003). The embodied field. *British Gestalt Journal,* 12(1): 6–14.

Kernis, M. H. (2003). Toward a conceptualization of optimal self-esteem. *Psychological Inquiry, 14:* 1–26.

Kets de Vries, M. F. R. (2005). Leadership group coaching in action: The Zen of creating high performance teams. *Academy of Management Executives, 19, (1):* 61–76.

Kim, W. C. & Mauborgne, R. (1997). Fair process: Managing in the knowledge economy. *Harvard Business Review (July–August, 1997).*

Kohut, H. (1984). *How does Analysis Cure?* A. Goldberg (Ed.). Chicago: The University of Chicago Press.

Kolb, F. & Fry, D. (1975). Towards an applied theory of experiential learning. In: C. L. Cooper (Ed.). *Theories of Group Processes.* London: Wiley, pp. 33–57.

Kotter, J. P. (1996). *Leading Change.* Boston, MA: Harvard Business School Press.

Kotter, J., & Heskett, J. (1992). *Corporate Culture and Performance.* New York: The Free Press.

Kramer, K., & Gawlick, M. (2003). *Martin Buber's I and Thou: Practicing Living Dialogue.* New York: Paulist Press.

Laloux, F. (2014). *Reinventing Organisations.* Belgium: Nelson Parker.

LeakySquid.com (2014). *Very cool optical illusion.* [image] Available online at: www.leakysquid.com/2014/05/very-cool-optical-illusion.html#links [Accessed 21st April 2017].

Leary-Joyce, J. (2014). *The Fertile Void: Gestalt Coaching at Work*. London: AoEC Press.

Lee, H., Padmanabhan, V., & Whang, S. (1997). Information distortion in supply chain: The bullwhip effect. *Management Science, 43(4):* 546–558.

Lee, R. (1995). Gestalt and shame: The foundation for a clearer understanding of field dynamics. *British Gestalt Journal, 4(1):* 15–21.

Lee, R. (1996). Shame and the gestalt model. In: R. Lee & G. Wheeler (Eds.). *The Voice of Shame: Silence and Connection in Psychotherapy*. San Francisco, CA: Jossey-Bass, pp. 3–21.

Lee, R. & Wheeler, G. (1996). *The voice of shame—Silence and connection in psychotherapy*. San Francisco, CA: Jossey-Bass.

Levine Bar-Yoseph, T. (Ed.) (2005). *The Bridge: Dialogues Across Cultures*. New Orleans, LA: Gestalt Institute Press.

Levy, D. (2000). Applications and limitations of complexity theory in organization theory and strategy. In: J. Rabin, G. J. Miller & W. B. Hildreth (Eds.). *Handbook of Strategic Management (2nd ed)*. New York: Marcel Dekker.

Lewin, K. (1926). Vorsatz, wille und bedürfnis [Intention, will and need]. *Psychologische Forschung, 7:* 330–385.

Lewin, K. (1935). *A Dynamic Theory of Personality*. New York: McGraw-Hill.

Lewin, K. (1936). *Principles of Topological Psychology*. New York: McGraw-Hill.

Lewin, K. (1948). *Resolving Social Conflicts; Selected Papers on Group Dynamics*. Gertrude W. Lewin (Ed.). New York: Harper & Row.

Lewin, K. (1948 [1997]). *Resolving Social Conflicts/Field Theory in Social Science*. Washington, DC: American Psychological Association.

Lewin, K. (1951). *Field Theory in Social Science; Selected Theoretical Papers*. D. Cartwright (Ed.). New York: Harper & Row.

Liebhart, M. & Garcia-Lorenzo, L. (2010). Between planned and emergent change: Decision maker's perceptions of managing change in organisations. *International Journal of Knowledge, Culture and Change Management, 10(5):* 214–225.

Livne-Tarandach, R. & Bartunek, J. (2009). A new horizon for organizational change and development scholarship: Connecting planned and emergent change. In: R. Woodman, W. Pasmore & A. Shani (Eds.). *Research in Organizational Change & Development*, 17. Oxford: Emerald Group Publishing.

Lukensmeyer, C. (1997). Power, change & authenticity: A political & gestalt perspective. *British Gestalt Journal, 6(1):* 4–16.

MacKewn, J. (1997). *Developing Gestalt Counselling*. London: Sage Publications.

Marmgren, L. (2014). *People at Work: Gestalt Methodology and Management*. Books On Demand.

Marmgren, L. (1998). Change: some speculations based on comparing gestalt and complexity theory. *Gestalt Review, 21 (1):* 28–47.

Marshak, R. J. & Bushe, G. R. (2013). An introduction to advances in dialogic organization development. *OD Practitioner, 45(1):* 54–59.

Martin, R. L. (2016). M&A: The one thing you need to get right. *Harvard Business Review, June:* 43–46.

Maurer, R. (2005). Gestalt approaches with organizations and large systems. In: L. Woldt & S. Toman (Eds). *Gestalt Therapy: History, Theory and Practice.* London: Sage Publications.

Mead, G. (1934). *Mind Self and Society from the Standpoint of a Social Behaviorist.* Chicago, IL: University of Chicago.

Melnick, J. & Roos, S. (2007). The myth of closure. *Gestalt Review, 11(2):* 90–107.

Melnick, J., & Nevis, E. C. (Eds) (2009). *Mending the World: Social Healing Interventions by Gestalt Practitioners Worldwide.* Wellfleet, MA: Gestalt International Study Centre Publication.

Meulmeester, F. (2006). *Changing is standing still.* Utrecht: Brave New books.

Montuori, A. (1998). Postmodern systems theory, epistemology, and environment: The challenge of reconceptualization. *Best Papers of the Proceedings of the Academy of Management Conference,* Boston, August 1997, CD-ROM.

Nevis, E. (1980). *Gestalt Awareness Process in Organizational Assessment.* Cambridge, MA: MA Institute of Technology.

Nevis, E. (1987). *Organizational Consulting: A Gestalt Approach.* Cambridge MA: Gestalt Institute of Cleveland Press.

Nevis, S. M., Backman, S. A., & Nevis, E. C. (2003). Connecting strategic and intimate interactions. *Gestalt International Study Center, 7(2):* 134–146.

NTL Institute (2014). *The NTL Handbook of Organization Development and Change (2nd ed.).* Hoboken, NJ: Wiley.

O'Neill, M. B. (2000). *Executive Coaching with Backbone and Heart.* San Francisco, CA: Jossey Bass.

Ogden, P., Minton, K., & Pain, C. (2006). *Trauma and the Body: A Sensorimotor Approach to Psychotherapy.* New York: W.W. Norton.

Olson, E. E. & Eoyang, G. H. (2001). *Facilitating Organizational Change: Lessons from Complexity Science.* San Francisco, CA: Jossey-Bass/Pfeiffer.

Opengart, R. (2005). Emotional intelligence and emotion work: Examining constructs from an interdisciplinary framework. *Human Resource Development Review, 4(1):* 49–62.

Parlett, M. (1997). The unified field in practice. *Gestalt Review, 1, 1:* 16–33.

Parlett, M. (2000). Editorial. *British Gestalt Journal Vol. 9(2).*

Parlett, M. (2015). *Future Sense: Five Explorations of Whole Intelligence for a World That's Waking Up.* Leicestershire: Matador.

Perls, F. S. (1947). *Ego, Hunger and Aggression*. New York: Random House.

Perls, F. S. (1969). *Gestalt Therapy Verbatim*. Moab, UT: Real People Press.

Perls, F. S. (1973). *The Gestalt Approach and Eyewitness to Therapy*. Palo Alto, CA: Science and Behavior Books, Bantam Books edition.

Perls, F. S. (1976). *The Gestalt Approach and Eye Witness to Therapy*. New York: Bantam Books.

Perls, L. (1978). Concepts and misconceptions of Gestalt therapy. *Voices, 14(3)*: 31–36.

Perls, F. S., Hefferline, R. F., & Goodman, P. (1951 [1994]). *Gestalt Therapy: Excitement and Growth in the Human Personality*. New York: The Gestalt Journal Press.

Phillips, L. (2011). *The Promise of Dialogue: The Dialogic Turn in the Production and Communication of Knowledge*. Amsterdam: John Benjamins.

Polster, E., & Polster, M. (1973). *Gestalt Therapy Integrated: Contours of Theory & Practice*. New York: Brunner/Mazel.

Rainey Tolbert, M. A. (2004). What is gestalt OSD? All about the O, the S, the D … and of course, gestalt. *OD Practitioner, 36 (4)*: 6–10.

Rainey, M. & Jones, B. (2014). Use of self as an OD practitioner. In: B. Jones & M. Brazzel (Eds.). *The NTL Handbook of Organization Development and Change (2nd ed.)*. San Francisco, CA: Wiley, pp. 105–126.

Rask, G. (2014). *Meetings with Meaning: A Guide to Strategic Collaboration*. Sweden: Vulkan.

Rhodes, C. (2000). Doing knowledge at work: Dialogue, Monologue and power in organizational learning. In: J. Garrick & C. Rhodes (Eds.). *Research and Knowledge at Work: Case Studies and Innovative Strategies*. London: Routledge, pp. 217–231.

Rittell, H. & Webber, M. (1973). Dilemmas in a general theory of planning. *Policy Sciences, 4*: 155–169.

Robine, J-M. (2011). *On the Occasion of an Other*. Gouldsboro, ME: The Gestalt Journal Press.

Rogers, C. R. (1951). *Client-centered Therapy: Its Current Practice, Implementation and Theory*. Boston, MA: Houghton Mifflin.

Ronall, R. (2008). Intensive gestalt workshops: Experiences in community: In: Feder & Frew (Eds). *Beyond the Hot Seat Revisited: Gestalt Approaches to Group*. New Orleans, LA: The Gestalt Institute Press.

Rothwell, W. J. & Sullivan, L. (2005). Models for change. In: R. Sullivan, & G. N. McLean (Eds.), *Practicing Organization Development: A Guide for Consultants*. San Diego, CA: Pfeiffer, pp. 39–418.

Rubin, E. (1958). Figure and ground. In: D. C. Beardslee & M. Wertheimer (Eds.). *Readings in Perception*. Princeton, NJ: Van Nostrand, pp. 194–203 (original work published 1915).

Sackman, S., Eggenhofer-Rehart, P., & Friesl, M. (2009). Sustainable change: Long term effects towards developing a Learning organization. *Journal of Applied Behavioural Science, 45*: 521–549.

Sapriel, L. (1998). Can gestalt therapy, self-psychology & intersubjectivity theory be integrated? *British Gestalt Journal, 7(1)*: 33–44.

Sassoli de Bianchi, M. (2015). God may not play dice, but human observers surely do. *Foundations of Science, 20(1)*: 77–105.

Scharmer, O. (2000). *Presencing: Learning from the Future as It Emerges: On the Tacit Dimension of Leading Revolutionary Change*. Available online at: www. ottoscharmer.com/sites/default/files/2000_Presencing.pdf [Accessed 6th April 2017].

Scharmer, O. (2009). *Theory U: Leading from the Future as it Emerges*. San Francisco, CA: Berrett-Koehler Publishers.

Schein, E. (2013). *The Humble Inquiry*. San Francisco, CA: Berrett-Kohler.

Senge, P. (1990). *The Fifth Discipline*. New York: Doubleday.

Senge, P., Scharmer, C.O., Jaworski, J., & Flowers, B. S. (2004). *Presence: Human Purpose and the Field of the Future*. Cambridge, MA: The Society for Organisational Learning.

Siegel, D. J. (1999). *The Developing Mind: How Relationships and The Brain Interact to Shape Who We Are*. New York: Guildford Press.

Siegel, D. J. (2007). *The Mindful Brain: Reflection and Attunement in the Cultivation of Well-being*. New York: W. W. Norton.

Silani, G., Lamm, C., Ruff, C. & Singer, T. (2013). Right supramarginal gyrus is crucial to overcome emotional egocentricity bias in social judgments. *The Journal of Neuroscience, 33(39)*. Available online at: www.jneurosci. org/content/33/39/15466 [Accessed 2nd April 2017].

Sills, C. L. (2012). An introduction to gestalt. London: Sage.

Siminovitch, D. (2017). *A Gestalt Coaching Primer: The Path Towards Awareness IQ*. Toronto: Gestalt Coaching Works.

Smith, E. W. L. (1976). The roots of gestalt therapy. In: E. W. L. Smith (Ed.). *The Growing Edge of Gestalt Therapy*. New York: Brunner/Mazel, pp. 3–36.

Smuts, J. C. (1926). *Holism and Evolution*. The Gestalt Press.

Spinelli, E. (1989). *The Interpreted World: An Introduction to Phenomenological Psychology*. London: Sage Publications.

Spretnak, C. (2011). *Relational Reality*. Topsham, ME: Green Horizon Books.

Stacey, R., Griffin, D., & Shaw, P. (2000). *Complexity and Management: Fad or Radical Challenge to Systems Thinking*. London: Routledge.

Staemmler F. M. (1997). On cultivating uncertainty: An attitude for gestalt therapists. *British Gestalt Journal, 6 (1)*: 40–48.

Staemmler, F. M. (2016). Taking another turn: The relational turn in gestalt therapy revisited. *British Gestalt Journal, 25(2)*: 3–19.

Steiber, A. (2014). *The Google Model—Management for Continuous Innovation in a Rapidly Changing World.* London: Springer.

Stern D. N. (2004). *The Present Moment in Psychotherapy and Everyday Life.* New York: Norton & Company.

Stevenson, H. (2008). Emergence: The gestalt approach to change. Available online at: www.clevelandconsultinggroup.com/articles/emergence-gestalt-approach-to-change.php [Accessed 10th April 2017].

Stewart, J., Zediker, K. & Black, L. (2004). Relationships among philosophies of dialogue. In: R. Anderson, L. Baxter, K. Cissna (Eds.). *Theorizing Difference in Communication Studies.* London: Sage, pp. 21–38.

Stolorow, R. D., Brandchaft, B. & Atwood, G. (1987). *Psychoanalytic Treatment: An Intersubjective Approach.* Hillsdale, NJ: The Analytic Press.

Tangney, J. (1995). Shame and guilt in interpersonal relationships. In: J. Tangney & K. Fischer (Ed.). *Self-Conscious Emotions: The Psychology of Shame, Guilt, Embarrassment, and Pride.* New York: Guilford Press, pp. 114–139.

The Economist Special Report (April 2015) *To Have and to Hold.*

The Economist Special Report (November 2004) *Family Business: Passing on the Crown.*

Truskie, S. (1999). *Leadership in High-performance Organizational Cultures.* London: Quorom Books.

Van Eron, A. & Burke, W. W. (1995). Separation. In W. Rothwell, R. Sullivan, & G. N. McLean (Eds.). *Practicing Organization Development: A Guide for Consultants.* San Diego: Pfeiffer, pp. 395–418.

Waldrop, M. M. (1992). *Complexity: The Emerging Science at the Edge of Order and Chaos.* New York: Simon and Schuster.

Waterman, R. H., Peters, T. J., & Julien, R. P. (1980). Structure is not organization. *Business Horizons 23(3):* 14.

Weick, K. & Quinn, R. E. (1999). Organisational change & development. *Annual Review of Psychology, 50:* 361–386.

Weisbord, M. R. (1976). Organizational diagnosis: Six places to look for trouble with or without a theory. *Group & Organization Studies, 1(4):* 430–447.

Westoby, P. (2014). Theorising dialogue for community development practice—an exploration of crucial thinkers. *Journal of Dialogue Studies,* 2 (1): 69–86.

Whitehead, A. N. (1920). *The Concept of Nature.* Cambridge: Cambridge University Press, 1986.

Wheatley, M. (1999). *Leadership & The New Science: Discovering Order in a Chaotic World.* San Francisco, CA: Berrett-Koehler.

Wheatley, M., & Frieze, D. (2011). *Walk Out Walk On: A Learning Journey into Communities Daring to Live the Future Now.* San Francisco, CA: Berrett-Koehler Publishers.

Wheeler, G. (1991). *Gestalt Reconsidered: A New Approach to Contact and Resistance.* New York: Gardner.

White, W. (2008). The interlocutor's dilemma: The place of strategy in dialogic theory. *Communication Theory, 18:* 5–26.

Wollants, G. (2012). *Gestalt Therapy: Therapy of the Situation.* London: Sage.

Yontef, G. M. (1982). Gestalt therapy: Its inheritance from gestalt psychology. *Gestalt Therapy, 4(1/2):* 23–39.

Yontef, G. M. (2002). The relational attitude in gestalt therapy theory and practice. *International Gestalt Journal 25/1:* 15–35.

Yontef, G., & Friedemann, S. (2016). Dialogue and experiment. *British Gestalt Journal, 25(1):* 9–21.

Yontef, G. M. (1993). *Awareness, Dialogue & Process.* New York: The Gestalt Journal Press.

Zahavi, D. (2005). *Subjectivity and Selfhood: Investigating the First-Person Perspective.* Cambridge, MA: The MIT Press/A Bradford Book.

Zeigarnik, B. (1938). On finished and unfinished tasks. In: W. D. Ellis (Ed.). *A Source Book of Gestalt Psychology.* New York: Harcourt, pp. 300–314.

Zinker, J. (1994). *In Search of Good Form: Gestalt Therapy with Couples.* San Francisco, CA: Jossey-Bass.

Zinker, J. (1977). *Creative Process in Gestalt Therapy.* New York: Vintage Books.

INDEX

For Product Safety Concerns and Information please contact our EU
representative GPSR@taylorandfrancis.com
Taylor & Francis Verlag GmbH, Kaufingerstraße 24, 80331 München, Germany

www.ingramcontent.com/pod-product-compliance
Lightning Source LLC
Chambersburg PA
CBHW070611270326
41926CB00013B/2502

9 7 8 1 7 8 2 2 0 5 2 3 4